WITHDRAWN

New Dimensions in
Student Personnel
Administration

New Dimensions in Student Personnel Administration

edited by

ORLEY R. HERRON, JR.

President
Greenville College

INTERNATIONAL TEXTBOOK COMPANY
an Intext *publisher—Scranton, Pennsylvania 18515*

the *International series in*

GUIDANCE AND COUNSELING

consulting editor

the late **R. WRAY STROWIG**

University of Wisconsin

ISBN   *0-7002-2312-6*

Library of Congress Catalog Card Number: 75-127073

Preface

The college campus has been in a state of ferment in recent years and student personnel administrators have been in the main stream of action. The challenges of the day are requiring a knowledge and charisma unknown in other years. How the student personnel administrator meets this challenge may determine the future well-being of our great institutions of higher learning. This book is designed to provide insight in several areas of concern in student personnel administration. The contributors to this book represent a wealth of experience in the arena of student personnel, and I am indebted to them for their expertise. There are many others who assisted in a variety of ways so that the book could be completed. I wish to pay tribute to the extremely adept President of Indiana State University, Dr. Alan C Rankin, who has demonstrated an unusual sophistication in dealing with the students of today and his generous and continued support in this document is gratefully acknowledged. The Vice-Presidents of Indiana State University and my close associates were most helpful with their insights and life styles in college administration: Dr. Charles W. Hardaway, Vice-President for General Affairs and University Secretary; Mr. J. Kenneth Moulton, Vice-President for Business Affairs and Treasurer; Dr. Wayne E. Schomer, Vice-President for Development and Public Affairs; Dr. John W. Truitt, Vice-President for Student Affairs, who contributed significantly in his four chapters; and Dr. Maurice K. Townsend, Vice-President for Academic Affairs. The Board of Trustees of Indiana State University has presented an excellent model of emulation by its forward approach of having three student observers officially attend the monthly board meetings: the President of Student Government, the Vice-President of Student Government, and the Editor of the campus newspaper. Indiana State University's Board of Trustees is to be commended for the erudition it exhibits in student affairs and, in my judgment, the Board presents a standard that should be adopted by governing boards across the country.

The staff of International Textbook led by its exceptional educational editor, John Dugan, Jr., was a tremendous help in all the multifaceted vectors of this book. A special word of commendation should be accorded the late Dr. R. Wray Strowig, former Consulting Editor in Guidance and Counseling of the International Textbook Company. He contributed in many ways to this effort and the legacy of his influence will remain in the lives of the vast number of students he taught in his distinguished career.

Others who should be cited for their guidance and able assistance in exemplifying styles of lay leadership in dealing with the youth of today and serve as a reservoir of understanding:

Dr. David Burnham, friend and dynamic pastor of the Chapel of Fir Hill, Akron, Ohio, which is situated near the campus of the University of Akron. His discernment in the area of student affairs is most commendable.

Mr. Jack Morgan, owner of Intermountain Surgical Supply Company at Boise, Idaho, who is an astute statesman of the dilemmas of the universities in modern society.

Mr. William Kidd, former football coach, New Philadelphia High School, New Philadelphia, Ohio, and member of the Ohio Coaches Hall of Fame, who continues his tradition as an unusual teacher and builder of men.

Dr. Donald Morgan, professor, California State Polytechnic College, San Luis Obispo, California. His sophisticated studies with the government provide invaluable insights to the nature of administration.

Mr. Harvey Chrouser, Athletic Director, Wheaton College, Wheaton, Illinois, whose innovative programs in working with youth have been recognized nationally.

Mr. Tom Winters of Louisville, Kentucky, connoisseur of state and public relationships, who was most helpful with his sage advice.

Mr. Niles Herron, Vice-President of the American Investment Corporation, Los Angeles, California. His outstanding expertise on lay advisory boards has provided a valuable service to student personnel administrators.

Mr. Dale Morgan, world traveler and successful business leader of Whittier, California, who has given innumerable hours to the development and understanding of youth.

Many accolades should be given to my typist, Roberta Bowers, who typed the manuscript so expeditiously and efficiently, a continuation of the standard of quality she began in the typing of my first book with International, *The Role of the Trustee.* It should be added that since that first book she has graduated with a Masters degree in guidance and counseling.

This book is dedicated to Dr. Walter F. Johnson, Professor of Education, Michigan State University, who is a distinguished leader and pioneer in Student Personnel Administration. His enviable record in developing executives in the Student Personnel area is greatly acknowledged and is so recognized by this dedication. Four of the contributing authors of this book have enjoyed his tutelage and wise counsel. Dr. Johnson's variegated skills have been widely acclaimed and the American Personnel and Guidance Association honored his outstanding career by electing him as President in 1958.

Finally and most importantly, I wish to pay tribute to my wife Donna who has been a compatriot with me through the years of college administration. Her advice, love, patience, support, faith, and respect are a constant source of inspiration.

ORLEY R. HERRON, JR.

Greenville, Illinois
July, 1970

Contents

1   *New Dimensions: An Overview*
    Orley R. Herron, Jr.   1

    Living and Learning Centers. In-Service Education. Counseling.
    Student Government. Organization and Administration of Student
    Personnel Services. Campus Ministry. Dropouts. Student Subcultures.
    Values. Campus Security. Junior Colleges. Financial Aids. Con-
    gressional Response to the College Campus. The Future.

2   *A Nation on the Move*
    Mark O. Hatfield   21

3   *The Image of Today's Student*
    John W. Truitt   29

    Political. Social. Education. Economics. Religion. Summary.

4   *University Posture and Student Protest—The Second Round*
    John W. Truitt   43

    Introduction. University Posture. Anticipation and Prevention of
    Confrontations. Confrontations and Disruptive Actions. Due Process
    and Fair Hearing. Summary.

5   *Diverse Views That Contain the Basis for Student Unrest and*
    Agitation
    John W. Truitt   61

    Introduction. Black Power. The New Left. Private-Versus-Public-
    Life Concept. Student Power. Summary.

6   *Student Values—A New Approach*
        Patrick H. Ratterman **76**

7   *The Changing Role of the Counselor in Modern Society*
        C. Eugene Walker **86**

8   *Helping the Student Understand Himself*
        R. Wray Strowig **94**

        The Self Viewed Pragmatically. The Conditions of Aiding Student
        Self-Understanding. Conclusion. References.

9   *The Behavior Therapies: Alternatives and Additions to Traditional*
        Counseling Approaches
        Milton Wolpin and C. Eugene Walker **107**

10 *Student Personnel Administrators and the Campus Ministry*
        Wayne W. Hoffman **120**

        How Does the Student Personnel Administrator Look at the Campus
        Ministry? The Structure of Campus Ministry. How Campus Ministry
        Views the University. The Student and the Campus Ministry.

11 *Living and Learning Centers*
        Donald V. Adams **128**

        Living and Learning at Michigan State University. The Role of the
        Student Personnel Worker in Living-Learning Residence Halls.
        Summary.

12 *Information Systems in Student Personnel Administration*
        William R. Osmon **139**

        Introduction. What Is an Information System? A proposed Student
        Research Information System (SRIS). Student Research Informa-
        tion System (SRIS). Research and Operations Applications. Sum-
        mary.

13 *Dropouts: Recent Studies—Implications and Observations*
        William Hannah **156**

        Studies on College Attrition. Summary. References.

14 *New Dimensions in Junior College Student Personnel*
Administration
    John R. Fawcett, Jr. and Jack E. Campbell 179

    Introduction. Philosophy Underlying Junior College Student Personnel Administration. Areas of Junior College Student Personnel Work. Organization and Administration. Summary and Conclusions. Bibliography.

15 *In-Service Education*
    John W. Truitt and Richard A. Gross 209

    The Need for In-Service Education in Student Personnel Work. General Principles of In-Service Education Programs. Development of an In-Service Education Program. Selected In-Service Education Activities. Summary. Bibliography.

Appendix   *Student Bill of Rights* 231

Index 241

1

New Dimensions: An Overview

Orley R. Herron, Jr.*

The role of the college administrator has assumed new dimensions. The feelings of good will shared by so many students and administrators in the past have been replaced on many campuses by attitudes of distrust and indifference. This is a period in educational history of action. The antiestablishmentarians are being seen and heard clearly. One dean of students remarked that "We live as does an alcoholic, from day to day. We hope we can simply get through the day without some type of student disturbance that would seriously upset the task of the university here."

Colleges old and new, liberal and conservative, traditional and progressive, are being placed in tortuous confrontations. The results have left many a campus with more tension and turmoil than ever before. University administrators are seeking new strategies to combat the trials of the times and the student agitators are continuing to bring strong force and resistance to the university's power structure. It is apparent that old approaches to new problems are not going to work, and it requires the ingenuity of the finest academic minds to chart higher education on a course of progress and reward.

*Dr. Orley R. Herron, Jr., holds the B.A. from Wheaton College, Wheaton, Illinois, M.A. and Ph.D. from Michigan State University. Prior to his present appointment as President of Greenville College, he served as Assistant to the President at Indiana State University, the Director of the Doctoral Program in Student Personnel at the University of Mississippi, Dean of Students at Westmont College, Santa Barbara, California, and Head Resident Advisor at Michigan State University. Dr. Herron is the author of several books including *The Role of the Trustee, Input/Output,* and the author of numerous articles in the field of higher education.

The electronic and written media have brought the disorder on the campus into the living room so that the general public becomes eyewitnesses to the actions. No more can friend or foe suppress the news; it is instant action and the results are vibrating across the country. The student unrest that has plagued the campus is not to be resolved with simple solutions. It is a complex dilemma—conditioned by multifaceted vectors that must be understood if reason and order are going to exist on the campus again. Cracking a student over the head may bring blood, but more often than not it fails to bring understanding. Yet the universities cannot let the dissidents control, and the use of force may be the only way to stop the onslaughts until the warring groups can interact in a proper way together.

The price of keeping a campus open amidst difficulty may be high, but our great universities must not be brought to a halt by the guerrilla tactics that have been evidenced on so many campuses. Such disruption and disorders point out vividly that higher education and its growth need a thoroughgoing reevaluation. Walter Moberly said in the *Crisis in the University*, "If you want a bomb, the chemistry department will teach you how to make it; if you want a cathedral, the department of architecture will teach you how to build it; if you want a healthy body, the departments of physiology and medicine will teach you how to tend it. But, when you ask whether or why you should want bombs or cathedrals or healthy bodies, the university on this score remains dumb and silent."

The university of today must be relevant to the needs of society. It must preserve its prerogative to be the transmitter of the important traditions of society, but it must also be the *avant-garde* of the new world and the future. Too often higher education in its mission to preserve the past has stagnated itself in useless reflection and utilized energies in areas that could have been directed elsewhere. Higher education must be the laboratory for the future and in that role a major and viable leader in society. Progress requires innovation and innovation can cause tension, but tension is a hallmark of excellence when properly directed. Campuses should not shun tension that is characteristic of positive change.

What must the role of the university be in an era of change? What are the dimensions necessary for the progress and well-being of institutions of higher learning? Should certain dimensions and directions be advocated if a university is to march ahead? Are there pitfalls and dangers to be avoided? What answers and solutions can be found to meet the demands of a tense and tenacious student population as well as a restless faculty? This book is designed to answer questions like these. Some of the topics identified have been in existence a very long time, but all have taken on new meaning, relevance, and new dimensions.

LIVING AND LEARNING CENTERS

Living and learning centers, the subject of the chapter by Dr. Adams, represent a dimension very new to the college environment. The concept is historic in that this style of living was typical of the early institutions of higher learning. Yet, in a day of explosive unrest it has become an answer to the impersonality and computer-card orientation of the multiversity. The philosophy of the living and learning centers is basic and quite clear.

The university feels that the student's place of residence should be more than a "pad." This concept involves the premise that a student's out-of-classroom activities should be contributory to his educational experience. In this way his academic experience can be extended so that it is not just an in-classroom affair which concludes after each class period. Since a student spends approximately a third or more of his time in his place of residence, it follows that the residence should be given a new context and outlook as a learning experience. University administrators have found it difficult to locate satisfactory housing units for their student population short of constructing new ones. The construction of housing units for higher education is big business and the million-dollar mistakes in such edifices are more than apparent. A number of universities such as Michigan State have been pioneers in advocating the living and learning context, and many of these have followed suit by establishing an environment where the facilities provide the avenue by which optimum learning can transpire. These housing units are furnished with classrooms, academic offices, chemistry labs, lecture rooms, seminar lounges, libraries, typing rooms, electronic lecture playback from a computer center, counseling rooms, reading carrels, fine-arts rooms, and student senate chambers, as well as snack bars, dance floors, television rooms, radio rooms, and dining hall facilities for the total occupancy of the unit. Some of these units are semiluxurious hotels—almost self-contained colleges packed into one giant facility. The staff is trained for such innovation and is quite capable of meeting the varied needs of the students.

The philosophy of living and learning centers has had tremendous success in many institutions. The centers are normally coed, so that the classes as well as the social activities reflect a coed university setting. I feel that coed residence halls are excellent and a norm for the major university campus. Housing segregated by sex, race, or academic class is not the ideal for institutions of higher learning. Housing officials should be cognizant of building residence halls and housing units that are flexible and allow for innovation and change. Too often housing units are outdated before they are actually constructed. A residence hall should reflect the character of an institution and be an important factor in the education of its residents.

Administrators should exercise care in selecting the architects. Some architects may design a beautiful-looking building that is weak in function. Universities that have not constructed coed living and learning complexes should consider going in that direction. Experience with those now in existence has been favorable and proves that such a design is worthy of consideration.

IN-SERVICE EDUCATION

The chapter on in-service education is essential for any book on student personnel. The consistent, systematic upgrading of student personnel workers is required if an institution expects to go forward. The results of student personnel workers not trained for the position is a legacy that must be eliminated. Few institutions have established a program of educational improvement for their staffs. Dr. Gross and Dr. Truitt write from personal experience because their staffs have been involved in excellent in-service education programs and reflect their "perceptive efforts."

The framework of their programs are fine models for emulation by other institutions. They have proposed ways of initiating and implementing an in-service education program which I feel is worthy of adoption. In-service education need not be cumbersome or expensive to be effective, but it must be adequately developed to maintain the level of excellence its nature requires. In-service education is a new dimension in the field of student personnel. Professional growth programs can be designed for both large or small institutions and can provide the interaction necessary for good programming.

Dr. Gross and Dr. Truitt state that "Broadly conceived, in-service education encompasses all phases of student personnel work that contribute to continuing professional development and competence. The program includes activities, planned in accordance with specific objectives intended to enhance the professional growth and competence of a student personnel staff, both individually and collectively."

In-service education will compliment a student personnel staff. Wise student personnel administrators will introduce in-service education programs that will assist student personnel staffs to meet the challenges of our times. I urge more administrators to adopt such programs, and I am quite confident that the results will be significant enough to warrant their continuance.

COUNSELING

Counseling is an important area of student personnel administration. The program that may be initiated and administered by the student personnel department will vary greatly from one institution to another. Considerable discussion has transpired on the roles and types of efforts that can be extended in the area of counseling. In all areas of campus life student personnel administrators must guard against taking away meaningful experiences between a faculty member and a student by providing a smorgasbord of specialists. Many of the student problems will best be served by the faculty-student interaction. Some student personnel departments are so highly specialized that faculty members quickly refer any student problems to the student personnel specialist instead of dealing with the problem themselves.

Recent counseling research has demonstrated that it does not require a vast sophistication in training to do a good job. The increasing suicide rates on college campuses, the deviations that continue to occur, and the personality conflicts that grow all need to be given attention by concerned members of the academic and administrative communities. It is quite true that with bulging student enrollments and larger class sizes students are going to be increasingly independent in their academic pursuits. Not always independent by choice, but by reason of the lack of adequate personnel to deal with the students' personal and emotional needs. Students are asking very basic questions—simple in nature but serious to their future—such as, Who am I? Where am I going? They are searching for fuller and more meaningful relationships. They want to understand their role in society; they want to be relevant and relate appropriately to the challenges of the times. Students are impatient with the red tape of bureaucracy and the hypocrisy that appears in some segments of society. Far from being apathetic, they want to respond to the needs of society and to contribute in ways that provide progressive change. Being stopped and stifled in that goal inspires them to challenge the hierarchies with strong force and deviant behavior patterns.

Realizing this, a number of universities have provided unique and practical ways to satisfy the pressing emotional demands of students. Some universities have installed twenty-four-hour telephone counseling services which initially began as a weekend service and now have grown into a seven-days-a-week affair. On many campuses student-trained counselors live in residence halls and assist both undergraduate and graduate students in a variety of ways. Some universities have programmed seminar sessions for their faculty to train them in basic counseling techniques. The results of those efforts have paid handsome dividends in their relationships to students. Institutions should adopt a plan which could be easily implemented on their campus in training their staffs to help students.

The style of approach to counseling—whether directive, nondirective, eclectic, or behaviorist—may not be as important in the years ahead as men have claimed it to be previously. Guidance as we know it could be replaced almost totally by computers, which may obtain a more thorough and accurate overview of such things as personal abilities and vocational choice. Informational systems are undergoing such revolutionary changes that it takes constant care lest the information input be improperly disseminated. Elimination of the human factor and the one-to-one relationship may never be accomplished in our lifetime. Student personnel approaches to counseling must be equal to the times and the environmental pressures.

Dr. Walker has written one chapter and coauthored another with Dr. Wolpin pertaining to the field of counseling. His insight through counseling, teaching, and administration bring new perspective and vision to his writing. He gives an overview of the changing role of the counselor in modern society, which is an important phase of understanding in any student personnel program. The second chapter, "The Behavior Therapies: Alternatives and Additions to Traditional Counseling Approaches," provides a fascinating survey of modern trends. I think it is quite apparent that the modern-age student needs assistance, whether formal or informal. Total campus involvement in their needs demands our attention, and we must provide solutions by utilizing the resources available on a college campus. To relegate counseling to a few is to disregard the potential and deny students vital opportunities for help.

A college student personnel administrator realizes that we accept students just as they are. We do not ask them to leave their problems at home. We accept students and seek to provide services to meet their needs that may come to light immediately or in later days in their college sojourn. College administrators and faculty members should yearly reexamine the resources available on their campus. Providing psychiatric staff and psychologically trained individuals is one answer, but the faculty members themselves possibly hold the key to a more adequate solution for the students. The specialists can resolve the most serious problems; the lesser problems must be handled by the faculty and staff.

STUDENT GOVERNMENT

The trend to appoint students on major policy making committees is a wise one. Previously, students had been appointed in a token manner on committees that had little importance in the decision making of an institution. Now students serve on policy-making committees such as academic affairs or the Board of Trustees. In most institutions the student members serve with a high sense of responsibility and purpose.

Student governments have taken on new importance today. On many campuses they have been the target of student agitators because of the ineffectiveness of their government. Some administrators have erred in responding to these agitators by granting new powers to these splinter groups before evaluating the role of student government on the campus. Student government needs a major overhaul or we will see its demise. Because of the confrontations, the student personnel administrator may wonder whether the student government is a friend or foe. To strengthen student government the student personnel administrator should take time to assess the student leadership on his campus, meet weekly with the leaders of student government, and review the areas that need wise counsel and attention.

Good student body presidents require careful and systematic interaction with the members of the administration. The student body president is elected to represent the students, and the student personnel administrator is normally delegated by the university president with the authority to work with student leaders. A degree of understanding and expertise engendered by these two forces may well depend on which type of environment is produced on campus. The relationship should be one of mutual respect and support for achieving objectives that will enhance the learning and living experiences of students. It should also provide opportunities for decision making that are important for the institution and society as well. Students will be led only to the degree they want to be led, and our task is to raise their goals of leadership and give them realistic standards for achievement. Trying to achieve unrealistic goals is not only frustrating and disheartening to students but can wreck and undermine the continuity of capable leadership. In this day of concern it is not surprising that many campuses are having difficulty in attracting candidates to run for student government offices. Some elections have been made farcical by the type of candidate placed in nomination and the kind of campaigns such candidates follow. Some political slates have offered topless dancers, pedigree dogs, and other types of nonacademic diversions, yet these candidates have fared surprisingly well at the polls.

It is indicative of the displeasure the students have with the stoic, unchanging student governments that have done so little in the way of positive action on the campuses. The institution and its members must share responsibility in letting this type of do-nothing organization be perpetuated. The weaknesses, inequalities, and loopholes of student government need to be corrected; and the student personnel administrator can be of major assistance in bringing about the change. Certain underlying principles of working with student government must be understood in this day of cataclysmic student revolution.

First, student government should be given clearly defined prerogatives and powers within the college setting. Exactly what can students do and what can they not do? Second, the student officers should be the acknowledged official student governing agent within the institution. However, if the group is not representative of the variegated groups on campus, then its structure should be modified to be more democratic and representative. If the university grants charters to splinter groups and other organizations, they should be under the umbrella of student government. If not, excessive division and competition for power will emerge. Third, the relationship between the administration, faculty, and student government should be one of mutual trust and understanding. Frankness and courtesy can be exhibited as they strive to solve common problems and achieve cooperative solutions. Distrust and divisiveness will also destroy purposeful relationships. Openness between the student leaders, faculty, and administrators must always prevail. When a breakdown occurs the channels of communication are curbed and trouble is on its way. Fourth, the university should utilize its resources to support the development and continuance of a strong, progressive student government. Government that is active, involved, and guided by democratic checks and balances will be an exciting operation to observe. The leadership can be dynamic and diplomatic in its approach to the issues at hand. Fifth, student affairs committees at the board level would eliminate some of the misunderstandings in policy formulation that arise between student leaders and trustees. Many trustees are willing to participate in this arrangement, and the success of the boards that have done so merits highest recognition.

ORGANIZATION AND ADMINISTRATION OF STUDENT PERSONNEL SERVICES

The staffing of student personnel offices is becoming quite complicated in the quest to meet the various needs of students and other groups within the university. Yet a detailed analysis of the purpose and philosophy of student personnel service is essential before an organization can be built. Crucial to the establishment of a student personnel staff is the definition of the objectives of the program which must be an outgrowth of the objectives of an institution. Student personnel programs developed in contrast to the primary objectives of an institution will create havoc. In fact, it will eventually bring a major confrontation within the university which could have been avoided had the program been structured properly.

Student personnel services or student affairs exist to be of service to the university and primary to the students. Their task is to see that a student utilizes his capabilities in achieving the objectives he is required to accomplish at the institution. The student personnel program is designed to assist the student in making a satisfactory adjustment to the institution and to promote the environment in which he can pursue his academic goals with the least amount of difficulty.

The organization of staffs differ widely as to size, scope, and nature of the institution. Some institutions spend vast amounts of money to build student personnel programs and others fund it in very miserly fashion. Institutions should not slight the funding of a program because it is vital to academic health and progress. Good programs are flexible and should be annually audited to determine whether they are functioning in the most optimum manner to achieve the institutional objectives so defined. If they are not, then they must be revised. Staffs that are hesitant to change may regret that decisions when the structure is buried and broken by the sophistication and pressures of today's student.

A student personnel program must never be designed so that it distracts from the academic program. A dean of students should periodically evaluate his activity program and see if it is fractioning the students time so severely that he cannot accomplish the main purpose of going to college—to obtain an academic education.

The objectives of student affairs programs should be set forth clearly and understood by those who participate in its execution. The following objectives illustrate how a student affairs program can be designed into a tripart operation. A fourth aspect of this particular program would include consulting services if further organization expansion is warranted.

OBJECTIVES OF STUDENT AFFAIRS[1]

1. To stimulate students to integrate formal and informal learning, encouraging education of the "whole man" by emphasizing the interdependence of the concepts learned in the classroom and the discoveries made through out-of-class experiences.

[1]From Student Affairs Organization Chart, Indiana State University, Terre Haute, Indiana

2. To provide enrichment experiences for all students by developing student programs, encouraging student participation, and providing special services for students who need individual attention.
3. To encourage relationships among professors, administrative officials, and students which will enhance increased communications and provide bases for decision making by all groups.
4. To create a climate in which each student may have equal access to all the educational opportunities of the university.
5. To encourage an atmosphere in which each student may seek self-identification and to create avenues through which he may express his individuality.
6. To establish a climate in which each student can be challenged to higher levels of intellectual development and personal and moral maturity.

OBJECTIVES OF STUDENT LIFE

1. To assist students in their growth and development by providing opportunities for them to exercise their sense of responsibility, their leadership potential, and their interpersonal relationship abilities.
2. To operate as a service agency for students, faculty, parents, and other administrative officials.
3. To provide opportunities for one-to-one relationships between administrative officials and students to discuss concerns of the students.
4. To develop a style of relationship among students, faculty, and staff which encourages frequency of inter-action and the strengthening of commitments in areas of common interest.
5. To provide opportunities for broad student participation in the governance of the university in areas where students can make valuable contributions.
6. To strive for a high quality of student participation and leadership in the life of the university.

OBJECTIVES OF STUDENT ADMINISTRATIVE SERVICES

1. To provide admission, registration, student research, testing and related services to students, faculty and administrative officers.
2. To establish and maintain a Student Information System with common and unique student data readily available for administrative and academic decision making.
3. To provide a special coordinated program between academic offices and student administrative services based upon the comprehensive Student Information System.

4. To conduct student research and provide comprehensive data to the university community for immediate and long-range planning.
5. To coordinate and design information processing, retrieval, and flow for all areas of student affairs.
6. To interpret the educational opportunities of Indiana State University to prospective students.

The staffing of a student service area can become quite difficult. Top people are hard to find, and the competition for their talents is very keen. Student personnel staffs that are good are usually highly trained, well paid, and possess exceptional morale. Expertise in student affairs does not come by accident; it is a result of a strong program geared to fit people for this work. The role of the student affairs division requires skills and techniques gained by experience and training tailored to the problems of that department. Graduate schools need to revise their programs in student personnel and higher education so that the graduates are ready to assume executive positions.

Institutions and deans of students have been caught off guard too often when their campus erupted because of lack of ability and understanding in the basic needs and objectives of students in higher education.

Student personnel staffs must be organized so that experimentation, research, and professional growth can take place. Lower- and middle-management employees can destroy a potentially powerful program by lack of morale and motivation. Don't let staffs professionally stagnate and be caught in the mire of discontent because of lack of professional reward. The student personnel leaders should be and must be professionals in people-to-people problems. They cannot let their own staffs be torn by personality strife and division. Interest and incentive can be coupled by the opportunities for professional advancement and the furthering of academic growth. Words of encouragement and gratitude should be given frequently to the staff. A dean or vice-president can get so caught up in the triviality of internal and external administrative detail that he fails to see the need to upgrade his staff, say a kind word to them, or clarify the direction in which the student personnel program is going. If the dean of students is not careful, he will develop a staff of frustrated, disenchanted, distressed people who in turn must deal with students possessing similar concerns.

A new office has been created on many university campuses, called *ombudsman*. The role of the ombudsman has taken on new and important dimensions in university life. He is troubleshooter for the university and plays a major role in curbing strife. In the early days after the creation of this office, quite a number of deans of students were opposed to this position; it was a threat to many of them because of their wide powers in student affairs. Some ombudsmen did in fact create more division than harmony. Recent results have proven that the dean of students and the ombudsman can live in harmony and play mutually supportive roles.

Maintaining the titles of dean of women and dean of men is quickly becoming outdated, and such titles should be changed to reflect the alterations in their roles. The new concepts presuppose that it is important for staffs to be resourceful in handling the varied problems that come to them. In the past, deans of men and deans of women were relegated and assigned to the problems of students of their own sex. This is not the approach in advanced student personnel programming. In the new realignment of duties and responsibilities men can deal with women student problems, and vice versa. It has worked out splendidly, and it is an approach that should be followed. Some institutions may still persist stoically in maintaining a dean of men and dean of women with a rationale that serves their purposes. I do not support that position and feel that the concept of those roles is inappropriate for programs that aspire to excellence and relevance.

CAMPUS MINISTRY

The role of the campus ministry is in a state of flux. The spiritual values of a college student are important and cannot be neglected in the pursuit of other developing programs. It is true that the state university cannot get into the business of religion but they can permit campus clergymen to minister in their unique ways to the students. There have been some excellent groups and organizations on the college campus in recent years. Campus Crusade for Christ and Inter-Varsity Christian Fellowship are two vital organizations that have been most effective on college and university campuses. Their approach is very clear—"to meet the spiritual needs of the college students." The groups are well organized, properly supervised, and have a place on campuses today. They are cooperative in their approach to the administration and normally have faculty and administrators participating in their programs. The student personnel worker should be supportive to them because of the transforming results that have taken place through their ministries. How to provide opportunities for the wide and varied denominations and faiths on campus is a tough question.

In response to the spiritual need of students, some institutions have leased land at one dollar a year so that religious organizations could build centers for their students. The Baptists, Methodists, Presbyterians, and Roman Catholics have been most aggressive in this effort. The early institutions of higher learning fostered spiritual values because of their religious moorings, and the institutions of modern society should provide an avenue for exploring spiritual values.

DROPOUTS

Higher education is becoming a right rather than a privilege. In high schools the question is not Are you going to college, but Where are you going to college? The pressure to attend college is growing, and some students are entering institutions of higher education ill-prepared to make the adjustments necessary for satisfactory performance. The results of not being ready can be evidenced by dropouts, low grades, behavior pattern change, and the like. College administrators are concerned about this and are seeking ways to remedy the situation. Yet the dropout rate continues to rise and, as Dr. Hannah states, has developed "into enormous proportions." The reasons for withdrawal take on new importance and demand significant attention from student personnel administrators. Some of the surface reasons for dropouts are quickly evident, but the subsurface causes need to be determined and then solved. Withdrawal may be the proper and appropriate step a student should take, but it should be a step made only after careful discussion. College administrators have permitted many a student to withdraw without an exit interview with the student who is intent on leaving. The dropout phenomenon is not new to student personnel workers, but its importance is of great concern in an age of constant pressure and change. The percentage of dropouts is a dimension that must be dealt with. Dr. Hannah is well qualified to review the implications of the dropouts and report some observations regarding it. His review is thorough, and his observations are most worthy of consideration.

STUDENT SUBCULTURES

Minority groups, and in particular black students, have risen to new heights of concern. Though black students represent only a small percentage of the total student population, their presence, as well as their demands, is being widely felt. Their search for recognition and identity on the college campus has been significant. Their demands for separate living facilities following the struggle for integration is being questioned by the Health, Education, and Welfare Department, and rightly so. Black history classes, black student forums, new black fraternities, black student unions, swahili courses, Soul Week, black student week, Afro-

American studies, black academic journals, new black sororities, and Black Panther organizations are a few outgrowths of the student interests. Many of their requests are not being met, and their frustrations from this have led to major student confrontations and unrest.

There are some things that can be done to lessen tension in black-white relationships. Emanuel T. Newsome, Assistant Dean of Student Life at Indiana State University, and the author investigated one area which we hold to be crucial to easing tension—the Board of Trustees.

George Romney insisted when he became Governor of Michigan that at least one black person be appointed to each university board in the state. His declaration is important because it is indicative of a new trend emerging in higher education. Black people long deprived from the sacred chamber of the decision makers of academia on predominantly white campuses are now being thrust into the centers of control. It is our supposition that every board of trustees across the nation should take note of the Michigan trend and seek to appoint a minimum of one black person on their college and university boards. We surveyed by telephone a number of university trustees and administrators to elicit their reaction to having Negroes on governing boards. Dr. James Miller, President of Western Michigan University, advocated in the interview that "We need blacks in all positions, not just in one area." His words have been translated into action and he now can testify that "at Western Michigan University, blacks are on the Alumni Board of Trustees, the University Board of Trustees, and the Athletic Board of Control."

John Hannah, former President of Michigan State University and former Chairman of the National Commission on Civil Rights, was also interviewed. He reiterated what so many others concluded, that "The deprivation of blacks for over one hundred years has to be made up and therefore blacks should be in decision-making positions." Dr. Hannah affirmed that "It is very important that qualified blacks be on the board of regents or trustees."

Higher education has, however, been one of the excellent avenues for a black person to succeed. The athletic field has escalated many a Negro to great fame and reward. However, the Ford Foundation report has noted sadly that few Negroes go on to complete the doctorate degree. The Foundation's substantial grants may serve as a breakthrough to help alleviate this condition.

The question today is not to just give blacks equal opportunity but to see that equal results are actualized. It is the results that will strengthen or lessen their place in society. Programs have begun and should continue which are designed to eliminate difficulties in the education of black students. This program should dovetail with a total effort to eliminate difference in our populace regardless of skin color. The

American ideal and our democratic philosophy demand that we do no less.

The left-wing Students for a Democratic Society have developed significant power in the past few years. They have created a great deal of difficulty on many college campuses and have gained the attention of university administrators through their dissident action. Students, however, are beginning to make protests in other ways apart from such negative approaches.

> •Six blind students at the University of North Carolina demanded blind professors and Braille textbooks. Although they admitted their protests were made "to take the wind out of the black student movement," they also suggested "blinding everyone so no one would know what's black and what's white." ˙
>
> •A group of students at Queens College, New York, who called themselves Irish Revolutionaries Interested in Scholastic Help (IRISH) issued a series of demands to the college and then took over a campus building used for storage. Their demands included the observance of St. Patrick's Day as a holiday and the establishment of a Gaelic studies program.
>
> •A group of students at the University of Wisconsin at Madison presented a list of demands from the "Homophiles of Madison" requesting the establishment of a homosexual studies department and the institution of "gay" social events.
>
> •A new counterrevolutionary organization has been formed at Wichita State University; the group calls itself SPASM, the Society for the Prevention of Asinine Student Movements.[2]

Counterrevolutionary groups designed to stem the tide of forces geared to disrupt campuses are springing up across the country. Legislators have reacted strongly to the student dissidents (many of whom are out-of-state residents) and have recommended strong measures to deal with them, such as (1) cut nonresidence enrollment, (2) prohibit the universities from recruiting nonresident students except athletes, (3) put legislators and governors on the board of trustees, and (4) eliminate tenure for faculty members and require the dismissal of professors taking part in disruptive demonstrations.[3]

Today, from within and without the academic community, support is being engendered for a tough stand against campus disorders. The student personnel worker must do all he can to gain knowledge of their subcultures and try to understand their aims.

[2] *The Chronicle of Higher Education*, Vol. 3, No. 13 (March 10, 1969), p. 8.
[3] *Ibid.*, p. 1.

VALUES

Are today's students different from those of yesterday? Is the philosophy of the "new morality" being spoken about just "old morality" having greater news coverage. Have young people today lost their sense of dedication and commitment to the nation amidst a tone of criticism and rejection? Are students set on destroying viable institutions such as higher education institutions because of their irrelevancy and lack of response to the needs of society? Are students rebelling against the institutions who seek to maintain the status quo in the age of dynamic change? These are only a few questions one can raise in a period when the values of students are undergoing examination and critical review. Probably at no time in American history have the young people wanted to be more active and participate in the affairs of the world.

Many a business has geared their products to the youth because of tremendous market represented by them. The values perpetuated and internalized by the student will influence society and their numbers are increasing everyday. The college student is in a "see-it-now" age. He no longer waits for information, but can see fashions, war, and sports on "instant replay" and in color. Little can be hidden from his view, and his values will reflect the dynamics and the depression of an accelerating age.

Institutions of higher education must wisely rethink their role, in influencing values of college students. Do students come to college with built-in values too late to modify, and too limited to identify adequately? Or are institutions programming in such a way as to perpetuate a limited value system or a distorted and unrealistic one? Is the mission of higher education to instill new values in students, or to instill new meaning and understanding in the value patterns students bring with them to college? And if so, how does one go about doing that?

What effect do the social activities, the competitive intercollegiate sports, the curriculum, the faculty, the students, the state legislators, the administrators, and the donors have upon the students? Does a TV commercial have more subconscious influence than a history professor? It is safe to say that traditional influences that once affected students may be in the process of tremendous change because of the dynamics of the age in which we live. The Rev. Patrick Ratterman speaks on the issue of values in a most provocative and helpful manner in Chapter 6.

CAMPUS SECURITY

The increase in student population coupled with the student power trend has brought on new dimensions to the area of campus security.

Some campuses have contracted special police agencies to handle their campus security. (Some groups of students have mockingly labeled them "Rent-a-Cop.")

Many campuses have grown to the size of a large city, and such growth has made the campus share the problems of a city. Thefts, drugs, fights, suicides, sexual deviance, and vehicular accidents are some results of the growth phenomenon.

A few years ago campus security was concerned with panty raids. Such raids are of little importance today in view of the devastating and destructive riots that have recently transpired on college campuses. Campus security police must be trained in campus riot control, yet with the knowledge that their presence could be the spark that could ignite a major student disturbance. The tragedy of campus security is that too often universities pay standard or minimum wages to their staffs and thus cannot attract the finest people. A total review of the campus security salary structure is needed. The old adage "You get what you pay for" is not far removed from the truth in this instance.

Universities have often staffed their campus security offices with retired or about-to-retire policemen or officers who moonlight for extra money. The student personnel administrator and the chief of campus security need a continuous and careful communication between their areas. Lack of such is a welcome mat to disaster.

The flow of traffic, the security of buildings, and the protection of life and property are becoming a greater responsibility for the campus police force. Students are questioning the use of guns by the campus police and their concerns have become stronger each day. There is a definite and growing need for campus police on most American college campuses.

The style of response that comes from the campus security during a confrontation is very important. How they act and react may escalate, modify, or calm a student uprising. Student personnel administrators must have a "battle plan" ready, for if they do not they are in trouble. The logistics of what to do and what not to do must be completely understood between the administrator and the police.

Probably no agency is more misunderstood or maligned or in need of a better image than the campus security force. College administrators are obligated to make the necessary changes to obtain the finest campus security program available. Good security costs money, and institutions that try to get by with a minimum wage and a slim staff may find themselves in a far more costly situation in the future.

The student personnel administrator is faced with a penetrating question—What should be the role of the campus police today? How can they be properly oriented to higher education as it differs from that in a normal city? What about the use of weapons? What are the rights of students and how can they be protected? When is force needed? Who should supervise the security program? These are only a few of the important questions in such a strategic area of concern.

JUNIOR COLLEGES

The rapid growth of the junior college system is one of the great hallmarks of education in America. The pace for new junior colleges has been accelerated to meet the demands of an escalating student population. The outgrowth of all of this is bulging student enrollments and the vast need for a program geared to the junior college student. Student personnel administrators are in great demand on the junior college campuses and these administrators must design programs relevant to the student of today. Junior college enrollment varies from an institution with one or two thousand to a large institution with enrollment in the tens of thousands.

Most student personnel administrators are not being trained in the graduate schools to direct the programs as they should be. New and careful studies must be undertaken to discover what type of administrator is needed for the student personnel department on the junior college campus.

Dr. Fawcett and Dr. Campbell present a unique survey of the student personnel administrator at the junior college; the chapter should be reviewed carefully.

FINANCIAL AIDS

It was only a few years ago that a dean of students could assign a staff member part-time to financial aids. That has drastically changed today. A financial aid program is a large and significant adjunct to the student personnel program. Some universities handle millions of dollars in either grants, loans, scholarships, or work-study programs to help students meet their college expenses.

The administration of a financial aid program requires a sophistication unknown in past years. Due to the auditing, accounting, and business techniques required, some programs are now under the supervision of the Business Office. As more students seek college admission and costs continue to rise, so will the financial aid program.

The complications and intricacies of a financial aid program are quite extensive, and college administrations should seek to employ a most capable administrator to supervise its activities. Institutions that place ill-trained people to assume the responsibility of a financial aid program are doing a great disservice to the student, the institution, the public, and higher education. The financial aid program is so important that it merits the wisest administration.

CONGRESSIONAL RESPONSE TO THE COLLEGE CAMPUS

Institutions of higher learning are being faced with critical analyses by the members of Congress. The riots and other college disorders have elicited a responsive chord in Congress, and congressmen are reviewing legislative ways and means to combat the disorders. A number of administrators unaccustomed to congressional review have been appearing before state, senate, or congressional special study committees.

Senator Hatfield, of Oregon, a longtime member of various legislative bodies, and a former college student personnel dean, presents an overview of the result of the 1960's and the challenge of the 1970's. He speaks from a platform of experience as a legislator and educator, and his frequent visits to college campuses have made him cognizant of the issues of higher education.

THE FUTURE

College administrators can look forward to a fascinating and rewarding future. The areas of their concern will be a test for the years ahead. It is most likely that the role of the deans will be drastically changed, possibly to the extent of removing the position entirely.

The rapidly changing technological, scientific, and educational advancements will play a major role in the colleges of the future. Their impact will greatly benefit colleges, and colleges will be more closely related to society than before. Students will be more independent, self-reliant, and more exposed to sophisticated electronic media.

International programs may be replaced with field trips to space—to the moon or planets. The future, however, will still be involved with people, and knowing this colleges can expect people problems no matter how sophisticated mechanically and technologically they become. There will still be the problems of dealing with humans, involving interpersonal and intrapersonal relationships. There will be wider concentrations of populations to create larger complexes of cities so that there will be clustering of campuses involving new and varied dimensions.

To meet the demands of the future, campuses must be (1) innovative, (2) flexible, and (3) experimental. They must not be tied to archaic tradition but geared to change to make their institution, society, and the world a finer place in which to dwell. One of the greatest tasks of the future will be to allow the individuality and self-identity of the student to emerge. If not, institutions will not be a complement but a hindrance to the well-being of society. Student personnel administrators must play a vital part in the long-range planning of an institution so that they will be equal and ready to meet the student populations of the many tomorrows.

Too often institutions are so involved with the everyday activities and in putting the fires out of confrontation that they cannot prepare for the future. Administrators must insist on wise and adequate planning for the 1980's and the 1990's and beyond.

The future is a challenge to young and old, and the college administrator must be ready, willing, and prepared to meet the unknown. In a day when research is so advanced, the answers for tomorrow are not so far away as it may have seemed in years gone by.

The mission of institutions of higher learning is to lead society into the future and not be led by the future.

2

A Nation on the Move

Mark O. Hatfield*

The decade of the sixties began with an ambitious call to get this nation moving again. And we did begin to move. We set a goal of reaching the moon before the decade expired. The Peace Corps was established. Major civil rights legislation was passed by Congress. New programs for aid to the developing nations were initiated. The two superpowers agreed to ban the testing of nuclear weapons. In short, the decade of the sixties began with a surge of vitality and activism.

During those crusading years of vision and optimism, who would have predicted that the decade would end as it now has?

Before this decade began, the late President Eisenhower utilized the National Guard to enforce the order of the federal courts to desegregate the school system. The army went south to support equal rights for the blacks.

And, as the decade ended, it was commonplace for armed forces to be called into our northern cities to quell the rebellious uprisings of black communities. Only a short time ago, the nation's capital was a garrison, torn asunder by violence and hatred that was the expression of racial hostility. That was five years after the triumphant civil rights

*Senator Mark O. Hatfield holds the B.A. from Willamette University in Salem, Oregon, M.A. from Stanford University and has received twenty-seven honorary doctorate degrees. His distinguished and varied background include being Associate Professor of Political Science and Dean of Students at Willamette University as well as a trustee at Willamette and George Fox College. Senator Hatfield is the former Governor of the State of Oregon and presently serves as United States Senator from Oregon. He is author of the book *Not Quite So Simple* as well as many articles of special interest which have appeared in national and international documents.

march on Washington that culminated in the passage of the civil rights bill and predictions of racial harmony and peace in its wake.

At the beginning of the decade of the sixties, idealistic students and liberals migrated south during the summers to purge those areas of their racist social structures. By the middle of the decade, they had returned north, deciding to cleanse their own communities of the effects of racial bigotry. And by the end of the decade, they were finally looking within themselves, recognizing their own need for conversion.

The first President of the decade—a "liberal Democrat"—campaigned on the assertion that our nation was threatened by a "missile gap" and promised steps to insure our military security. As the sixties drew to a close, even retired marine generals warned about the extent of "militarism" in America.

When the decade of the sixties opened, there were about six hundred unknown military technicians in the obscure land of Vietnam. But part of our nation's movement in the early sixties was the creation of counterinsurgency forces—the Green Berets—to quell guerrilla warfare throughout the globe. Their first major test was Vietnam. This was the beginning of an unimaginable involvement of American troops which totaled nearly half a million as the decade came to an end.

Students, generally apathetic during the 1950's, became activistic as the sixties began, and alienated as the sixties ended.

The decade had witnessed more creative programs, government crusades, legislative efforts, and massive appropriations than any previous time in our history. Yet, polarization, unrest, and turmoil have not abated but rather grown far more severe.

Why have we found ourselves in this ironic, frustrating, and threatening condition? Where have all our well-intentioned efforts brought us? How have our benevolent social programs for both our country and the world failed?

Essentially, we have failed in our understanding of man. We have not discovered how to live with ourselves.

Our nation needs more than new programs; we even need more than restructured institutions. Fundamentally, we need revitalized, renewed people.

We have not adequatly understood the nature of our problems. We have looked at only the outward, material aspects of society's ills. But the real issue is the alienation felt by growing numbers of people— alienation from both society's institutions and from themselves. People today are experiencing a profound sense of personal irrelevance; they feel that what they think, say, or do really doesn't matter to anyone and cannot change their situation.

Consider our large urban areas, for instance. It is commonplace to believe that the foremost need of urban areas is massive government programs to provide jobs, education, and housing for the residents. Some even go a step further and claim that restructured institutions—such as decentralized schools—are the necessary and essential actions required to solve the urban plight. The validity and urgent need of such measures is unquestionable.

Yet the real urban crisis is a crisis of human relationships. The most fundamental issue is the deterioration of trust. The greatest need is the restoration of concern, dignity, and hope.

There will never be a final solution to the urban crisis until the attitudes and commitments of individual people are transformed—until both black and white can overcome the indifference and hostility toward each other, and take those steps of risk toward authentic human relationships, establishing bonds of trust and compassion. The confrontation and self-searching inevitably involved will be far more difficult —but far more important—than the most ambitious programs for rebuilding the physical conditions of our urban areas.

There are many other examples of how the solutions to our contemporary problems must involve the change of people's attitudes and values. The dominance of unquestioned military spending in our federal budget is not likely to be curtailed, for instance, until people value the bonds of humanity more than the barriers of ideology. In order to insure a rational use of our natural resources, people must value their relationship to nature as much as their admiration of technology. The point I wish to emphasize is not that government programs have been unimportant or useless; on the contrary, I have long been a supporter of aggressive government action to meet the challenges faced by our society. But I am convinced that the true solutions to our current problems require a far deeper degree of insight—one that will understand the human dimension and recognize the essential importance of changing people.

What is required at this point in history, then, is not new programs so much as new perspectives. We must learn to interpret the events of our day with greater comprehension and deeper wisdom. To begin, we must remold our image of man.

The technological revolution has profoundly affected our view of man. The temptation to judge man according to standardized, quantitative measures has never been greater. The methodology of science and technology convinces us that man, like any other phenomenon, can be objectively studied, analyzed, and measured by empirical scrutiny until he is fully understood and completely predictable. Thus man has become interpreted and understood through those aspects of his existence and can be easily and empirically measured.

But through this process, the passion and inner feelings of man lose their significance. The only things that count are the things that can be counted. Man's material conditions become more important than his personal experience.

Further, when social unrest or turmoil is observed, we then look for material solutions: Blacks in the inner city do not have enough money; impoverished nations of the world must simply increase their gross national product. When pure economic solutions do not pacify unrest, then we resort to the application of concrete force: The rebellious Vietnamese will be quelled by a sufficient number of bombs; turmoil in the cities will be halted by a massive show of strength.

But all the while we have failed to understand the roots of man's passion, the pain of his alienation, the determination of his will, and the searching of his spirit.

We have believed the computer printouts that have continually predicted a quick end to the Vietnam War; we do not understand what motivates the Vietnamese teenagers who stand on rooftops and shoot at our supersonic jets with World War II rifles. We are puzzled when countries like Nigeria and Pakistan—countries which we regarded as models of successful economic growth—are torn apart by internal violence. We are insulted and perplexed by Peru's defiant willingness to rupture harmonious relationships, embarrass us, and even risk the suspension of our benevolent aid.

And in our own society, when material prosperity and technological progress have reached unprecedented heights, we cannot account for the restlessness, the loss of faith, and the emptiness that so many feel; and we are confused by the frantic, exotic search by some for new forms of self-fulfillment and expression.

Some on our college campuses seem to understand best the plight of our time. They had led the call for new values, not just new appropriations. They have challenged the empty promises of hollow political rhetoric with the continuing, unabated realities of human suffering and misery. They have searched for a new life style, for deeper meaning and lasting commitments for their lives. They have rejected our society's hot pursuit of materialism and searched for a higher reality, for a more worthy and self-fulfilling existence. They have recognized the futility and injustice of the senseless war in Southeast Asia, and they have plead against the reliance on military might for the solutions to fundamentally human problems.

But while there is substantial unanimity on our campuses concerning the ills of our present society and the goals to be pursued, there is increasing discord concerning the means to be utilized.

The debates that rage in college residence halls today—arguments about violence and nonviolence, confrontation and negotiation, revolution and evolution, freedom and responsibility—these touch upon the most important questions facing contemporary society. What is more, we are no longer engaged in a merely academic or theoretical consideration of these issues, but are confronted with live realities that compel us to make decisions and commitments.

The major portion of my professional life that has not been devoted to political activity has been spent on the university campus. What the university community is concerned about, I try to be concerned about. Therefore, I want earnestly to share with you my views about the dynamics of change in our universities and in contemporary society.

The revolutionary premise of change is that power will not be given up willingly by those who hold it. Therefore, it must be seized by those who, because of their assured self-righteousness, believe they should possess the power. The corollary, currently popularized by Herbert Marcuse and others, is that whenever one cooperates within present Western "democratic" structures, he is given the illusion of having some influence and voice, but is actually being "pacified." As you might expect, on the whole I reject these premises.

Mahatma Gandhi, who led India's successful nonviolent revolution for independence, said that "the means is the end in the making." I agree.

Violent, anarchistic means to promote change, whether successful or not, will likely result in a violent end.

I am fully aware of those who protest against violence. After all, they charge, the real violence in our land today is being committed by those institutions and people who carry out the war, sustain poverty, and tacitly condone racism. There is substantial truth in these charges. But I do not believe in "an eye for an eye, and a tooth for a tooth."

Those who choose to carry their protest, regardless of its virtue, to the point of aggressive, coercive disruption, and destruction only invite the application of counterforce. In any resort to violence today, the side best equipped and best trained in violence will win, regardless of the relative justice of the issues involved. Further, current polls show that campus disorder is becoming the chief concern of our nation's population. I do not have to state how those of the reactionary right will find it difficult to resist making expedient political gain by exploiting popular feeling on this issue.

It is paramount that students today develop an effective strategy of influence. The danger I fear is that the idealism and vision of students, needed so desperately by our deteriorating society, will be rejected because of a cloak of anarchism and a glamorized faith in romanticized revolutionary myths.

Those who have changed history have known how to unify popular feeling and how to infiltrate society's power structure. The effective means of change in a postindustrial society like ours is such unified force of public conviction combined with the impact of those who can enter into the power structure without selling out of its premises and presuppositions.

The need of this day, then, is for students to speak out in unified protest against society's intolerable injustices and inequities where they exist, and to support political insurgents who will infiltrate all levels of influence and power, setting forth their alternative vision of the future. Students must remain uncompromising about their convictions and ideals. But they must also become flexible and adaptable enough to develop effective tactics that truly promote and do not inhibit the realization of their goals.

Most revolutionaries argue that existing structures and institutions must be abolished so that new life can spring up from the ruins. I must admit that under certain conditions I would concur with that premise. For instance,

The draft should be abolished.
Our paternalistic welfare system should be dismantled.
The Electoral College should be eliminated.
The power of political conventions to nominate Presidential candidates should be abolished.

It is clear that some structures and institutions in society cannot be reformed. After all, you do not reform inequity, you abolish it.

Let me take the draft as an example. Prominent political liberals have advocated draft reform. To me, that is like advocating slavery reform. We are asked to believe that the lottery is an equitable compromise to the present draft law. Let me ask you—what would you think of one who, during the last century, advocated replacing slavery— which was involuntary servitude—with a lottery system? Would that have changed the matter any? Would that have been a step toward justice? As far as the draft is concerned, I am a committed abolitionist. I know that during their time, abolitionists were considered too extreme, too radical; but I believe they were right. Inequity, as I said, must be abolished, not reformed.

The plight of our welfare structure is similar. Despite our well-intended social benevolence, and despite our investment of vast sums of money, our present welfare structure only deepens the dependency, hostility, and resentment of the poor toward their society. We must find new structures and avenues for creatively involving all citizens in the production and benefits of our economic abundance.

It is popularly accepted by almost everyone except many members of Congress that the Electoral College is an archaic, undemocratic institution that has no more right to exist in our modern technological society than the pony express. But I want to go further than even those colleagues of mine who have recommended electoral reform. We are told that the political conventions can be reformed and made truly democratic and responsive. Efforts to that end are being talked about in each party. But I remain dubious. I believe that this structure cannot be adequately reformed. There is no reason why our candidates have to be chosen by political conventions. There are many reasons why they should not be. I believe that it is time to let the people truly choose their candidates for President. Far too long the conventions have been the political brokerage firms and the people have had no controlling interest or certain influence. Let us establish a Direct National Primary Election and grant the people their true democratic voice. There are, of course, questions of political economics which would have to be resolved by such a proposal. But the real question at stake is whether we can afford democracy. Certainly, it seems the measures such as free television time for candidates and tax credits for campaign contributions could make it possible for any candidate, rich or poor, to have an equal opportunity to run for President.

In summary, there are institutions, structures, and policies in our society which we should attempt to abolish rather than reform. But such ends can be only achieved through efforts that exploit the viability of our democratic procedures for reaching decisions.

The politicalization of the nation's youth during the last election was the most encouraging sign of the decade of the sixties. But it must continue into the seventies. For the present there are specific political goals which can be influenced by the concerned involvement of youth. The draft, election change, congressional reform, military spending, the Vietnam War—these are only a few examples of pressing, relevant issues that can be dramatically influenced by student conviction and action.

Students today question whether there is either reason or wisdom in adhering to our democratic process. Their doubts have come because they best know its failures, and their hopes for its fulfillment have been stronger than any. I believe that students feel alienated from our political process not because they fail to believe in democracy, but because they do believe, and have seen it fail to function adequately.

But history has given to this generation the primary responsibility for determining most of our future. Although they feel alienated and victimized by the sixties, they have the opportunity to reshape our nation's life in the seventies.

It is my firm conviction that with the passionate involvement of youth, our structures of political life can be shaken, disturbed, and revitalized sufficiently to establish their greater relevance to people, enhancing human freedom and encouraging social responsibility during the next decade. Without youth, they will fossilize, becoming the obstacle rather than the instrument of change.

The seventies can be marked by creative perspectives and a whole new understanding of our nation's priorities that will result in significant progress toward full justice, restored sanity, and even lasting peace—at home and throughout the world. But the seventies could also be the time when alienation increases, polarization becomes more severe, and the tactics of political repression are perfected.

In this decade it is my hope that students will focus attention on how to change the values held by those in our society, transform the attitudes and views of individual people, and help establish authentic human relationships between the polarized segments of our society. Then institutions can be restructured or created that will truly serve the needs and hopes of people.

During the seventies we can direct our technology toward the service of human need, replace coercive power with meaningful participation, control military force by moral strength, and embrace worthy purposes to give meaning to our lives. If the future is to be open to these possibilities, it will require the commitment of converted persons. Students are the ones who must lead, for they have considered what it means to be human; they place their values in the sacredness of life, and they can discover the depth and roots of man's spirit.

3

The Image of Today's Student

John W. Truitt*

One of the games that Eric Berne left out of his fascinating book Games People Play, is the game that is played whenever I am identified as The Vice-President for Student Affairs. The game goes something like this. "I wouldn't have your job for anything in the world. You are the victim of hostile, youthful, agitating students." I play this game with anyone who can hold me stationary for any given length of time, such as the barber who has me captured in the chair, the waitress who has me glued to my table in the restaurant, even the shoeshine man who begins shining of my shoes. And lo and behold, this game is also played in a less personal way with illustrious educators and other public figures at national and regional conventions. After commiserating with me as the victim, they inevitably get around to their solutions to the ills of the younger generation, especially the college student. I have always noticed that there is a quantitative element about these solutions. The quantitative dimensions run from one answer to approximately ten, and are at times inversely proportional to the degree of sound thinking and thoughtful concern. Today it's *your* turn to become the victim in the

*Dr. John W. Truitt holds the B.S. degree in Social Studies and the M.Ed. degree in Guidance Education from Mississippi State University and the Ed.D. degree in Educational and Personnel Administration from Michigan State University. Dr. Truitt is currently Vice-President for Student Affairs and Professor of Education at Indiana State University. Prior to coming to Indiana State University he was Director of the Men's Division of Student Affairs at Michigan State University. His design of an in-service education program and his organizational manuals have been widely utilized by student affairs staffs across the country. Dr. Truitt is a frequent speaker at national academic organizations and his writings have made significant contributions to student personnel work in higher education.

game that people play regarding solutions to unsolvable problems.

The height of intellectual conceit would be for one to portray himself as an expert on the present breed of college student. In fact, the height of conceit may be further characterized as claiming to be an expert on any phase of the younger generation. The huge numbers of students—each with his own individual life style, aims, inspirations, desires, and hopes for the future—defy sophisticated research, not only on them as individuals but on the many areas of concern that they internalize. Normally when anyone queries me concerning university students, my immediate reply is "Which student are you talking about?" I say this in jest, but also with some reasonable amount of seriousness, simply because this is the age of the individual, and the avenues through which individuality can be expressed have never been more proliferate. Those who deal with students daily know all too well the hazards of posing as experts on college students, and it is with this trepidation that I present to you today some of my views concerning this very complex and overgeneralized topic. The basis of this chapter will be to highlight those areas and views that deal with the sociology of today's breed of college student, and the conflict between his generation and those earlier generations which he considers to be the Establishment. In highlighting these conflicts, I hope to discuss briefly some of the new ethics and moral pressures which are operative in the younger generation. In addition, I hope to describe, rather than analyze, the genesis of the activist student in the university today.

One can hardly pick up a newspaper, educational journal, or national magazine without seeing an article about the younger generation and its attitude toward some phase of American life. The topic of today's college student has been analyzed in innumerable ways, so the problem posed by this task was to develop a style of presentation that would be meaningful to those who deal with college students. It is for this reason that I have chosen to briefly describe some of the issues in the larger society, and the student concerns regarding these issues as they are reflected within the university community. It is the agreement or disagreement with the basic tenets of the systems of society that determines to which group the 1969 breed of college student belongs—those students whose interests and objectives are compatible with the larger society; those students who make up the great body who are quietly disillusioned with the deficiencies in the larger society; those students who support the activists but do not participate themselves; and those activist students who are aggressively opposed to the basic tenets of much of society.

For point of orientation, the context in which we are discussing the present breed of college student should be established. We are talking largely about those students from appromximately 17 to 29 years of age. In 1965, there were 4.2 million students in higher education. It has been predicted by the U.S. Office of Education that by 1975 higher education will enroll 8.5 million students. These figures indicate a doubling of the college population in the ten-year period, 1965–1975.

Every source of information concerning the college student indicates that the vast majority are diligently pursuing a higher education, are conducting themselves in harmony with university regulations, state and national laws, and have committed themselves to the furtherance of a democratic American society. However, it is not these youths who convey the image of today's college student in the news media, in the courts, in much of the political agitation, and in demonstrations on and off campus. The 1969 college student image is portrayed by a minority of students who are disillusioned and discontented with the lack of progress of educational reform and societal change. This chapter concerns itself with these groups in an effort to capture the image of today's college student, but in this effort we do not mean to insist that all college students follow these styles.

POLITICAL

The National Scene

I think it is safe to say that most college students feel that vote disenfranchisement is a legitimate problem. This feeling is manifested by the eighteen-year-old vote issue and is based upon many factors; but the most often heard is that if young people are old enough to fight, they are old enough to vote. Young people resent what they consider the self-serving interests of the political system. Once a politician is "in," he can keep himself "in" by means of the patronage system and other existing means. This and other factors lead young people to feel that there is something basically dishonest about the political system of this country. They feel that many political figures achieve success not because of their own attributes but because of "deals" they make which are compromises in principles. The younger generation views these as deficiencies in the moral fiber of the older establishment. The feeling prevails among the younger generation that the majority in political power has too great a control over those with opposition political views. The establishment itself is really not flexible in its perceptivity to the views of the minority, as set forth in the ideal form of a republic democracy. They point as examples to the fate of the political figures who are the spokesmen for the younger generation.

Young people's alliance with reform, especially reform which is in violation of the concept of law and order, and the older generation's revering of law and order more than they revere reform, are in severe conflict. Examples can be seen in Mayor Lindsay's initial defeat in the primary by a law-and-order candidate, in the defeat of a Negro candidate in Los Angeles in a law-and-order campaign, and in the victory of a former Minneapolis detective as mayor on a law-and-order ticket. These and other examples indicate that the pendulum is swinging back and the older generation is exercising extreme control over the political system to reinforce their concept of law and order.

The younger generation resents the fact that the older generation can commit the younger even to death (the Vietnam War) without the younger generation having much to say about the basic political system that makes the decision about the Vietnam War, etc. This has led to great soul searching on the part of college students, resulting in a variety of individual and group expressions of their allegiance to their conscience or to the national cause.

The University Scene

Since about 1960 universities in this country have been attacked both verbally and physically by students who are members of organizations possessing a political philosophy known as the New Left. Much of this agitation is related to the civil rights movement, and enthusiasm was further engendered by the emphasis on youth by John F. Kennedy, Robert Kennedy, and Eugene McCarthy—when this type of idealism was attached to the national political system. Since about 1960 great criticism has been generated regarding the political posture of the federal government, society in general, and the authority symbols within the university community.

Often within a university the same group of students will be the driving force behind more than one radical organization; but the most prevalent of all New Left national student groups is the Students for a Democratic Society. This group has received the most nationwide attention and has been labeled as the instigator of revolts at many universities. The Students for a Democratic Society have been able to organize and recruit critics of both the university and society to express disenchantment, and have been opportunistic in taking advantage of general student unrest to glean credit for much agitation that they did not initially promote. While they cannot agree upon a substitute model for campus or noncampus societal structure, they have successfully adapted the techniques which prove so successful for the blacks in fighting the laws and customs which they believe are discriminatory.

Many of the New Left organizations do not associate with and express contempt for student governments who try to work through organized channels for the betterment of the university. At those institutions where the student government is strong and is able to affect programs that give the average student a sense of participation in university affairs, the New Left organizations have been limited to nonuniversity issues.

SOCIAL

The National Scene

In spite of the American dream and the excellent examples of upward social mobility, the chances of anyone moving from more than one social class in his lifetime are severely limited. In years past there were a number of avenues of upward mobility. Railroad fortunes, explorations for oil by wildcat companies, emergence from the working class as union leaders with salaries of $125,000 and up—these avenues are pretty much dissipated. There is still the avenue in which the professional athlete can move from a low socioeconomic background and gain a wide reputation and great financial reward for physical feats. There are a few avenues open in the scientific and technical world through means of education; but by and large the day of the rugged individualist is about over. This the youth of America credit to the adult generation in the sense that everyone but the poor wishes to preserve their own status and believes that any great mobility of the social classes infringes on the older generation's status quo.

While the avenues of upward mobility have lessened in recent years, the avenues of lateral mobility from a socioeconomic standpoint have increased. This results in both opportunity and frustration. Opportunity is manifested in the chance for gainful employment and professional advancement outside of one's own community or in many different parts of the country, as when the university graduate does not return to his community but seeks opportunity elsewhere. The disadvantage of frustration is apparent in the large groups of individuals who, seeing no hope for upward mobility and a share in the better things of life, use lateral mobility to congregate in areas which serves only to highlight their common ills. The black ghettos in the northern cities have become a refuge for millions of black Americans—many of them from southern regions of the United States. Their chances in these areas for gainful employment and for increased education turn out to be no more than they were in their previous localities. It is these kinds of social problems which cause the present-day young person to say that the American dream is really a façade which creates the relationship between many affluent white groups—who are highly critical of the present social system—and the minority groups, who are the victims of this social system. It is along that relationship between the affluent white groups and the nonaffluent minority groups that much hostility toward the present social system erupts.

The whole problem of minority groups in the context of the general society and upward mobility is one that has caused great repercussions in the last fifteen years—in fact, has done so periodically since the beginning of American society. The present plights of the Afro-American or American Negro, Mexican-American, Chinese-American, Puerto Rican, Indian and Eskimo are all great social problems that our present society has not been able to deal with effectively. The younger generation does not understand why, with our great capacity to put men on the moon and to perform miracles in practically every area of life, the adult society is so unconcerned or inept in the problems of so-called underprivileged and minority groups.

It is not news to say that a conflict of generations exists even within the minority groups. This conflict is most prevalent in the largest minority group in America—the American Negro. The goals of the older generation of blacks are based on an integrated society where the black man achieves advancement based on his talent and ability and not on the basis of race. This is in opposition to many of the young blacks who are engaged heatedly in separatist movements. Many of the younger generation of Afro-Americans are faced with the great dilemma of deciding their own course of action along the continuum from the Martin Luther King concept of love to the Malcolm X concept of a separate state for the black American.

The University Scene

A review of the black power movement in the universities indicates that the black students have demonstrated great hostility toward the symbols of authority, discrimination, and racial bias. Hostilities which have built up over a period of time, as a result of prejudice in the greater society, have been transferred into the universities. In those instances where physical violence and destruction of property by black students have occurred, the goal inevitably has been the destruction of things they feel are the authority symbols of a built-in system of prejudice.

The black students come to the campus expecting to see some of the most learned people in the world. They express the view that if the leaders of the intellectual world do not understand them and their problems, then certainly they cannot expect to have a chance in society. They feel frustrated and lost when the hopes and expectations they had about the university as an answer to their problems come crashing down upon them. Their hopes are high and the performance of the university falls far short of their expectations. This involves frustration; frustration leads to hostility; and hostility leads, many times, to a "striking out" which may take the form of disruptive actions.

EDUCATION

The National Scene

One of the things that is perplexing to the younger generation is the fact that the same educational system is expected to produce the men who make peace and the men who wage war, and the weapons and materials with which that war is waged.

The younger generation feels that the older generation, through education, has the means to find effective solutions to some of the world's great problems. The present-day multiplicity of information has made the gap between information and knowledge ever greater. Each individual today probably knows proportionately less of the amount of information available than he did a hundred years ago. The problems resulting when man is called upon to make decisions out of this greater and more confused data only serve to alienate young people.

Young people have a conflict with the older generation about the goals of education. This grows out of a concept of education as a goal for all people—as compared with the process of education which lasts a lifetime. As expressed by the older generation, the basic point in this disagreement is "a sense of time" which youthful intellectuals often do not possess. A university degree is only a starting point and not the realization of a dream in itself. While the completion of four years of college may, to many young people, be the realization of a dream in itself, it is in reality that point in time when his productive role in society commences.

The University Scene

A major conflict existing at most institutions can best be described as the conflict regarding the role of the university in providing proper guidance and control of students, and at the same time maintaining an atmosphere conducive to their freedom to learn and experiment in the process of growing toward full maturity. The areas of conflict then are those rules, regulations, and policies which the university deems necessary for proper exercise of its responsibility and that the students insist is their private life.

The philosophy conflict is characterized by three groups of students. One group is concerned with increased involvement in the governance of the institution. This means that these students desire and expect to have greater authority in the affairs of the university—not only to serve on the committees which deal with student affairs, but also to have a role in policy-making decisions of faculty committees, the Faculty Senate, and the Board of Trustees. The object used to achieve these goals is student power. This phenomenon has been directed at increased attempts to secure additional student rights. The tactic is one of confrontation of the established authorities. The goal is participation in the policy making at every level in the university.

This increased desire to have greater participation in the affairs of the university is coupled with the desire of a second group to shorten the range of concern between the student and the university. This concept indicates that the university should shorten the range of concern which it has for students, and that the university should neither provide nor expect anything from students outside this agreed-upon range of concern. Many persons indicate that this range should cover only the academic areas, while others indicate that the dividing point is the on-campus–off-campus line. This group of students wants less, not more, involvement with the university. Their goal is student rights and freedoms.

The third and by far the largest group of students believes in the constructive concept of student power and seeks representation on committees, especially in the academic area. They expect university officials to take their opinions seriously, because they are deeply concerned by the irrelevance of education to the present-day world. They feel that the curriculum is oriented to internal systems of academic and not to the realities of the later part of the twentieth or the first part of the twenty-first century. This group seeks constructive educational reform. Their goal is a meaningful education. There is every indication that this is an area where the great pressure will be applied by students in the future.

One of the major conflicts between various segments of the younger generation itself evolves around change and the concept of change. Most young people agree that change is necessary, and most intelligent people would indicate that changes are taking place in every arena of American life. There is very little difference of opinion regarding this concept of change itself, but there is a great difference of opinion regarding a desirable rate of change. A small group of active and verbal youth, supported by an even larger group of nonactive and nonverbal youth, seek change at a revolutionary rate. The vast majority of youth, however, although they want change and reform of the educational and other societal systems, would change at a rate that does not affect their stability and point of orientation at any given time. Persons in power are then put in a position of refereeing this rate-of-change controversy, and in many instances the demands of a small group of vocal and active youth are institutionalized and made binding on the vast majority of people everywhere, and thereby mass havoc is created.

Education is an agent for change, and at the same time is an agent of preserving the reflections of the past as well as projections for the future. The clarity of the future of education is determined greatly by the historical, developmental processes of its own history. Education as a process is unique in society and its existence depends directly upon the concept of "freedom of inquiry." While the preservation of this concept necessarily demands a "cloistered" atmosphere, free from the political influences of society, the educational system nevertheless is a product and an integral part of society. The great conflict arises from the dualism between education operating as the leadership bulwark of societal reforms or responding to the goals of a society which operates at an adulterating rather that at the ideal level which most young people envision. Many students are critical of this because they do not have the benefit of a sense of history but make judgments at a given point in time with their own set of evaluative standards. One of the contributions that students do make to education is the induction of originality and fresh ideas. Students become quite frustrated when these become part of the ongoing process and the fruits of their contributions are not visible until long after they leave the institution. The university students normally want instant response and instant remedies to result from their solutions to many of education's or society's great problems.

The concept of fairness is probably one of the greatest challenges with which college students have to deal. While they desire it for all people, they have a hard time defining it in reality. Basic to this concept is *due process*—the term used to describe the method of adjudication of students who create conduct situations. Students have a great ambiguity regarding the term due process, the basis of which comes from civil law and not university authorities.

The courts, through the last seventy-five years, have ruled that students enter into an agreement with the university at the time of their enrollment. The university has the authority to insist that students abide by university regulations and take prescribed courses necessary for a degree in their chosen field. The university can also expect students to abide by the regulations that relate specifically to the behavior standards that concern their roles as students. This is called the *contract theory,* and is accepted by courts as the universities' inherent authority to make regulations and enforce these regulations by disciplining students. Courts have ruled repeatedly that this concept is a valid one. In fact, no court has ever ruled otherwise. Therefore, the power of the institution to discipline students is a separate concept from the right of the students to have fair hearings before final disciplinary action is taken. The courts have ruled that all students *should* have a fair hearing before disciplinary action can be taken.

Disagreement still exists regarding the criteria which constitute a fair hearing and the differences between a fair hearing for students and a legal hearing in a civil court.

Several recent court cases have addressed themselves to this topic, but the most thorough analysis was presented by the United States District Court for the Western District of Missouri, September 19, 1968. The court *en banc* issued a "General Order on Judicial Standards of Procedure." The order clearly indicates the differences, and the rationale for the diffrences, between university disciplinary due process and civil court hearing procedures.

ECONOMICS

The National Scene

One of the major conflicts between the younger and older generations is reflected in the high priority that the younger puts on human qualities and the high priority that the older generation places on material wealth. The young do not understand the older generation's preoccupation with material gain as the measure of success when social ills are evident in every city and state in the nation.

Many youth firmly believe that business is a "dirty game" and very few honest businessmen become successful. Students of 1969 many times resent the fact that the rules of the business establishment leave very little room for originality and creativity. They feel they must "toe the line" or not achieve within the company. They feel that promotion and financial benefits are derived from being an establishment clog in an establishment system.

The concept of big business, big government—in fact, big bureaucracy—has turned many students off with relation to the economic system of American society. They indicate their concerns about the industrial-military complex, which they feel is prolonging the war and diverting monies from domestic programs which badly need it, and the industrial-educational complex, in which the university contracts research for industry to produce war materials. It is not an unusual comment to be heard from a number of undergraduate and graduate students in the liberal arts and other related areas that the major cause of the trouble in this country is big business. They believe that the federal government has become a party to the merging of industries which has resulted in the furtherance of monopolistic trends of allowing holding corporations to own an array of complexes of industries. They feel very strongly that the bureaucracy of government with its ineffi- ciency, permits these mergers which create unfair competition for their smaller competitors.

The younger generation feels that the economic system of America is a frontal challenge to the individual rights of man and is also aloof to the ideals of compassion, concern, and human dignity.

The University Scene

The question of who should go to college and for what reasons is not only a social question but basically an economic one. The point has been raised by many groups that each person is an economic unit of society. He is either a contributing or a noncontributing member, in which case others shoulder his share of the burden by providing for him. The last twenty-five years have seen a large increase in the number of students enrolled in institutions of higher education who in other times could not. This influx has resulted in large, expensive universities where the cost is becoming increasingly prohibitive for students and their parents. This has brought about a crisis in many areas of private education and has caused the taxpayer to take a careful look at the rising cost of public higher education. Efforts by the federal government as well as most state governments to make higher education a possibility for everyone with ability have fallen far short of what is needed.

While college students have not always found favor with many of the systems of society, students realize that education and especially higher education is a necessary prerequisite for the future. Students feel the economic priorities of business are reversed, and that more concern should be shown for developing people and providing services than putting all their resources into material goods.

The economic facts of life are that in a land where the gross national product is almost a trillion dollars, millions of Americans cannot attend college for economic reasons.

RELIGION

The National Scene

The student generation views most of the organized institutions of religion as not being relevant to today's society. The organized church as a whole for too long was so busy defending God and the Church against attacks on the Scripture and against the proponents of the the- ory of evolution that it was unaware of events taking place around it. Ghettos were growing, the number of divorces and broken homes were increasing, the crime rate was accelerating, and poverty was more widespread than ever. When the Church began to become aware of conditions, its first concentrated effort was apparent in civil rights. Young people are watching carefully now to see if organized religion is capable of the kinds of social action which the younger generation feels imperative.

Most young people do not reject God but do reject the caricatures of God they see portrayed through human lives, particularly in the adult generation. They see God through people, and they see the hypocrisies which are purported to represent God through people.

One group of the younger generation, this generation which *is* more sophisticated than any who have preceded it, questions man-made rules and regulations as presented by organized religion. They see too often religion becoming a restricting, guilt-producing crutch to young people, even to the extent that psychiatric assistance is needed to enable them to stand on their own feet.

The University Scene

One of the most striking characteristics of the college student is the sophistication with which he portrays his carefree and open attitudes about many of the spiritual issues that might concern him. The contradiction of this open attitude, this particular style, is the great amount of traffic in counseling centers, psychiatric clinics and student health services all across the United States. It has been estimated by experts that approximately 10 percent of the college population could profit effectively from psychiatric service. Counselors, psychiatrists, and psychologists indicate that the genesis of the greater share of these problems is in students' deep-seated spiritual-value syndromes. In a survey completed by the Rober Research Associates in May 1969, in-depth interviews were conducted with a large sample of students across the United States regarding their beliefs in God, organized religion, church attendance, and several other issues of a relative nature. The study found that a majority of those surveyed believe in God, and a majority indicated that they attended church regularly or occasionally. It was concluded by this study, however, that organized religion fared less well than God. While a majority saw religion as an important part of their lives, many of the students indicated that organized religion had not been keeping up with the times until recently. The study indicated that 39 percent of those interviewed who classify themselves as antiestablishmentarian believe in God, either as a supreme being or as a governing force. And 49 percent of those students who were very active in student political activities still clung to a substantial religious belief. Forty-two percent of the antiestablishmentarian's thought that organized religion has already become, or is beginning to become, a dynamic force in the modern world.

A number of paradoxes exist in the ethics of college students and in the moral pressures that result from these ethics. One of these is situational ethics. When students are thrown into new experiences, especially in those areas where they have to make decisions based on the circumstances or conditions that confront them, there is a conflict between their circumstances as they see them and the overriding authority or value system governing such actions. This conflict poses a critical problem to many. Many students argue that decisions should be reached in terms of what is best for an individual whether or not the university regulation, public law or moral law is an overriding contradicting principle.

Students have great concern for fairness for other students; yet they will tolerate academic dishonesty of a wide variety and type. The "cheat-to-compete" philosophy is accepted by many students who at the same time are greatly intolerant of dishonesty among business executives and ridicule people who violate public trust in political positions. Students feel that if they have to make the choice between being true to their friends or being true to any institution, they would betray the institution rather than their friends.

Students are more open regarding their sex roles as males and females, and this has led to the general assumption that more sexual promiscuity exists among today's college students than in other generations. This is not borne out by reliable data. There is a feeling among some university students that the only valid moral decisions are self-made decisions in which they reject all authority and base their decision on the situation and their own desires.

SUMMARY

Meanwhile back at Computerville U., the students have some problems, concerns, and doubts which all generations encounter. Regardless of how involved students become in the great issues of society or educational reform, or how many idealistic worlds they are going to conquer, they are active members in the maturity span between adolescence and adulthood. Students have a natural and inexhaustible desire to achieve personal status, prestige, sense of belonging, and a sense of being needed. One of the basic tasks of all students is striving towards self-identity, self-assurance, self-insight, and self-esteem, and one of the major roles of the university is to assist students in achieving a sense of identity in this manner. This is the only way they will be able to express their own values and achieve perceptive relationships with others. The transformation is not a sudden one and many persons cannot make this transition without firm support at given times from those who care for and respect them most.

Dana L. Farnsworth, M.D., Director of University Health Services at Harvard University, in a paper presented to the Jesuit Educational Association Workshop in Denver, Colorado, in July 1965, identified seven unfinished developmental tasks of college-age students: (1) changing from relations of dependence upon one's parents and older people to those of independence; (2) dealing with authority; (3) learning to deal with uncertainty and ambiguity, particularly in matters involving the balance between love and hate; (4) developing a mature sexuality; (5) finding security and developing feelings of competence and obtaining prestige or esteem; (6) developing standards and values; and (7) obtaining essential knowledge of delicate and complex matters. If these are not achieved at the same time that students are achieving academic success, they make decisions about themselves based on inadequate knowledge and are forced to project their future into a world where they have had little or no experience.

The diversification of goals of the college student is almost unlimited; but one thing can be said of these goals. Because of the present level of prosperity, their goals differ markedly from the goals of other generations. The goals of this generation are more idealistic than any preceding generation. Today's student is not pushing the panic button with regard to the American society, but is sending up signals that necessary changes should receive first priority.

4

University Posture and
Student Protest—
The Second Round

John W. Truitt*

INTRODUCTION

One problem that has characterized the concerns of institutions of higher education in dealing with potential student protest is that the students who originate a protest have the initiative, so that a university's first action is always a reaction. This was especially true in the years following the student upheavals at the University of California at Berkeley in 1964. Many university officials indicated that there was something different about institutions such as the University of California, and upheavals of this type would not occur at their institution. This assumption has been dispelled by the widespread student unrest in practically all institutions of higher education. It is true that the larger and more prestigious institutions get a great deal of publicity but the potential for student unrest is evident on any campus. A careful study of the methods that have been used in an effort to preserve the ongoing operation of several institutions where confrontation and later disruptive action have taken place indicate that other institutions of higher

*Dr. John W. Truitt holds the B.S. degree in Social Studies and the M.Ed. degree in Guidance Education from Mississippi State University and the Ed.D. degree in Educational and Personnel Administration from Michigan State University. Dr. Truitt is currently Vice-President for Student Affairs and Professor of Education at Indiana State University. Prior to coming to Indiana State University he was Director of the Men's Division of Student Affairs at Michigan State University. His design of an in-service education program and his organizational manuals have been widely utilized by student affairs staffs across the country. Dr. Truitt is a frequent speaker at national academic organizations and his writings have made significant contributions to student personnel work in higher education.

education could profit from the trial-and-error methods used in these first years of student disruption. The lessons learned are in many areas: (1) the lack of policies which clearly state the agreed-upon relationship of students, faculty, and administrators within the university; (2) the techniques for dialogue prior to confrontations; (3) the use of campus police; (4) the bringing onto the campus additional police support; and (5) the legal basis for some of the actions of students as well as the university, which can now be more clearly identified after numerous court cases which resulted from these earlier disruptions.

The purpose of this chapter is to discuss (1) the posture of the university as it relates to the division of labor and cooperation within the university, (2) the points of stress that lead to confrontation which can arise in almost any institution, (3) some of the methods that have been utilized in dealing with the confrontations, (4) the legal methods utilized in dealing with individuals who create disruptive action, (5) the methods of adjudication of individuals who are identified in disruptive action, and (6) a brief description of the concept of due process as it has been defined by civil law.

UNIVERSITY POSTURE

At any given time in the history of higher education, the activities within the university usually express the stress and strain of the times outside the university and today is no exception. The silent young generations of the fifties are now the turbulent young generations of the sixties and every indication is that this will continue to be the case well into the seventies. A number of changes have begun to take place within the university to bring about honest open discussion of those issues which might otherwise generate emotional and irrational behavior. Because of the transitory nature of students, the basic role of students, faculty, and administrators should be defined so that the responsibilities and obligations can be understood in reaching a consensus on any given issue. This basis for cooperation and coordination among and between these three should have built-in consideration for the responsiblity of each group.

It is only from this common basis that agreement can be reached which will reflect the joint efforts of all concerned about the nature of the process of education necessary for the university to fulfill its purposes. A basic example of the kind of common understanding needed is found in the concept of peaceful dissent through freedom of expression within the university community. As an example of such cooperation, one state institution in the Midwest has arrived at the following policy after considerable discussion and dialogue by several divergent groups. The policy was drafted and refined by a committee of students, faculty, and administrators, and was adopted by the Faculty Senate, the Student Government Association, and approved by the university Board of Trustees.

POLICIES GUARANTEEING THE RIGHT OF EXPRESSION OF STUDENTS

The University believes that the right of expression is as necessary as the right of inquiry and that both must be preserved as essential to the pursuit and dissemination of knowledge and truth. Consequently, students, individually and collectively, may express their views through the normal faculty, administrative, and student channels of communication. Students also may express their views by demonstrating peacefully for concepts they wish to make known, and the University will make every reasonable effort to protect that right.

The University also has an equal and simultaneous obligation to protect the rights and freedoms of students who do not choose to participate in a demonstration. Similarly, the University is obliged to protect its property and to prohibit interference with scheduled activities of students, University personnel, and guests on the campus.

[The University] is aware of the need for forbearance on its part in tolerance of peaceful demonstrations, protests or other expressions of student attitudes. The University recognizes the fact that expression of opinion through demonstration or protest may, on occasion, lead to inconvenience and interruption of University activities or functions; therefore orderly and peaceful demonstrations are not forbidden unless they disrupt, as later defined in this policy, University functions or activities. The University has an obligation to assure the safety of individuals, the protection of property, and the continuity of the educational process. The object of this statement is, therefore, to provide through explicit reasonable limitations on expression a context in which expression may be protected and in which violent actions are avoided.

In order to meet all of the above obligations, the actions listed below are defined as exceeding the limits of appropriate expression or peaceful demonstration and are in violation of University policy for individuals or groups:

1. Actions which endanger the safety and well-being of individuals.
2. Actions which destroy property.
3. Actions which disrupt, by physical or auditory means, the ongoing operations of the University or interfere with the rights of other individuals in their exercise of expression. (This is designed to protect administrative, faculty, and student functions such as classes, libraries, public and private meetings, health services, recreational activities, and on-campus recruitment. See also regulations regarding facilities priorities.)

Individuals holding views hostile to those presented by persons participating in a peaceful demonstration, protest or other expression of student attitudes are subject to the same policies.

The initial judgment of the permissible limits of student expression should be made by the faculty member, administrator, or other University representative in charge of a specific University facility or function. Any member of the University community who believes the permissible limits of student expression have been exceeded may lodge a complaint to the University official in charge of the specific facility or function. If after observation of the situation, the person in charge of a facility or function determines that said situation is no longer peaceful and orderly, he should:

1. request, not direct, the students to desist from the activities causing the disturbance and allow a reasonable amount of time for such action to occur. In the event of the failure of his efforts at persuasion, he should inform the Office of Safety and Security of the nature of the disturbance and remain on the scene, except for extreme duress, until the arrival of the Security police.
2. elect when he believes personal safety or well-being will be endangered by direct involvement with the demonstrators to inform immediately the Office of Safety and Security or the Office of Student Affairs.

Adjudication

1. Violations of these limitations subject students to due process disciplinary action by the University.
2. University disciplinary sanctions for students found guilty of disrupting legitimate University functions may range in severity from admonition to permanent expulsion.
3. Students involved in disruptive behavior will have their alleged offenses adjudicated in the same manner as those of students involved in other violations of University policy. This includes appeal or referral to the Student Conduct Hearing Committee.
4. Any charges by the University for violation of this policy must be made within thirty days after the alleged violation.

This type of policy is necessary because it defines the rights of individual students in terms of peaceful dissent, and at the same time defines disruptive actions which infringe on the rights of others in the university community. It is extremely important that there be some common understanding of the demarcation between these extremely subtle and difficult concepts.

The freedom of expression and student power concepts for a period of time obscured the necessity for another general university policy which is vital and is a type of policy that has been adopted by many institutions. This policy relates to the use of university facilities and the purpose for which they can be utilized. A number of universities have policies that deal with space utilization, assignment of offices and classrooms, and activities scheduling for use of students, but these policies were not designed to cover the broad based situations of illegal utilization of university buildings and facilities. An example of this type policy was adopted after considerable dialogue and discussion among students, faculty, and administrators.

POLICIES REGARDING THE PRIORITIES FOR USE OF
UNIVERSITY BUILDINGS AND FACILITIES

I. Policies Regarding the Use of University Buildings and Facilities. Every faculty group and every officially recognized student organization has the right to the use of University facilities on a space-available basis for the purpose of holding meetings or conducting activities consistent with the objectives of that organization. Use of any facility is determined by the President or University officials designated by him according to the following priorities.

A. *Permanent Academic and Office Space.* Department chairman will submit requests for special needs of a permanent nature, such as space for faculty offices, research, and instructional laboratories, to the University Space Committee. Priorities will be assigned in accordance with the amount of space available. The department chairman to whom specific areas are assigned will then assume jurisdiction over these areas.

B. *Student Activities Space.* Student Activities space of a general nature is available in the (union, university lodge, and convention center). Space for social events, such as dances, movies, organizational meetings, and other such activities will be reserved through the director of the particular activity involved.

C. *General Instructional Space.*
   1. General classroom areas in the academic buildings, including the auditoriums in X Hall and X Hall, are not assigned to any specific academic department. These areas are under the jurisdiction of the Registrar's Office for assignment of regularly scheduled classes and are available for meetings and study purposes only on a temporary basis.
   2. General instructional space other than classrooms, such as tennis courts, athletic fields, the (recreation center), and library study rooms, may be requisitioned for use by making application to the specific department to which the desired space has been assigned.

D. *General Buildings and Grounds Space.*
   1. Every person with legitimate business at the University has the privilege of free access to the public areas of the buildings and grounds during those hours when they are open, such hours to be determined by the President or a University official designated by him. These areas are defined to include sidewalks, closed streets, entrances to buildings, corridors in classrooms and office buildings, library reading rooms, and common areas in the residence halls and the Union.
   2. The President or a University official designated by him may deny this privilege of free access to an individual or group which disrupts the normal operation of the University.

II. Right of Usage.
Use of space for purposes other than those for which it has been designated will not be allowed. Neither will individuals or groups

be permitted to interrupt the use of space after it has been duly assigned, without permission of the President or a University official designated by him.

This general university policy is a companion policy to the freedom of expression because they both relate to the same goal, although they are designed to cover two separate areas. The common goal of both policies is to keep the university open and operating for the purposes for which it was founded, and at the same time to protect the rights of individuals who wish to peacefully protest any of its activities, programs, and methods of operation. The above policy was also drafted by a committee of students, faculty, and administrators, and adopted by the Faculty Senate, Student Government Association, and approved by the University Board of Trustees.

The matter of posture within the university community also involves the philosophy of student participation in the governance of the university, because this issue will largely determine the scope and the degree of the concept of student power. There is great variance from institution to institution regarding the degree of student participation in the affairs of the university. This changes from year to year, and the following concepts may be helpful in determining the criteria on which an official university posture may be stabilized.

1. Should students be involved in the governance of the institution because personal involvement could possibly provide the best possible type of communication?
2. Can students contribute fresh ideas to both the administrative and the academic processes of university endeavors?
3. Should students be given the experience of experimenting on the university campus with some of the great issues which still need solution in the larger society?
4. Should students expect to be accepted as junior colleagues in the academic endeavor?
5. Should students seek shared responsibility and authority in the administrative affairs of the university up to and including presence at boards of trustees' meetings?
6. Do students support more actively those university affairs in which they participate in formulating?
7. Does the involvement of students at multilevels academically and administratively tend to provide for constructive methods of change and lessen the possibility of illegitimate student leadership?
8. Does student involvement provide students with a better understanding of the complex and difficult problems the university faces?

This is not an inclusive list of the concepts that one could utilize in arriving at a definite philosophy of student participation, but the point should be reiterated that this decision is basic before a number of other decisions can be made regarding the posture and style of operation within the university.

ANTICIPATION AND PREVENTION OF CONFRONTATIONS

There is every indication that institutions of higher education which do not maintain constant communication with students can expect misunderstandings and rumors on emotional issues to surface frequently. While good communication does not always alleviate confrontations and protests over issues within the university, it does provide for a basis of understanding, especially with proponents of points of view which may develop into pressure points of confrontation. Regularly scheduled dialogues with students and others about the problems of stress and unrest on campuses should prove helpful. One of the major objectives of widespread and constant communication and dialogue is to prevent the hard core of any student dissident group from dealing directly and unilaterally with administration or faculty for their own purposes and not for those of the student body in general.

It is virtually impossible to deal with points of stress unless they are fully identified. This identification should occur before the confrontation has polarized itself into unalterable positions. The tensions of these issues are often submerged like icebergs—very little of the real issues are identifiable unless one is in constant communication with the dynamics of campus life. The identification and analysis of these pressure points by administration, faculty, and students are essential in determining the course of action that will lead to possible solutions or conciliations.

In addition to the normal administrative, student, and faculty relationships that grow out of daily activities, a number of other methods can be used in trying to promote better understanding and communication. These must be tailored to circumstances within a particular university, but three general methods are available to any institution.

The first method is the involvement of students in the decision-making machinery of the institution. There are two basic points that would assist in the clarification of this method of communication. One is the responsibility of involvement. This indicates that students should have a chance to be involved at all levels of the basic decision-making machinery of the institution. To achieve this stance, the methods and channels of communication in which they may have their ideas discussed should be clear to students. The second point relates to the responsibility for outcomes. In this area, because of the nature of the decision-making process, the students usually have less influence in final outcomes than in the input areas. Responsibility is delegated by the trustees to administrators, to faculties through Faculty Constitutions, and to students through Student Government Constitutions. But the transitory nature of students dictates that the responsiblity for outcomes tends to be more heavily weighted in faculty, administrators, and then students.

The second method employed by many universities to affect better communication, especially the kind of communication that relates to grievances regarding issues within the university, is the human relations committee or the ombudsman concept. The nature and scope of the jurisdiction of this committee or person is usually defined as listening to and investigating the complaints of students and other members of the university community. In most situations avenues of compromise and conciliation are utilized; but if this is unsuccessful, action is instituted in an effort to resolve the conflict. There are approximately fifty persons with the title of ombudsman in universities in the United States at this time, and the number is still increasing; and there are even larger numbers of human relations committees. The ombudsman concept, and the human relations committees provide impartial offices where students and others may seek recourse for what they feel are injustices when all other channels have been exhausted.

The third method of communication is described as the feedback system accompanied by an in-service education program for university staff regarding potential pressure points. The basic principle involved in this is anticipation and prevention by dealing with the sources of the possible confrontations rather than waiting until the difficulty is at a hostile point. The system usually begins with staff meetings with specific discussions on the pressure points anticipated for the following year, based upon the experience of the past year together with the tone and the information received from state and national conventions and other sources. Once a list of possible points of confrontation has been identified, the most pressing sources of conflicts are assigned to a research team involving staff members, and in some cases, faculty and students. The issues underlying these conflicts are explored, in-depth papers prepared, and these papers discussed in staff seminars. Finally the papers are distributed to all members of the staff to be used as a basis for discussion and dialogue between and among individual student leaders and groups of students about issues involved. In this manner the responsibility is directed toward the total staff because everyone has a role in preventing potential campus protest regardless of where the protest occurs. Constant reevaluation of these pressure points should be made to reflect student concern because the dynamics of campus life are constantly in a state of change.

The exact methods of coping with student unrest are impossible to delineate even when specific details of a situation are known. It should be emphasized that many aspects of student unrest have no solution that can possibly satisfy persons who hold extreme views on either side of any particular issue. Regardless of the degree of success of mediation or solutions in any given issue, the primary role in dealing with the problem must be to preserve the atmosphere in which the university's major task may take place. Many of the protests of students have a great deal of legitimacy. Therefore, preserving the ongoing operation of the university does not mean promoting the status quo, but making changes where appropriate changes should be made, at the same time preserving the necessary atmosphere in order that all members of the university can have opportunity for access to teaching, learning, and research.

The concepts that have been discussed so far could serve as a basis to perfect a style of relationship with students which will give support to the majority of students. This is vital because without common clarifications to the student body, the vocal minority can create illusions which make it difficult for the majority of the students to make their own evaluations based on the objective facts regarding any issue. This is closely related to other matters of communication, because both sides of a given issue of any stress situation should be made available to the student body in general.

Another problem must be recognized in the university's posture in dealing with the large numbers of students who are present on most college campuses. This organizational pattern of universities was adapted from business, government, and the military in the early part of this century. There is sufficient evidence to indicate that the present type of organizational structure will not suffice to meet the types of dynamic problems on present-day campuses. One of the problems associated with the system of rewards in the present organizational structure is that the young inexperienced student personnel worker functions at the student level where much of the student stress occurs. The relationship between this young junior staff member and the student establishes a pattern of relationship which is valid only when there are no problems of stress present.

The high level of difficulty in making decisions regarding the day-to-day concerns of student unrest and agitation places an overwhelming burden on these young inexperienced staff members. This has made the neophyte staff member merely a referral agent, and student leaders must wait for answers to return from sources higher in the organizational structure than the person they work with every day. Impatient student leaders and groups consider this red tape, stalling tactics, or methods to distract them from their goals. Students are then encouraged to circumvent the established channels and use power plays to confront the officials they know will make the final decisions. Rethinking of who should deal directly with students seems to be in order as a result of growing enrollments, increased complexity of university life, and the great diversity of value systems resulting from increasing opportunities for persons from a broader spectrum of the social and economic levels of society to come to institutions of higher education.

Circumstances point to the fact that those persons in the upper and middle levels of university organizational structure, with the prestige and status which accompany their position, should seek ways that they may have daily contact with students. Part of the need for this has resulted from the gradual withdrawal of faculty members from meaningful relationships with students outside the classroom. This integration of junior and senior staff would strengthen the junior staff members' image in the eyes of many student leaders and would enhance his professional ability by participaing in team-effort decision making. New concepts which may include new titles, different salary structures, and additional status seem to be some of the elements that need to be evaluated carefully to place more experienced staff workers in daily contact with students.

CONFRONTATIONS AND DISRUPTIVE ACTIONS

The dynamics of the larger society as well as the university community make it inevitable that differences of opinion will arise and that points of stress occur between opposing groups with different views on any particular issue. The circumstances of institutions of higher education will vary greatly with regard to the susceptibility of student unrest and agitation, and the style of working with these problems must vary to fit the particular institution and situation. Yet much of the tension problems will arise from the parietal rules (which might be referred to as the private-versus-public-life concept), the disenchantment of black students with university concerns about their welfare and need for black identity, and the black studies program (which they feel is necessary to give them emotional support and identification as black students), the aberrations of the organized advocates of radical leftists ideas and actions, the student power groups who seek either constructive or destructive changes in university decisions and methods of university decision making, and the role of the student in the decision-making process of the institution—including the area of academics.

A number of preventive measures can be undertaken, and constant communication along open avenues for dialogue and discussion regarding differences of opinion concerning issues can be utilized. But there is no certain method or set of processes that can prevent peaceful confrontations from spilling over into disruptive action. For many university officials who are responsible for these matters, this raises the dilemma of determining the appropriate actions dealing with the confrontation and disruptive action when and if it becomes a reality.

If one were to glean as much information as possible from all of the confrontations of the past few years, it would still be impossible to arrive at an exact method to handle confrontations. Each set of circumstances underlying any given confrontation is decidedly unique, and the dynamics of the situation must dictate the style of handling that confrontation. It is extremely important, however, that this matter be given careful thought and a set of procedures be formulated that could be put into action if a confrontation should occur. Procedures identifying the official who is in charge of the strategy, the role of the campus police, who is to determine when outside assistance is needed, the wording of the statement that should be made at the appropriate time to the students, the matter of recording this statement for future reference in case the students fail to obey the order, and the method of handling the arrests if necessary—are all concepts which should be part of the predetermined procedures by university officials.

A review of styles of dealing with confrontations on college campuses indicates three distinct methods. One is the persuasion method. This is an attempt to deal with the underlying issues reflected by the confrontation. It presupposes a strong effort to persuade dissident students from carrying out their stated plan of action or to cease from infringing upon the rights of other individuals. The basic ingredients in this approach are dialogue and discussion to evaluate the issues involved, with the goal of arriving at alternate methods of reaching full consensus on divergent issues.

A second method utilized by many institutions is direct arrest. This method is especially necessary when the nature of the disturbance endangers human life or physical property and immediate action is demanded. This method of arrest has some danger of escalating the controversy but has been used effectively where the disturbance involves a small number of people and where the action is taken promptly. It has not proved effective when used as a delayed means to eject massive numbers of participants from sit-ins and illegal possession of university facilities. The third method to be discussed has proved to be more successful in handling this kind of disruptive action.

A third method, now being used by many institutions in regards to sit-ins, lie-ins, and other kinds of seizing of facilities with accompanying disruptive behavior, is the injuction method. An injunction is a writ formed according to the circumstances of the case commanding an act which the court regards as essential to justice. The function of an injunction is to restrain action or interferences of some kind and to furnish preventive relief against irreparable mischief or injury or to preserve the status quo. If the students do not desist from their activities when the injunction is issued by the court and is served by an officer, they are automatically in contempt of court and subject themselves to immediate arrest. After the arrest, the court will usually determine with another hearing whether the temporary injunction should be made permanent. It should be stressed that the injunction and the arrest of those who fail to comply with the injunction are not in themselves part of the original offense which cause the injunction to be issued. The injunction serves merely to keep a general situation from proceeding further or to prevent a situation from happening when there is evidence to indicate that specific individuals are causing or plan to create disruptive action. The charges that the university might bring against persons who participate in disruptive action are a separate matter and due process in the civil court or a fair hearing before the university are not affected by the injunction.

DUE PROCESS AND FAIR HEARING

The concept of due process is a legal one and is often used in the wrong context when it is used to describe disciplinary hearings within the university. The courts have ruled for years that the relationship between students and universities gives the universities authority to judge matters of student behavior. Universities have the authority to take disciplinary action, including expulsion and suspension of students, but courts have ruled that universities must give the student a fair hearing and have set forth what constitutes a fair hearing. One of the most clarifying rulings that has been handed down in this regard was made in the United States District Court for the Western District of Missouri, on September 19, 1968. The court sitting *en banc* issued a "General Order on Judicial Standards of Procedure and Substance in Review of Student Discipline in Tax Supported Institutions of Higher Education." This document spelled out the relationship between Courts and Education, Lawful Missions of Tax Supported Higher Education, Provisional Procedure and Jurisdictional Standards, Obligations of a Student, and the Nature of Student Conduct Compared to Criminal Law. The court defined a fair hearing in the following manner.

Three minimal requirements apply in cases of severe discipline, growing out of fundamental conceptions of fairness implicit in procedural due process. First, the student should be given adequate notice in writing of the specific ground or grounds and the nature of the evidence on which the disciplinary proceedings are based. Second, the students should be given an opportunity for hearing in which the disciplinary authority provides a fair opportunity for hearing of the student's position, explanations and evidence. The third requirement is that no disciplinary action be taken on grounds which are not supported by any substantial evidence. . . .

There is no general requirement that procedural due process in student disciplinary cases provide for legal representation, a public hearing, confrontation and cross-examination of witnesses, warnings about privileges, self-incrimination, application of principles of former or double jeopardy, compulsory production of witnesses, or any of the remaining features of federal criminal jurisprudence.

A fair hearing, then, is a hearing before duly constituted authorities of the university and can be a simple or an elaborate procedure, based upon the policies of the university. The minimum procedures for a fair hearing are that the student should be (1) informed of the charges, written or verbally; (2) given the names of the principal witnesses; (3) allowed a fair opportunity to defend himself by presenting his own witnesses; (4) given the opportunity to state his side of the situation before those judging him reach a final decision; and (5) given the appellate route of appeal in case the original judgment is to discipline him.

A few universities use the elaborate procedures which follow strictly the technical rules in legal hearing. The following are legal rules which the courts do not require the universities to utilize in order to accord the student a fair hearing: (1) the degree of proof; (2) the burden of proof; (3) cross examination of witnesses; and (4) representation by legal counsel. Most universities today have a procedure which they follow to give students a fair hearing before disciplinary action is to be taken against them.

There is much pressure by groups in higher education, as well as groups outside the university, who defend the legalistic due process approach as being synonymous with the fair hearing approach used by most institutions of higher education. There have been many legal decisions indicating that these are not synonymous and the Missouri court decision specifically spelled out the difference between these two concepts.

The attempted analogy of student discipline to criminal proceedings against adults and juveniles is not sound. . . .

By judicial mandate to impose upon the academic community in student discipline the intricate, time consuming, sophisticated procedures, rules and safeguards of criminal law would frustrate the teaching process and render the institutional control impotent.

Much of the rationale used by courts in arriving at clear decisions regarding the authority of the university is the voluntary nature of the relationship between the student and the university. Once admitted, the student and the university operate on an agreement of mutual responsibility and obligation. This is known as the *contract theory.* In regards to this theory, the Missouri court stated:

> The voluntary attendance of a student in such institutions is a voluntary entrance into the academic community. By such voluntary entrance, the student voluntarily assumes obligations of performance and behavior reasonably imposed by the institution of choice relevant to its lawful missions, processes, and functions. These obligations are generally much higher than those imposed on citizens by the civil and criminal law.

Institutions of higher education are required by state law or by trustees of a private corporation to formulate all policies and regulations necessary for the operation of the institution. The legality of this is further substantiated by court rulings. Again the Missouri court stated:

> Standards so established may apply to student behavior on and off the campus when relevant to any lawful mission, process, or function of the institution. By such standards of student conduct the institution may prohibit any action or omission which impairs, interfers with, or obstructs the missions, processes, and functions of the institution.
> Standards so established may require scholastic attainments higher than the average of the population and may require superior ethical and moral behavior. In establishing standards of behavior, the institution is not limited to the standards or the forms of criminal laws.

The courts through the last seventy-five years have ruled that students enter into an agreement with the university at the time of their enrollment. Universities have the authority to insist that students abide by university regulations and take prescribed courses necessary for a degree of their choosing. No court has ever held that this concept is not a valid one. The concept of authority of the institution to discipline students is a separate concern from the right of the student to to have a fair hearing. This concept has been validated many times. One of the most forceful of these was the *Goldberg v. Regents of California,* 248 A.C.A. 1015, 57 Cal. Rptr. 463 (1967).

This case affirms the university's right to discipline students. The case resulted from dismissal of one student and the suspension of three others in what is now called the "Filthy Speech Movement." One quote from the appellate court of California in handing down this ruling further clarifies the university's responsibilities in this area of its educational process.

Broadly stated, the function of the university is to impart learning and to advance the boundaries of knowledge. This carries with it the administrative responsibility to control and regulate that conduct and behavior of the students which tends to impede, obstruct or threaten the achievements of its educational goals. Thus, the university has the power to formulate and enforce rules of student conduct that are appropriate and necessary to the maintenance of order and propriety, considering the accepted norms of social behavior of the community, where such rules are reasonably necessary to further the university's educational goals.

Historically, the academic community has been unique in having its own standards, rewards and punishment. Its members have been allowed to go about their business of teaching and learning largely free of outside interference. To compel such a community to recognize and enforce precisely the same standards and penalties that prevail in the broader social community would serve neither the special needs and interests of the educational institutions nor the ultimate advantages that society derives therefrom. Thus, in an academic community, greater freedoms and greater restrictions may prevail than in society at large, and the subtle fixing of these limits should, in a large measure, be left to the educational institution itself.

We hold that in this case, the university's disciplinary action was a proper exercise of its inherent general powers to maintain order on the campus and to exclude therefrom those who are detrimental to its well-being.

As a result of recent student demonstrations on college campuses, the federal government as well as various state governments have passed laws dealing with conditions of disruptions and seizure of university buildings. Some federal laws prohibit students who are guilty of participating in campus disruptive action from receiving financial aids, fellowships, etc. Many state laws have been passed to make some kinds of regulations into laws in an effort to regulate the behavior of students. Many state legislatures did not invade the authority and responsibility of the Boards of Trustees but took the position that the authority and responsibility of these boards should be clarified. There is ample evidence to indicate that these clarifications were considered to be a mandate by lawmakers with the possibility that future laws limiting the authority of Trustees would be forthcoming if these mandates were not executed. Two examples of these types of laws were passed by the state legislature of a Midwestern state in 1969. The first law is a clarification of the powers, duties, and responsibilities of the various boards of Trustees.

SECTION I. It is the purpose of this act to recognize and define certain powers, duties and responsibilities of the boards of trustees of the several universities of the State of _____which are supported by appropriations made by the General Assembly. The powers, duties and responsibilities referred to by this act are not intended to include all powers, duties and responsibilities of the several boards and nothing contained in this act shall be deemed to diminish or abrogate any other of the powers, duties or responsibilities of the respective boards specifically conferred by statute or properly implied thereby.

SECTION 2. The boards of (names of state universities) each as to its respective institution, shall have the power and duty:

(a) To govern the disposition and method and purpose of use of the property owned, used or occupied by the institution, including the governance of travel over and the assembly upon such property;

(b) To govern, by specific regulation and other lawful means, the conduct of students, faculty, employees and others while upon the property owned by or used or occupied by the institution;

(c) To govern, by lawful means, the conduct of its students, faculty and employees, wherever such conduct might occur, to the end of preventing unlawful or objectionable acts which seriously threaten the ability of the institution to maintain its facilities available for performance of its educational activities or which are in violation of the reasonable rules and standards of the institution designed to protect the academic community from unlawful conduct or conduct which presents a serious threat to person or property of the academic community;

(d) To dismiss, suspend or otherwise punish any student, faculty member or employee of the institution who violates the institution's rules or standards of conduct, after determination of guilt by lawful proceedings;

(e) To prescribe the fees, tuition and charges necessary or convenient to the furthering of the purposes of the institution and to collect the same;

(f) To prescribe the conditions and standards of admission of students upon such bases as are in its opinion in the best interests of the State and the institution;

(g) To prescribe the curricula and courses of study offered by the institution and to define the standards of proficiency and satisfaction within such curricula and courses;

(h) To award financial aid to needy students and award scholarships in encouragement of excellence of achievement out of the available resources of the institution as shall seem desirable and in the best interests of the institution and its students;

(i) To cooperate with other institutions to the end of better assuring the availability and utilization of its total resources and opportunities to provide excellent educational opportunity for all persons.

SECTION 3. Conduct which constitutes a violation of the rules of the instituton may be punished after determination of guilt by lawful procedures, without regard to whether such conduct also constitutes an offense under the criminal laws of any state or of the United States or whether it might result in civil liability of the violator to other persons.

SECTION 4. The individual governing boards are responsible to fulfill the powers, and duties conferred upon each by law. Each such board is authorized to employ such officers, faculty, employees, consultants and counsel as it may deem necessary or convenient to aid in the formulation and implementation of its policies and to execute its will within its particular institution. To such end each board may delegate to such persons and to others such authority as it may possess. Provided, that no manner of delegation shall be irrevocable and such delegated authority may be exercised only at the pleasure of such board and subject to its approval.

SECTION 5. Nothing in this act shall be deemed to discourage or disparage the status of students, faculty and other persons or the valid concerns of the public in matters of policy and of management of the universities of this State.

SECTION 6. The provisions of this act shall be considered separable and in the event any provision, or the exercise of any power contained herein with respect to any person, shall be declared illegal, such invalidity shall not affect any other portion of this act which can be given effect.

SECTION 7. The provisions of this act shall be applicable to each university declared by the General Assembly to be a university of State, now or hereafter created.

SECTION 8. Whereas an emergency exists for the immediate taking effect of this act, the same shall be in force from and after its passage.

The second law is related to the problems of trespass and illegal seizure of university facilities.

SECTION 1. It shall be a misdemeanor for any person intentionally to damage any property, real or personal, of any institution established for the purpose of the education of students enrolled therein.

SECTION 2. It shall be a misdemeanor for any person to go upon or remain upon any part of the real property of any institution established for the purpose of the education of students enrolled therein in violation of any rule or regulation of any such institution for the purpose of interfering with the lawful use of such property by others or in such manner as to have the effect of denying or interfering with the lawful use of such property by others.

SECTION 3. It shall be a misdemeanor for any person to refuse to leave the premises of any institution established for the purpose of the education of students enrolled therein when so requested, regardless of the reason, by the duly constituted officials of any such institution.

SECTION 4. It shall be a misdemeanor for any person to go upon or remain within a public building for the purpose of interfering with the lawful use of such building by other persons or in such manner as to have the effect of denying to others the lawful use of such building.

SECTION 5. A person who commits a misdemeanor defined in this act shall be punished, upon conviction, by a fine of not to exceed five hundred dollars ($500) or by imprisonment for not to exceed six months, or by both fine and imprisonment.

SECTION 6. Nothing in this act shall be interpreted as affecting the right of any person to engage in any conduct not in violation of this act or any rule or regulation of any such institution, or of any institution established for the purpose of education of students to discharge any employee, or expel, suspend or otherwise punish any student, in accordance with its procedures for any conduct which may be a violation of any such rule or regulation of any such institution or rendered unlawful by this act or may otherwise be deemed a crime or misdemeanor.

SUMMARY

The college campus reflects the societal unrest brought about by the conflict between the younger and the older generation, highlighted by the war in Vietnam, the civil rights movement, the concern of the younger generation regarding big business and big government, the emphasis upon technology which many feel tends to dehumanize individuals, the problems of the curriculum being relevant, and the students great desire to be a participating member in the operation of the university. These and other concerns or issues within and without the university provide the seeds for student agitation and unrest.

The constant process of trying to keep universities open and operating for the purpose for which they were founded is the primary obligation of all connected with higher education. Concurrent with this responsibility is an obligation to see that the rights guaranteed to every citizen under the first amendment are not abused when maintaining the atmosphere of freedom of inquiry, teaching, and research. There is no absolute method of dealing effectively with these problems, but matters discussed in this chapter can provide a basis for a style of action that universities can develop and adapt to fit their own particular situation.

The responsibility of dealing with these problems is awesome and difficult. Several concepts are now more visible as a result of the experiences of universities for the past several years. Among these is the need for an agreed upon university posture. This could include many things but essential to this stance is the need to insure students a positive role in university affairs. This provides the best possibilities for students to participate in concert with faculty and administrations to arrive at a consensus regarding policies and procedures which constitute the basis for a university posture toward peaceful dissent and disruptive actions. This posture would have many components but should include at least an assurance of freedom of expression, a policy regarding use of facilities, methods of anticipation and prevention of confrontations, methods of dealing with disruptive actions, legal concepts regarding student behavior, and the concepts of guaranteeing students fair hearings.

These styles and techniques are the lessons learned as institutions of higher education following the opening round of student protests at the University of California at Berkeley in 1964, and they provide the best possibilities in this second round of student unrest.

5

Diverse Views That Contain the Basis for Student Unrest and Agitation*

John W. Truitt†

INTRODUCTION

Regardless of how isolated a student body may be from the mainstream of student unrest, the news media—television, newspapers, and radio—make not only the disruption, but also the techniques of disruption, available to everyone. There is reason to believe that student unrest and the techniques for manifesting this unrest will soon be obvious on most university campuses. It seems necessary for those who are responsible and concerned for the operation of the university to be aware of the forces underlying the potential unrest and agitation. Points of confrontation will have to be identified and the best possible thinking

*The explanations of some of the societal problems in this chapter are partial duplication of materials presented in Chapter 3. The reason for this duplication is one of emphasis; namely, that the problems of the black and of the New Left in the larger society and in the university setting grow out of the same larger societal issues, both contemporary and traditional. It is impossible to separate the attitudes of these groups within and outside of the university and indicate that their outlook toward the great issues of these times are markedly different.

†Dr. John W. Triutt holds the B.S. degree in Social Studies and the M.Ed. degree in Guidance Education from Mississippi State University and the Ed.D. degree in Educational and Personnel Administration from Michigan State University. Dr. Truitt is currently Vice-President for Student Affairs and Professor of Education at Indiana State University. Prior to coming to Indiana State University he was Director of the Men's Division of Student Affairs at Michigan State University. His design of an in-service education program and his organizational manuals have been widely utilized by student affairs staffs across the country. Dr. Truitt is a frequent speaker at national academic organizations and his writings have made significant contributions to student personnel work in higher educaton.

brought to bear on these issues, not only to promote intelligent discussion, but also to alleviate destructiveness.

To get an understanding of the nature of the problems that are occurring in universities across the country, four major areas of potential discontent will be described. These are present in some stage of development on every university campus, and each university should be aware of the nature and the intensity of concern of students at any given time. Understanding, communication, and the bringing together of members of the university community with diverse views in a forum of honest, open dialogue gives the best chance for solutions to these problems.

Factors underlying the areas of agitation and discontent are highly interrelated but each area will be briefly described to illustrate the focal points underlying each concept. The four areas of potential discontent are (1) the black power movement, (2) political agitation from the New Left, (3) the private-versus-public-life concept, and (4) student power.

BLACK POWER

To understand the black power movement on university campuses, one must be aware of two interdependent concepts. The first concept concerns the historical facts concerning the role of the Negro in American society with all of its related injustices. The second concept relates to the university community as a microcosm of the American society and the fact that all aspects of society are present in the university community.

It is the philosophy of the present-day black students that they must act collectively to fight discrimination and prejudice so that the barriers are removed for all blacks. The black students believe that the goals they seek should be available to all people who demonstrate the necessary ability, and that barriers should not exist which are based on race rather than on individual ability.

It is difficult to determine what percentage of the black students in American universities are involved in the black power movement, but it is safe to say that the percentage at any given institution is rather high. If they are not activists themselves, many will support the black activists in their efforts. Most of the black students that are sympathizers or activists in the black power movement tend to have militant attitudes toward many of the aspects of the university that do not respond readily to their desires. The philosophical continuum of all black students on college campuses probably ranges from Martin Luther King's concept of nonviolence to the separatist militant movement espoused by Malcolm X. It is difficult at any one time to determine how many students are involved at any given point on this continuum. There often are basic programs that the black student seeks such as a black studies program, black advisors, black professors, and more black students admitted to the institution, but the tension regarding the black power movement is more often related to specific instances which occur on campuses that lead to excitable and direct action by the black student.

Many of the black students who are leaders in the black power movement on college campuses grew up in ghettos in the larger cities, lived in neighborhoods which were all black, went to predominantly black schools, and were not able to see firsthand the contrast in the adult world of discrimination. Consequently, when the black student arrives on the college campus he receives a cultural shock when he is placed in a predominantly white-controlled society such as exists on most university campuses. Except in the black southern university, the Negro constitutes a very small portion of most university populations. He begins to see and experience firsthand many of the experiences that his parents had when they sought employment, loans, and other symbols related to keeping the black man in his subservient role. Most black students have been told that the best escape from the ghettos and the subservient roles forced on the Negro is through the avenue of education—especially a university degree. The black student comes to the campus expecting to see some of the most learned people in the world. These students express the view that if the leaders of the intellectual world do not understand them, they certainly do not have a chance in society. The black student finds the same symbols of prejudice at the university that his parents found in the larger society. He feels frustrated and lost when the hopes and expectations he had about the university as an answer to his problems comes crashing down upon him. His hopes are high and the performance of the university falls far short of his expectations.

A review of the black power movement in the universities indicates that the black students have demonstrated great hostility toward the symbols of discrimination and racial bias. At times this is not a refined hostility and many persons involved as targets are shocked and hurt because they feel they are unrelated to the problems. In those instances where physical violence and destruction of property by black students have occurred, the goal inevitably has been the destruction of things they feel are symbols of the built-in system of prejudice. Hostilities which have built up over a period of time, as a result of prejudice in the greater society, have been transferred into the universities. Consequently, most universities now have two student bodies—one black and one white.

The factors that lead to this separatism very often have been underlined by animosities that have repercussions from the white students. The polarization of black and white students provides a militant white backlash problem of disturbing proportions in many institutions.

Most black students would agree that the university has limited ability and resources and would have a difficult time solving most of the problems underlying the black power movement. But black students insist that barriers which keep them from being successful should be those based on requirements which affect them as individuals and not those which affect them because they are black. Black students feel that people in authority are dishonest until they are proven honest, and that talking about prejudices and discriminations means nothing. The only thing they understand is action. Black students indicate that if people in authority do nothing about racial discrimination or the symbols of racial discrimination, those people in fact agree with it.

The black students consider the university a citadel of equality. Their hopes and expectations of the university, and the limitations of the university to control people's acceptance of other people, provides a vacuum of expectancies which will be impossible to fill.

THE NEW LEFT

Since about 1960 students of the New Left have created much agitation that is aimed at the "Establishment"—the social, political, and governmental structures of the American society. The specific aspects of the establishment which have come under attack have been civil rights, the Vietnam War, the draft, the relationship between the government and the universities regarding ROTC training, and contracts between industries and universities. Paralleling the younger generation's disillusionment with these problems was a type of idealism that arose. This idealism in the early 1960's was diverted into political and social welfare channels by President John F. Kennedy's emphasis on youth. This partial harnessing of this enthusiasm was accomplished by volunteer projects, such as the Peace Corps, the VISTA programs, the Job Corps, and others. Since President Kennedy's death the movement has diverted its political posture to attacks upon the federal government, authority symbols in society and the university community. These New Left activists exhibit great unhappiness with the academic programs, with teaching, with the curriculum, and in fact, practically all areas of the university operation.

Many such students are confused in their objectives but do not have a better model for education or society than the ones that they are trying to disrupt and finally destroy. They believe that whatever will take the place of the present structures would be better than the traditional establishments which are the focal points of their dislike and agitation. The techniques that have been adopted by the Students for a Democratic Society on college campuses have been adapted from the techniques that have proved successful in the civil rights movement. There is some effort to adopt some of the tactics that are used by the Japanese students in their protests against the Japanese government.

The organizations most prevalent in terms of sowing seeds of destruction vary from institution to institution as well as from one section of the country to another. Many of these organizations have different names but similar objectives. Often within the university the same group of students will be the driving force behind more than one radical organization. The most prevalent of all New Left national student groups is the Students for a Democratic Society, which has received the most nationwide attention and was the instigator of the revolt at Columbia University in the spring of 1968. This organization has been responsible for the spark that has ignited student sit-ins and lie-ins and physical destructiveness in universities over the country.

Another organization that is at work in many institutions is the Radical Press. This is the organization that publishes an underground press, criticizing in writing the same kinds of authority symbols, methods used by the university administrators in their decision-making process, teaching, the curriculum, government contracts with the universities, Reserve Officers Training Corps, and other issues to which they are opposed. The local Radical Press are members of the National Liberation Press. The National Liberation Press does not determine the policy of the local organizations, but does furnish the local chapters copy and serves as a clearing house for materials concerning agitation written by leftist organizations throughout the United States and foreign countries.

The Students for a Democratic Society, as a national organization, is committed to four general areas: (1) agitation for alteration of the system of government in the United States, (2) liberation of the student from the authority of the university, (3) fight for equal rights for all persons, and (4) revision of the structure of the university so that students, faculty, and administrators are equal partners on all issues. The Students for a Democratic Society are devoted to bringing the university to a disruptive end; and in this respect they are different than many other New Left organizations. The style of operation of the Students for a Democratic Society, as it relates to the liberation of students from university control administratively and academically, was expressed by one member of the Students for a Democratic Society, in a speech at the national convention December 2, 1967 at Indiana University. The prepared portion of his presentation centered around four basic efforts of the Students for a Democratic Society in terms of their resistance within the university.

1. *Desanctification*—meaning that students and other members of the movement should challenge any institution, policy, procedure, or agency and not be deterred by tradition, status, prestige, or legal power and authority. In other words, nothing should be regarded as sacred.
2. *Deobfuscation*—meaning to cut through to the real significance and meaning of all policies, regulations, announcements, and verbalized statements. Participants in the resistance should require things to be in writing and then challenge them on the basis of meaning of words, insinuations, assumptions, and assumed power. Don't let authorities "con" you with words.
3. *Disengagement*—meaning that participants in the resistance must disengage themselves from institutional concerns, constraints imposed by membership in formal groups and from other limiting forces within society. Any resistance must depend on individuals who are free to act in accordance with the needs of specific situations and tactics and who can appeal to individuals on any basis which will gain their attention and win their support.
4. *Dismantlement*—meaning to tear apart institutions and other constraining agencies. The basis for rebuilding the new society will be established only by tearing apart the constraining and limiting pressures which now force students into certain molds, limit the power of universities to be truly free and which permit governments to be so corrupt and decadent as to wage an immoral war against the will of the people.

The Students for a Democratic Society has had a phenomenal growth in the past seven years and is believed to have at least 200 chapters on university campuses at the present time. The Students for a Democratic Society began in June 1962, and its creation was an outcome of a Port Huron (Michigan) convention of members of the New Left movement. From this conference came a document called the Port Huron Statement which was the first official statement creating the student division of the League for Industrial Democracy. The Port Huron Statement is a critique of American life and policy, and a description of how any New Left American must operate to overcome these political flaws. One major idea in the statement indicated that the university would be a fruitful place for a division of the New Left because the universities are a good recruiting ground for liberals and socialists. The statement further emphasized that these radicals could promote controversy within the university community with very few repercussions from university authorities.

It has been said that the New Left and the Students for a Democratic Society have been a cover for communist and socialist activities in the universities. While this statement has been generally agreed to even by J. Edgar Hoover Director of the Federal Bureau of Investigation, institutions have had difficulty in the identification of individuals who are professional communists in their New Left movements. However, many leaders of the national group do admit that communists are involved in the movement. The future of the Students for a Democratic Society in this country is dependent upon a variety of issues—number one being the Vietnam war. Another will be the avenue the university takes within the next few years in accepting student participation more fully in the role of operating the university. There seems to be a definite swing of the political pendulum in the country back toward the moderate, and even conservative, stands on issues created by young radicals. Many of the disturbances that have occurred in universities the last few years have received very little sympathy or support from the mainstream of student or adult life.

PRIVATE-VERSUS-PUBLIC-LIFE CONCEPT

This conflict can best be described as the conflict between the student and the university concerning parietal rules. The university on one hand with obligations and responsibilities stemming from the authority of the state legislature and the Board of Trustees, and in private universities from the Board of Trustees, must try to affect a style of relationship with students to provide proper guidance and control of student matters on the campus. The other side of the controversy is the student's insistence that he is a mature young adult and that he needs the freedom to experiment with his life at the same time that he is engaged in the pursuits of higher education. Issues which result from this private-versus-public-life concept range from hours for women in residence halls, no housing regulations for students, to no off-campus restrictions regarding behavioral problems of students.

Some universities place the obligation to provide proper guidance and control before the priority of maintaining an atmosphere of freedom to learn and experiment. There are many historical reasons for this, but one reason is the several adult publics which make demands upon the university. Students view the concept of freedom to learn and experiment as primary in their educational life and see the universities' responsibility to provide proper guidance and control as secondary. In fact, the major unrest in this area has been an outgrowth of the feelings students hold that they are adults and are mature enough to make their own decisions and do not desire or need the guidance and control the university imposes upon them.

The philosophical conflict can be described by two concepts. One is that many students want instant participation in the governance of the institution. They want greater authority and a greater share in the affairs of the university. Especially do they want the avenues of partici- pation open to them so their views will be heard in the faculty and administrative groups who make decisions regarding the university. Some insist that the student should be a junior partner in the operation of the university, including seats on the Board of Trustees. The other concept is expressed by the students who hold to the philosophical point of view that the university should have nothing to do with the student and his private life other than the academic programs. The university should provide very little and expect very little. The second group indicates that the university should shorten its range of concern with students.

The students' definition of the dividing line is what they consider their private life versus what they consider to be their legitimate rela- tionship with the university, which is their public life. From the student standpoint, the dividing line between a student's public life (legitimate relations with the university) and private life (which is considered not a concern of the university) is really in the student's mind. Students may abide by university policy but they might never accept these policies as the proper exercise of authority by the university.

From the university standpoint, the dividing line is where the uni- versity policies extend. This, then, is the student-university relationship where the students' public life ends and their private life begins. The basic philosophy conflict is that the university considers its responsibil- ity of proper guidance and control a prerequisite to the creation of an atmosphere conducive to freedom and learning. Students consider free- dom and experimentation as the first priority, with proper guidance and control something that may occur but not to be programmed in a defi- nite manner. The basic question is then asked, what point on the con- tinuum provides the optimum conditions for the best of both considerations?

Three polarized dividing lines related to the private-versus-public- life concept can be identified in universities in this country:

1. Students' legitimate relations with the university are in the aca- demic areas; everything outside of that is their private life.
2. Everything on campus is a part of the legitimate relation with the university; everything off campus is their private life.
3. Everything that the students do which reflects on their status in the university and the university itself is a part of their public life; everything outside of that is their private life.

Number one and number two are self-explanatory. If dividing line number three is the university's position, student violations involve evaluation on the part of the university officials. Many students do not like this because it means the dividing line is always subject to evaluation by these officials. The uneasiness of not having in writing the regulations or descriptions which define the university's dividing line is disconcerting and often leads to unrest and agitation.

Many institutions have been affected by the private-versus-public-life argument. While it loses the center of the stage from time to time, it is the focal point of the majority of student power and agitation in this country. The arguments presented by student power groups concerning this area of unrest are aided and advanced by the "normal" students, not necessarily the radical types who are concerned mostly with issues of a societal nature. This is a part of the natural growth toward freedom from authority of all kinds. The private-versus-public-life concept is a part of the normal growth pattern of all university-age students, regardless of their political ideology, and social or academic development. Most unrest occurs in this area because of the students' normal grasping with problems related to early maturity. Student power groups seek freedom from authority, not only from the university but from all traditional authority in society.

STUDENT POWER

One of the major problems that confronts student affairs and other university officials is determining at any given time the nature and extent of student power and unrest, faculty power and unrest, and other dynamics of the university scene. If the complexity of these problems presents a Pandora's box to university educators, one can visualize how perplexing this must be to alumni, legislators, parents, and the general public. There is ample evidence that the situation will increase in complexity in the future.

The factors which underlie student power are readily identified— large cities of students; students better prepared academically; traditional curriculum which reflects the past, not the future; alienation of students by the authority patterns of the establishments of business, industry, government, and education; twenty-five years of social upheavals and reforms; and a mass-communications system which has given students excellent portrayals of conflicts in world, national, and local problems, but very few solutions. Students bring to the campus great reservations about the world that adults have built; and, dissatisfied with established views, students set about devising their own solutions to these problems. The basic training ground for the techniques and solutions to these problems is the campus. The university's permissive atmosphere makes it an excellent arena for educational and social reforms, with resulting experimentation. The carrying out of these educational and social reform actions becomes what is now termed student power; and the direction these actions take makes student power either constructive or destructive.

Wide disagreement is prevalent among students regarding the style and techniques that should be utilized to achieve the goals of student power. One student power source believes in the confrontation of the established authorities of the university with a goal of destroying the established authority patterns, but with no clear model to replace the present structure. Another student power source believes in the constructive concept of student power, desiring increased participation on committees throughout the university at all levels, and expecting university officials to take their opinions and contributions seriously.

Two major emphases are evident in universities as they relate to this increased student participation. One is an attempt to secure additional student rights related to life outside class, and the second is for an active role in educational reform and change. Until a few years ago student power was evident only along the lines of traditional relationships that students had with administrators and faculty groups. Recent developments have not only increased student power in the traditional areas, but relationships have been pioneered in areas that had previously been the private inner sanctums of administrators or faculty members.

The old and the new relationships, with resulting student power, have been enhanced by two major developments. One is the dissipation of the concept of *in loco parentis* as a result of student effort to achieve emancipation from traditional authority. The second development is the student's evaluation of the present curriculum as irrelevant and archaic and a major force in perpetuating the society they hope to reshape. They feel their influence in the academic areas can bring about changes which will reflect the realities of society as viewed by their generation. Academic reforms have been advocated in one manner or another from practically everyone connected with the educational process. The specialists want more general education taught; the humanists feel that there has been a dehumanization of education since the scientific emphasis brought about by Sputnik in the late 1950's. Ethnic groups are pressing for areas of knowledge to be taught regarding their literature, history, and traditions. Students want a voice in what is taught. The list is endless, but in the center of stage of this conflict are students. They are the products of the university as well as the leading targets of the curriculum. Many of the causes which underlie these conflicts do not lend themselves to full analysis, but several of them can be identified. One is the population explosion; another is the information explosion; and a third one is the lack of ability to synthesize small bodies of new knowledge with large bodies now in existence which would increase the meaning of both. This promotes a fragmentation of the curriculum that discourages students and aborts the vitality of the learning process as it relates to the well-educated person. The real question then is, How does the university conceptualize these conflicts and arrive at a style of operation that satisfies her that she is proceeding along her most logical course in curriculum planning and development? These and other conflicts indicate why students have a great concern about being involved in the governance of the academic life of the university.

The basic relationship between students and the university does not give the students a right to participate in the governance of university affairs. The criterion set by the university for student participation is predicated on soundness from an educational standpoint. Therefore the question resolves itself around the educational desirability of allowing students to participate in the academic governance of the university in the areas in which they have a direct concern and to the degree that they can make a contribution. While this general assumption receives favorable approval in many quarters, it is the specifics—the extent and scope of involvement—that create the greatest problems and concerns; for example, whether students should participate, and to what extent, in (1) the selection of faculty members, (2) the dismissal of faculty members, (3) the promotion of faculty members, (4) the tenure policy of faculty members, (5) the selection of specific areas of the curriculum, and (6) changes in areas of study presently in the curriculum. The circumstances of each institution would determine the depth and scope of the participation of students in the governance of academic affairs, but from the experience of the last few years, general trends can be detected.

The general trend is that students are becoming more involved in a shared manner in the selection of administrative officials including presidents, academic deans, and department chairmen. The selection of faculty members, unless they are chosen for a special assignment, so far has not been greatly affected by this process. It is possible that the participation in the former is largely because of administrative or semi-administrative responsibilities, but strong student pressure exists in some universities to participate in the selection of new faculty members.

There is even stronger sentiment among students that they should participate in the dismissal of faculty members whom they feel are incompetent. As one can realize, this is a very difficult decision for students to make because they may be largely concerned with their relationship with the faculty member rather than his competence in his professional field. The reverse of this is often true. When tenure is not given to professors who are popular with students, this sometimes causes dissension and difficulty between students and the individuals within the university who must make those decisions.

A very definite feeling exists on the part of most students that incompetent professors should not be promoted or given tenure. While very few students are on promotion or tenure committees, in the next few years, a great pressure will increase to have participation in this process. Proponents of student power indicate that this is the cornerstone of involvement in academic affairs, and, that unless students have a share in this area of the academic program, the involvement in other areas will be of little significance. While students are extremely concerned about the curriculum and its relevancy to the realities of society they feel that the curriculum can never be better than the professors who teach it. Student power groups feel that the starting point for reforms are with the policies that are related to the employment, dismissal, promotion, tenure, and evaluation of faculty members. Students feel that this is the real objective of student power as it relates to the academic area.

Administrators often find themselves in a secondary role in this respect, and unless faculty power comes to some consensus concerning student power involvement in academic affairs, great inroads will result from the current efforts which student pressure groups are making.

These efforts lead to another assumption that needs exploring. It is often said that the basic relationship in an institution of higher education is the relationship between the professor and the student, or the teacher and the learner. As everyone knows, the basic freedom of a professor to conduct his class in a manner which is within the framework of his own competence, understanding, and style of teaching is called academic freedom. One of the basic questions in academic reform from a student power standpoint is, What is the role of the learner in the teacher-learner relationship within the confines of academic freedom? Are students natural partners in this relationship or does their participation depend upon being given a share in this responsibility by professors? Some of the more militant student power groups are now pressing for the right of participation, not a shared responsibility delegated by professors.

Another problem operating in the student-versus-faculty-power area is the nature of the faculty governments, which are usually of one-year duration, thereby giving it a rather fluid nature. Many faculty governments in one year hesitate to make commitments affecting the participation of student power groups in the governance of academic matters which would bind faculty governments for longer periods of

time to specific relationships. Students also have fluid types of government, but their concern for participation is to gain involvement in
endeavors where they have all to gain and nothing to lose from their
own traditional operations. Each student government is pledged to
increased involvement in the academic area. Students know these
efforts are breaking new ground by deeper penetration into areas which
heretofore have been free from student influence. Using these same
assumptions, this partially explains why administrations are being constantly pushed for a redefinition of relationships which would provide
for more involvement on the part of faculty and student groups in the
total university endeavor.

The implication of student power is that the present policy-making
system in most institutions of higher education needs to be changed. All
student power groups agree on this one fundamental principle, and
they differ only as to what methods are most effective in bringing about
changes which they feel are desirable. The traditional concept of *preparing people for the future* and the decision-making process within the
university giving credance to this objective are not acceptable to student power sources, because these eliminate any meaningful role or
contributions on the part of students at the present time. Student power
groups attack another traditional view on which universities are predicated—namely that some people know more than others and that the
process of education has an element of gradual development attached
to it. Student power sources do not accept this principle and find considerable fault not only with the directions and goals to which much of
this knowledge is applied, but with the old adage that wisdom is the
product of learning plus experience. Another implication for institutional policy concerning student power is that it would make inroads on
many assumptions of academic freedom. This would be a quest for
shared responsibility in curriculum planning, grading policies, and actual content and style of course presentation. Student influence in the
academic areas continues to produce new ideas which would symbolize
the thinking of the present generation, with regard to the problems
they now face and will continue to face after their formal education.
These ideas will be only partially valid but will provide decision makers
within the university with a continuing supply of innovations from each
present generation.

Changes in the administrative areas of policy making as the result
of student power will likely result in a shortening up of the range of
official relationships between the student and the university. Present
trends indicate that a description of this relationship must be published
in college catalogues and/or other university publications and made
available to the student prior to his enrollment at the university. Ele-

ments of student power together with other groups such as the Civil Liberties Union and the AAUP have forced, and will continue to force, the relationship outside of the classroom between students and the university. The implication of this for policy making is an increased written clarification of specific university policies and regulations, and published guidelines of implementation and a more legalistic adjudication process. One of the major developments that has been produced, and that will increase, is the acceptance of students as partners with shared authority and responsibilities in those areas dealing with student life. The integration of students with administrative and faculty officials could serve as a constructive alternative to a continuous series of administrative and student power confrontations. There seems to be a definite swing of the political pendulum in the country back toward the moderate, and even conservative, stands on issues created by young radicals. Many of the disturbances that have occurred in universities the last few years have received very little sympathy or support from the mainstream of student or adult life.

SUMMARY

This chapter is a description of some of the major movements that can be expected to develop or to continue at most institutions in the future. The appreciation and understanding of the concepts underlying these issues seem to be the best methods of developing a common criterion to serve as a university's posture during these troubled times.

One doesn't have to look closely to find the presence of student power on university campuses. The basic task at this time is to determine the scope and extent of student power and direct it into constructive channels. The welfare of the university is best served when this goal becomes a reality. If students are not actively involved in the planning and operation of the university to the extent that they can make a contribution, playing games with them is one way to create illegitimate leadership. These illegitimate groups confront the university with action designed to create disorder and agitation, and this is done outside the student govenmental structure and the normal channels of communication.

The concept of constructive student power where students see their role of participation as fruitful not only gives them a legitimate voice in affairs, but it also tends to dissolve the problem of communication which divides the university into a triad of special interests. This participation takes many forms but could be an honest approach to the involvement of students in order to bring new ideas, fresh opinions, and a voice for thousands of students who are unknown personally to those individuals who make decisions within the university.

The basic relationship between students and the university is a complicated matter and has ramifications for most aspects of the university. A common criterion needs to be formulated upon which judgments and expectancies between students and universities can be established. Many institutions, in trying to settle disruptive behavior situations, have found this common criterion absent. The absence of a common understanding provides a ready-made opportunity for dissident students and some faculty members to probe in one area after the other so that administrative officials must constantly deal with day-to-day problems rather than work toward long-range solutions that could promise better understanding and relations between students and the university.

If one lesson can be learned from other universities it is that the best thinking of all responsible and concerned for a university needs to be utilized in the reemphasizing of the university's common purposes and objectives. One major purpose surely involved is the preserving of the basic premises upon which the university was founded—teaching, learning, and research. This common posture also holds that the major purpose of the university can best be achieved by the faculty having the major responsibility for teaching and research, the student for learning, and the administration for providing the conditions and an atmosphere in which these can best take place. The complexity of university operation dictates participation by all in areas of common interest, but these collective efforts must serve as a valuable means to enhance increased effectiveness of faculty, students, and administrators in their primary obligations and responsibilities.

6

Student Values— A New Approach

Patrick H. Ratterman*

In today's society now undergoing such truly revolutionary change, how are student values being determined? It is tempting to say that in such an age the best index of developing student values is a catalogue of values that students have rejected. Students themselves are not always certain what they are for. They appear certain only with respect to what they are against. Moreover, present student values seem to be determined, or at least to become manifest, only as individual issues are perceived and stands are taken. In the course of the sixties the major issues with respect to which students have taken strong stands have concerned civil rights, Vietnam, poverty, and university reform. A brief review of the nature of student involvement in each of these issues may give some clues to the overall, more basic values upon which students are today basing their judgments.

The first student cause of the sixties concerned civil rights. Participation in the struggle to remedy the racial injustices of the South provided an almost perfect mixture of all that is essential to a student crusade. The oppressor and the oppressed were both easily identified. The goal was clear. The danger was real. Little coordination of effort was required. To participate one could ride, march, sit in, use a segregated drinking fountain or washroom, or exchange places for a semester

*The Rev. Patrick H. Ratterman, S.J., attended the University of Michigan for two years and was ordained to the priesthood in 1950 at the Jesuit House of Studies, West Baden, Indiana. Father Ratterman is currently Vice-President for Student Affairs of Xavier University, after serving 14 years as Dean of Men at the University. He is the author of the book the *Emerging Catholic University* and has published numerous articles on the subject of higher education.

on southern and northern campuses. Sustained sacrifice and a willingness to accept suffering were essential to the experience. As it turned out, the crusade provided a taste of success. A well-deserved sense of self-esteem was felt as the barriers of southern segregation began to totter. The injustices of a centuries old culture were successfully challenged. The spirit of "We shall Overcome" was felt for the first time by American students as a group. They would carry this spirit into other crusades.

One very singular consequence of student participation in the civil rights movement in the early sixties has perhaps not been given sufficient attention as it affected later student movements. Students who participated in the early phases of the civil rights struggle learned to identify with an oppressed and suffering people. White students who went south to participate in the civil rights movement learned to "think black." They shared not only the scanty food and shelter of the southern Negroes but their emotional life as well, their hopes and fears, their deeper hopelessness and shame. Translated into ballad and song, the experience was brought back to northern campuses and communicated to younger minds. Millions of high school and college students learned from sing-ins and phonograph records to identify with a segment of suffering and oppressed humanity in a language their parents could not understand.

It is without doubt an oversimplification to say that identification with a suffering people brought so many college students to take such serious offense with the conduct of the war in Vietnam. However, identification was certainly a factor. An older generation viewed America's first TV war as impassively as they watched a midnight movie, not perceiving the incongruity of full living color scenes of human suffering in Vietnam interspersed with blatant commercials for the products and services of the American economy of abundance. Many young people saw it differently. To them national commitment and security seemed abstract and remote. The issue for so many college students was the cost of the war in terms of human suffering. It is unimportant whether a U.S. military officer or some overimaginative war correspondent first said that a particular village in the war area "could be saved only by being destroyed." Many young people wondered if the observation did not apply to all of Vietnam. If that was the only way Vietnam could be saved, and this seemed increasingly to be the case, they questioned the morality of the entire saving operation. It is difficult for older people to understand but in the eyes of the young the atrocities of the Viet Cong, however well documented, did not begin to compare with the massive suffering which appeared unavoidable as a direct result of U.S. efforts to save Vietnam. Students identified with the suffering people of a nation that to them appeared to have been judged expendable in the cause of world peace.

Partly as a result of deepening interest in civil rights and partly as a consequence of our national involvement in Vietnam, student attention gradually focused on poverty in the United States, another source of human indignity and suffering. A substantial minority of students are obviously less impressed with theories of finance and government than they are with the inequities and inconsistencies that appear inevitable as a result of current economic and political practices. Such students reject the traditional vision of American success. They perceive wealth, comfort, and social status as blindfolds to injustice and suffering. They are more concerned than students of any previous generation with the poor who will never have an opportunity to share the nation's wealth because of the circumstances of their birth. They suspect that poverty has become institutionalized, seemingly an essential element for the successful functioning of some segments of the national economy.

With considerable campus support university reform has been added to the catalogue of issues on which students are taking a firm stand. The case against the university has many aspects. It is felt that at best the education given on campuses today is largely irrelevant to the needs of young people living in an age of revolutionary change. At worst, today's university education serves to reinforce the institutions of our society which perpetuate inequities and inconsistencies in the American way of life. It is an accepted campus view that American education has become subservient to American technology, that it operates as though it were totally unaware of, and unconcerned with, the social and cultural upheavals taking place just beyond the campus gates. As a corrective, students are demanding the right to play a more self-determining role both in their own educational development and in the policy determinations of the university itself.

This brief review of the stands taken by students within the last ten years with respect to civil rights, Vietnam, poverty, and university reform can perhaps provide some clues as to the basic factors which are determining student values today and are likely to influence student judgments in the foreseeable future. As a result of their involvement in the issues of the sixties, students today are certainly more perceptive of human deprivation and suffering than their campus predecessors, far more concerned with what offends human dignity or threatens human individuality in the larger society. They have indeed greater determination to overcome conditions that appear to perpetuate social inconsistencies and inequities, whatever reassessment this may involve of traditional American values or whatever readjustments may be required in our American way of life.

The attitude which has evolved in student minds with respect to the political, economic, and social institutions of American life is perhaps the most important factor to be weighed in determining present-day student values. The four major issues to which the student generation has addressed itself in the sixties have brought students into direct confrontation with what they regard as forms of American cultural institutionalism. Students see racial segregation as a cultural institution in the South, containment of a monolithic Communism at whatever cost to whatever people as institutionalized in American foreign policy, poverty as an institutionalized element of the national economy, and education as the institution which serves to reinforce all existing American values and other institutions. Because these institutions manifest a strong interdependence, there has developed among students a widespread distrust of *all* American institutions. In one way or another students suspect that all American institutions fit into a mutually reinforcing "system." "The system" is what students regard as ultimately responsible for all the inconsistencies, inequities, and injustices which are to be found in our American way of life.

Young people today regard with particular suspicion any institution that is big, powerful, wealthy, and impersonal—big government, big welfare, big business, big religion, big education. One reason why students so readily challenge authority today—or more simply just ignore it—is that authority is so often exercised in the name of institutions that are big, powerful, wealthy, and highly impersonal. For the same reason more radical segments of the student society are unimpressed by appeals for "law and order." They feel that the concept of law and order, itself a social institution, has frequently been used to protect and even institutionalize social injustices and inequities in American society. *Codes* of ethics and morality fall under the same censure. Students are inclined to suspect that ethical and moral codes, products of a former age, have not only themselves become institutionalized but are fostered by institutions—big, powerful, wealthy, and impersonal—which are either blind or hypocritically adjusted to the basic social ills of the day. A significant amount of student unrest, therefore, runs far deeper than the specific issues to which students have so far addressed themselves. Underneath the particular issues at hand there has begun to emerge a more generalized belief not only that the institutions of American society are the real *bête noire* of the nation's social ills, but more importantly that existing institutions are hopelessly inadequate to cure the ills which presently beset our American way of life.

It is impossible to estimate the present extent of student distrust of institutionalism in American life or to calculate the possible consequences of this distrust to American society. Followed to its logical conclusion and applied to causes, a complete repudiation of American institutions cannot but evolve into a truly revolutionary outlook. In its most extreme form such thinking terminates in "Burn, baby, burn! Whatever comes out of the ashes will be an improvement on what we have now." Such extreme revolutionary views are definitely to be found today on some American campuses. Moreover, universities themselves become the first targets of such radical thought. Universities must either be "ground to a halt" or reformed according to extreme radical ideals so they can become the agencies of revolution for other institutional reforms in the American society. This is the program which the extreme radical groups are presently attempting to promote on American campuses. The absolute number of such student revolutionaries is small indeed. But to what extent do their views influence or in part characterize a much larger body of student thought?

Before estimating the effect of radical student views on the larger student population another very important consideration must be weighed. Disturbing as the cultural revolution may be which is today ruminating on American campuses, there are strong indications that some of its values are rooted in the unfulfilled ideals of previous generations. The great religious and political documents of recent years, certainly in no way influenced by present student opinion, reflect a deep perception of the need for institutional reform in modern society. It is not altogether surprising therefore that there is strong faculty support for many radical student causes. Moreover, studies tend to indicate that the parents of today's campus radicals espouse liberal views that were considered quite radical in their own student days. In some cases radical students appear to be acting out latent parental frustrations. Mark Rudd, leader of the Columbia University student revolt, is referred to by his mother as, "My son, the revolutionary." His father has remarked, "I was a member of the depressed generation and my greatest concern has always been making a living. We're glad Mark has time to spend on activities and politics." (*Time*, May 31, 1967.) Mark Rudd's parents express a parental attitude which is probably more widespread than is generally suspected. Somehow checks and money orders from home continue to support bearded sons and beaded daughters however radical their campus politics.

Radical views are also more widely supported on campuses than is generally believed. Comfort is sometimes taken in the statistic that campus radicals constitute only a very small campus minority variously estimated at from 2 to 10 percent. It is then presumed that there exists a sharp break between this small minority of radicals and a 90 to 95 percent typical, fun-loving, basically conservative student population. Such estimates lead to the suggestion that problems of campus unrest could easily be resolved if the student (and faculty) members of radical organizations and cliques were summarily dismissed from all campuses. Such thinking reveals a very unrealistic estimate of student thinking. There simply does not exist any neat cutoff point distinguishing radicals from nonradicals among the student population. Radical student opinions are by no means limited to small revolutionary student organizations and cliques. While the largest proportion of students appear basically conservative, the number of students who share radical views on any particular issue is certainly many times greater than two to ten percent. The swing proportion of student opinion strings out in a continuum between the 2–10 percent radicals and the much larger percentage of conservative students. The proportions of this continuum are ever shifting depending on the issue at hand. On any particular issue the 2–10 percent radical minority can swell to a significantly larger percentage, at times to a majority. Moreover, since conservative students are seldom active or vocal in representing their views, otherwise uncommitted student opinion is likely to manifest itself on the radical side whenever it is expressed.

The possibility of some "outside influence" playing an important role in American radical student movements is being raised so strongly that some consideration must be given to the problem. The obvious "foreign influence" that most questioners have in mind is the international Communist conspiracy. One first wonders whether such a consideration is not another manifestation of the exaggerated American idealization of youth. American youth, it is assumed, could not possibly react with such distrust of our American way of life unless some outside influence were somehow leading it astray. The assumption can only be answered by pointing out that American youth is wonderful enough to be idealistic. By reason of its own idealism and its own inner dynamism it is quite capable of reacting forcefully against any injustices it perceives in American society without any outside help or influence.

However, a number of more serious observations must be made if possible Communist influence in American student movements is to be studied further. First, it should be noted that American students in general, and specifically campus radicals, explicitly repudiate authoritarianism in all governments, Communist as well as non-Communist. Authoritarian Communist governments do not escape the American student distrust of institutionalism. The expression, "Better Red than dead," has never found acceptance in American student movements. Authoritarian Communism has no attraction to American radical student movements. It is found repressive and uninspiring.

On the other hand, it would not be correct to assert that all American student radicals completely reject all aspects of Communism. The idealism of the youthful Marx, "to overthrow all conditions under which man is an oppressed, enslaved, destitute and despised being," expresses too clearly the radical student ideal to be rejected simply because of its source. Moreover, even though they reject the authoritarian governmental forms of existing Communist states, some American students undoubtedly envision as an ultimate ideal the classless society which Communism has so long promised but never produced. Without doubt some students will be watching to see if the "liberalized" Communistic states begin to approach the classless ideal.

One particular facet of the Communist movement is definitely having a direct influence on the activities of radical student movements on American campuses. Insofar as the more radical student movements definitely seek to revolutionize the entire American society they are not adverse to importing and adapting to the American circumstance the revolutionary methods and tactics developed by Communists. At least one radical student organization (Students for a Democratic Society) has widely distributed a handbook which explains in detail how the revolutionary tactics perfected by the Communists can be applied in taking over American universities. Communist revolutionary heroes such as Che Guevara have been adopted as patrons of such movements. How much influence the American Communist party itself has in the promotion of such tactics and heroes is questionable. Leaders of the radical student movements probably themselves do not know. While they claim to act with complete independence, they do not repudiate support from any quarter. Most university administrators and faculty members who work closely with students perceive very little direct Communist influence on American student movements. Many people who are not so closely associated with students feel that university officers are extremely naive in this matter.

One particular circumstance must be considered if the development of modern student values is to be understood. The sheer number of college and university students in the United States is a factor in determining the character of student judgments. At the present time there are almost eight million students on American campuses. Within a decade this number is expected to approach nine million. It is not insignificant that by 1972 the median age for voters in national elections will be twenty-six years. Thanks to the nation's superb news networks, student groups function with great unity even though a singleness of thought and action was not previously planned. A sense of corporate power is manifesting itself in student value judgments. As students are becoming aware that their value judgments are becoming increasingly important in the determination of national affairs, a greater self-assurance is apparent in their value decisions.

Michael Harrington[1] describes today's campus radicals as "A Prophetic Generation." The characterization is apt. A prophet speaks boldly. He sees issues in black and white without shades of grey. He speaks in terms of unquestionable absolutes. He is angry when these absolutes are not fully realized. The prophet does not ask. He demands. He knows. He is certain. He is convinced he speaks eternal truth. How many prophets will nine million students produce as this nine million becomes more self-assured in its value judgments. To what extent will this self-assurance affect the value judgments of this college generation? How many true prophets will they produce and how many false?

The second characteristic of student value judgments is that they are becoming increasingly critical of American society. This is not surprising. To criticize is but another facet of youth's idealism. Where reality does not match the ideal—and it never does—criticism is inevitable. Criticism of the American way of life by such an overwhelming number of students will provide a new and not altogether welcome experience for the nation. It is not something for which previous generations bargained as, with their own idealism, they labored to provide the opportunity of a college education for every young person in the nation. The criticism of students is already considered unreasonable and unfair, as indeed much of it undoubtedly is. Students are considered thoughtless and ungrateful, as indeed many of them are. Their actions are thought irresponsible as they heap their criticism on "the system" that pays the bills for their education, and some of their criticism is unquestionably very irresponsible. However, the ultimate price which any nation must pay that dares to educate its young is to bear with the critical attitude that education inevitably produces. A nation cannot teach its young people to dream and then stifle the hope that their dreams inspire.

The dreams and the hopes that the American education experience is presently producing in the young is a significant factor in student unrest. Most students in earlier generations, preparing to assume their places in the professional and business world, took little notice of the economic and social conditions of people less fortunate than themselves. Their dreams and hopes would be fulfilled by a reasonable measure of personal success and family security. But the American overall educational experience has changed all this. Now even before entering college many students are concerned about the poverty and suffering of other segments of the population. As the underprivileged and the oppressed of the nation strive to fulfill their "rising expectations," the students identify with their hopes and aspirations. As a consequence the

[1]From his introduction to *A Prophetic Minority* by Jack Newfield.

foment of the larger society is reflected and magnified on campuses. Students challenge every aspect of American life which appears in any way accountable for producing or perpetuating poverty, discrimination, or the sacrifice of human dignity.

Perhaps the American educational effort has produced too much too soon. Perhaps it has produced more critical thinking than the American culture is presently able to assimilate. The United States has never before had to contend with a university population acting out its function as social critic. Suddenly it must face with the largest student population ever produced by a single nation in the history of the world. It is difficult for the nation to comprehend that for these millions of students to be critical is for them to be themselves. And criticism, like charity, unfortunately begins at home.

A third characteristic that is influencing student value judgments today is a result of the urgency with which young people view the need for solutions to national problems. It is characteristic of youth to seek solutions NOW. Because the need for immediacy appears especially pressing today, students are becoming increasingly forceful in the expression of their views. This forcefulness sometimes manifests itself in violent forms.

Modern communications have made the problems of the nation, and of the world, extremely visible. There have always been peoples who were the victims of oppression and injustice in situations which sometimes have endured over generations and even centuries. Until recent times the problems of such peoples have always seemed remote and unreal. They could easily be overlooked, ignored, or forgotten. Today, however, there are no hidden problems. All at once the oppressions and injustices of the past have all become visible and horribly real. This sudden visibility of so many national problems provides a whole new dimension in student value decisions. Solutions which will "take time" cannot be considered. As students see it, time has run out. There is no more time. Solutions must be found now. Impatience and frustration are as common to youth as their idealism and critical character. Student impatience and frustration are mounting today as the institutional means available to solve national problems prove ponderous and slow, or positively resistant to change. Impatience and frustration lead easily to the employment of means that are forceful and, if necessary, violent.

What will be the response of the American culture to the forceful means which students are beginning to employ to bring change in the American society? Extreme attitudes are certain to polarize. As John W. Gardner has observed, our cultural institutions are "caught in a savage crossfire between uncritical lovers and unloving critics." The uncritical lovers tend to protect the institutions from life-giving criticism, "loving their rigidities more than their promise." On the other hand, the unloving critics are "skilled in demolition but untutored in the arts by which human institutions are nurtured and strengthened and made to flourish." *(Time,* June 14, 1968.) Can our colleges and universities produce NOW a determining balance of *loving critics,* a student generation not only with understanding of the values inherent in the basic institutions of American life but with the vision to see "their promise"?

7

The Changing Role of the Counselor in Modern Society

C. Eugene Walker*

It has become almost trite to marvel at the rapid changes taking place in our culture due to the rise of industrialism and technology. We cannot escape the fact that this century has seen a hitherto unimaginable increase in the tempo of change. The fact that such an observation has become trite only attests to its basic accuracy. The changes that took place from the discovery of the wheel to the horse-drawn carriage—which figured so prominently in the early years of the history of our nation—were relatively slight. However, with the invention of the internal combustion engine, the jet engine, and many new sources of power, the changes in transportation both in terms of the rapidity with which destinations can be reached and the increasingly distant destinations that we are striving for (e.g., in outer space) is truly remarkable.

In previous years a person could expect to be born, reared, and die essentially in the same world. The changes that took place were relatively small and gradual enough for the individual to assimilate and adjust to them. However, technology has developed at such a rapid rate that the infant today is born into a world that will no longer be in existence when he reaches school age, and when he is in school he will be educated in a technology and for a world that will no longer be in existence when he graduates. As Marshall McLuhan [1][1] has quipped, "If it works, it's obsolete."

*Dr. C. Eugene Walker holds a B.S. degree from Geneva College, M.S. and Ph.D. from Purdue University. Currently Dr. Walker is a consultant for the Veteran's Hospital and the Head Start Program, Waco, Texas and Assistant Professor of Psychology at Baylor University. Dr. Walker's extensive publications in the fields of higher education, counseling, and psychology have been widely received and highly acclaimed.
[1]Numbers in brackets indicate references at end of chapter.

While our world and our civilization are changing at a rapid pace, we more frail and recalcitrant human beings often find that we are unable to match the pace. We find ourselves with one foot in each world.

I recall an elderly couple from a small town in Ohio where I grew up. This couple had been born and reared in a society where the horse-drawn carriage was the main mode of transportation. At the time I knew them, they owned an automobile and were thoroughly acquainted and accustomed to its use. However, their phenomenological world and the cognitive map which they entertained of their surroundings had not changed since the horse-and-carriage days. Thus, when they decided to drive to Painesville, Ohio, which was some forty miles away, they would take their car to the garage mechanic to have it checked over and tuned up for the trip. To them, this trip was still a very major journey which could be undertaken only at infrequent intervals and with a great deal of preparation beforehand.

Another striking feature of our culture frequently commented upon is the profusion of affluence. We have become a people about to be overwhelmed by the productivity of the technology and industrial machine which we have built. We now have more free time and more products to consume than have any people or any civilization in history. While much of the world starves and struggles to eke out an existence, America wallows in fat and obesity is one of the most talked about national health problems. It is probably safe to say that the average American family has more wealth, more convenience, more entertainment, more opportunity for travel, better health care, and in general, a more comfortable and posh existence than did any of the kings or rulers of ancient empires who were noted for their conspicuous consumption.

Lest we think that this is a temporary state that we are in, we are assured by those in a position to forecast that what we can expect in the future is even more affluence, more free time on our hands, and more problems of increasing consumption.

As many observers of the American scene have commented, while this state of abundance might be expected to result in a full and enjoyable life, the exact opposite seems to be the case. People used to think that the rise of industrialization would be a great boon to humanity. It was thought that once freed from the sweat and toil of existence, man would be able to enjoy the finer things in life such as art, music, and literature, and be a happier, more fulfilled person. However, it is becoming increasingly apparent that no such thing is happening; in fact, one of the consequences of affluence in many cases seems to be increasing neuroticism [2].

When the country was in economic depression, and following that when the country was involved in a major war, people had little doubt about what their goals were. They knew where they fitted into the picture, what their responsibilities were, and what they had to do. They had a strong sense that others were dependent upon them; a strong sense of national community. The situation was difficult. Day-to-day existence was an end in itself. Things were relatively clear-cut; judgments were easy. There was a certain "rising to the occasion" and *esprit de corps* which carried people along.

However, in times such as we have today the necessities and even the desires of life are easily satisfied. Freed from the concern of day-to-day existence, people are forced to consider the questions "Who am I?" "Where am I going?" "What is really important?" and "What does life really mean?" When the answers to these questions are not readily forthcoming, the individual begins to realize that along with the luxurious and lavish consumption that he is afforded come numerous tensions and anxieties. There is the recurring necessity to change, to change again, and to be a part of a continually revising system. Since change is often difficult and threatening, people become neurotic and need therapeutic help.

Among previous generations there has always been a rather robust optimism among people that a utopian era, the best of all possible worlds, was just around the corner. Democracy and science could not fail to bring it to our doorstep. People were content that the future could contain nothing but good.

However, we now find ourselves in that future, and replacing our optimism is fear and anxiety. In place of the dynamic self-made man, the true individualist, we have the hippie, a collective individualist. The hippie is a greatly magnified version of the pain, the anxiety, and disenchantment that exists very widely in many people in our culture.

Basically, it would seem that we simply have not learned to live with affluence. Since there is little doubt that the prediction concerning increased affluence and increasing free time for the average individual is true, and, since it is also a fact of life that more and more people will not have skills that are marketable in our society, it becomes the job of the counselor, of the educator, of the minister, of everyone, to attempt to help people learn to deal with this situation.

Along with these changes in American society have come changes in the role of the counselor. The remainder of this chapter will trace the development of some of these changes over the last twenty or thirty years and note their relation to the developments taking place in society.

One of the most striking changes that one observes in the current status of counseling as compared with the work of the counselor or therapist of thirty years ago is the continual trend toward demystification of the counseling process. In the 1940's, when psychoanalysis was at its peak, the therapeutic relationship and the counseling room were considered a deep, dark, mysterious bastion in which resided a highly trained, thoroughly professional therapist who had gone through analysis himself, and who now was prepared to pass the wand of healing over all who came to him. The dangers of the dynamics and emotions that were supposedly unleashed in this secret chamber were emphasized, and therapy was considered a long, painful experience to be undertaken only by people who were "mentally ill."

In contrast, the counseling process is currently seen in a different light. Carl Rogers was an early forerunner in this process. What he left undone was completed by the existentialists and the behavior therapists. The end result is that the therapeutic and counseling relationship is seen as one of an open, honest, above-board, encounter between two human beings in which one attempts via principles of learning or through some relationship to effect a change in the behavior, attitudes, and feelings of the other. It is increasingly being recognized that there is nothing secret about this. The process can be studied objectively and communicated to others.

Partially as a result of this change, and partially as a result of various other movements within our culture, counseling is becoming more acceptable to more people. While it is still considerable, there is less stigma attached to people who go to a counselor or therapist. More people are realizing the need for counseling and therapy, and, while it is impossible to document, it appears quite possible that more people need therapy today than did in the past.

Another result of the change in attitude toward therapy has been the increasing recognition that nonprofessionals can be used effectively as psychotherapists. Rioch [3] trained mature housewives to do psychotherapy. While many were scandalized at the beginning of this project, most would now agree that she has been extremely successful and that this is an avenue that should be explored more and more in the future. Indeed, the Joint Commission on Mental Illness and Health recommended in its report [4] that college volunteer programs should be encouraged and expanded.

These programs, begun with Harvard students, have spread throughout the country [5]. They are not the typical volunteer program where the participants run errands, type letters, and do other types of menial work. Instead the students meet with individual patients and groups of patients for a type of therapy. The students are oriented and supervised by professional staff members. A variety of rationales are employed in the students' therapeutic work, including modeling, friendship, behavior modification, remotivation, interaction, and the like; but these young people are doing therapy and the patients seem

to benefit from it. In fact, one such program developed between Westmont College in Santa Barbara and Camarillo State Hospital eventually
led to successful experimentation with the use of selected high school
students in this role [6].

The college student programs seem to result in mutual benefit to all
concerned. The patients benefit therapeutically from the presence of
bright, young men and women who are concerned and eager to help.
The hospital staff enjoys the stimulation of having active youth around
doing things and asking questions. The students benefit by seeing in a
firsthand way what the world of mental illness and clinical psychology
is all about. This makes their textbooks and class lectures much more
meaningful and understandable.

The author has recently heard about a program in which older
juvenile delinquent boys are being trained in basic techniques of counseling with other individuals, and then used as counselors to younger
delinquent boys. The end result, it is hoped, will be that a marked and
significant change will occur in all of the boys [7].

While the use of such people as counselors may seem strange to
some, it should not be thought that this is just a stopgap measure due
to the shortage of truly professional manpower. In fact, it would appear
that, in most cases, these untrained counselors have a very definite
contribution to make. A study of school counseling [8] found that the
untrained counselors did better than the trained ones. Poser [9] found
the same thing with undergraduates doing group psychotherapy with
psychotic patients; and Carkhuff [10], in an extensive review of the
literature on nonprofessional counselors, concluded, "Evidence indicates that with or without training and/or supervision, the patients of
lay counselors do as well or better than the patients of professional
counselors."

It would, of course, be premature to say that training is completely
unnecessary to be a counselor, because, when the facts are all in, it will
undoubtedly be clear that good training is needed. But, it also appears
that there is much that can be accomplished under the right circumstances by those with little or no training.

In addition to the recognition of the role of nonprofessionals and
the growing willingness and openness to using them, there is more and
more recognition of the need to draw other people into the circle of
helpers. The role of the teacher is becoming increasingly seen as one
which can lead to the development of better emotional adjustment in
the student, in addition to teaching him subject matter. The growth of
the pastoral counseling movement is another evidence of this same
trend. Whereas the pastor of fifty or sixty years ago thought of his main
responsibility as preparing the Sunday sermon and making a few social
visits from time to time, the current minister feels that one of his most

pressing problems is to help his parishioners deal with the tensions and pressures of modern living. Ministers are taking courses in psychology and studying the techniques of counseling. In addition, journals have been established, books written, and internship programs begun to enable the minister to become a better counselor.

As Mowrer has pointed out [11], there is also a strong trend toward the development of natural resources in counseling. Numerous groups are springing up throughout the country in which individuals meet to discuss common problems, to offer support and help to each other, and to enable each other to cope with situations that are proving difficult for them. The leadership of Alcoholics Anonymous has been known and respected in this area for many years. There are similar organizations for a wide variety of people such as addicts, former mental hospital patients, prisoners, and so forth, as well as for the average person interested in exploring his feelings and relationships with others.

Along with these developments is an increasing realization by people in general and by counselors in particular that a more meaningful life and a life which is fulfilling will automatically result in better mental health [12]. The role of the counselor and therapist was previously thought of as dealing with sick people and, in some way, psychotherapeutically removing the sickness or the pain from them in order to get them back to what they used to be. It is now being seen much more clearly that the problem is not to attack the sickness so much as it is to help people to live a meaningful, rich, full life, both as a preventive and as a therapeutic measure [13]. Increasingly, the counselor is being faced with a client who has no major problem, who is able to cope with life in an adequate way, but who wants to find more fulfillment; who wants to have a more meaningful, rich, and fruitful existence. This is a different kind of problem and requires a different approach than many counselors have been trained for.

Some of the more recent developments of this sort are related to the rise of community psychology [14]. The counselor is increasingly being thought of as a consultant in a broad general way rather than as a therapist for individual patients. This job takes him into the community, to organizations, to groups, rather than to a small office where sick people are brought to him. Telephone counseling centers, suicide prevention centers, and crisis teams which make home visits to see families through problems on the spot are a part of this movement. A group of ministers recently established a telephone center where people may call at any time just to talk to them. Another group established a center where people may phone in and confess anything that they want to get off their chest. There are partial hospitalization plans where individuals sign themselves into a hospital during the day but spend their nights at home, or work during the day and spend nights at the hospital [15].

There are individuals who come to a hospital or see a private therapist for a weekend of therapy. The marathon group therapy movement is an example of this [16,17]. The old-model state hospitals are declining significantly in size and influence. Community clinics and outpatient care are increasingly becoming the treatment of choice. Mental health professionals are realizing that hospitals are very artificial environments in which to try to help people solve problems that basically have to do with interpersonal difficulties involving their families and neighbors. There is significant danger that removal from the community actually may make many people worse rather than better by stereotyping them into the role of a "mentally ill person" [18] and developing a dependence upon the hospital and its staff.

We are currently being forced to pay more than lip service to the fact that the problem of the mentally ill is the problem of all of us. We are moving to a point where the counselor will find his role and his job with relatively well-functioning and some not-so-well-functioning people who are attempting to face and cope with their environment and who are being supported *in the community* while they are seeking help [19,20].

The implications of these trends for the school or college counselor are clear. Counselors in these settings will undoubtedly find the trends here described familiar. The school counselor of the future will find more and more students who are at college because they need a college degree to survive; who are uncertain about who they are or where they are going, who, therefore, can't decide on a major or a career, who feel a deep sense of futility and frustration with trying to cope with an increasingly complex world; and, with a group of people who are more and more capable, more and more talented, but who still feel unfulfilled, and are searching for ways to lead a more meaningful and fruitful existence. The school counselor of the future will probably spend less of his time in the counseling center (though there will always be a need for personal counseling), and more and more of it in the dorms, in meetings with small spontaneous groups, in various campus movements, and in broader attempts to restructure the school environment along lines compatible with mental health.

REFERENCES

1. McLuhan, M. *Understanding Media.* New York: McGraw-Hill Book Company, 1964.
2. Schofield, W. *Psychotherapy: The Purchase of Friendship.* Englewood Cliffs, N.J.: Prentice-Hall, Inc., 1964.
3. Rioch, M. J., E. Elkes, A. A. Flint, B. S. Usdansky, R. G. Neuman, and E. Silber.

"National Institute of Mental Health Pilot Study in Training Mental Health Counselors," *American Journal of Orthopsychiatry*, 33 (1963),pp. 678-689.

4. Ewalt, J. R. *Action for Mental Health*. New York: Basic Books, Inc., 1961.

5. Umbarger, C. D., J. S. Dalsimer, A. P. Morrison, and P. R. Breggin. *College Students in a Mental Hospital*. New York: Grune & Stratton, Inc., 1962.

6. Walker, C. E., M. Wolpin, and L. Fellows. "The Use of High School and College Students as Therapists and Researchers in a State Mental Hospital," *Psychotherapy: Theory, Research, and Practice*, 4 (1967), pp. 186-188.

7. Jones, D. W. "The Treatment of Deviant Behavior by Youth Involvement in Public School." Ph.D. dissertation, University of Oregon, 1968.

8. Zunker, V. G., and W. F. Brown. "Comparative Effectiveness of Student and Professional Counselors," *Personnel and Guidance Journal*, 44 (1966), pp. 738-743.

9. Poser, E. G. "The Effect of Therapists' Training on Group Therapeutic Outcome," *Journal of Consulting Psychology*, 30 (1966), pp. 283-289.

10. Carkhuff, R. "Differential Functioning of Lay and Professional Helpers," *Journal of Counseling Psychology*, 15 (1968), pp. 117-126.

11. Mowrer, O. H. *New Group Therapy*. Princeton, N.J.: D. Van Nostrand Company, Inc., 1964.

12. Maslow, A. H. *Toward a Psychology of Being*. Princeton, N.J.: D. Van Nostrand Company, Inc., 1962.

13. Schutz, W. C. *Joy: Theory and Methods for Developing Human Potential*. New York: Grove Press, Inc., 1967.

14. Bellak, L. *Handbook of Community Psychiatry and Community Mental Health*. New York: Grune & Stratton, Inc., 1964.

15. Greenblatt, M., D. J. Levinson, G. L. Klerman, and J. R. Ewalt. *Mental Patients in Transition*. Springfield, Ill.: Charles C. Thomas, 1961.

16. Bach, G. R. *Intensive Group Psychotherapy*. New York: The Ronald Press, Inc., 1954.

17. Sohl, J. *The Lemon Eaters*. New York: Dell Publishing Co., Inc., 1967.

18. Sheff, T. J. *Being Mentally Ill: A Sociological Theory*. Chicago: Aldine Publishing Company, 1966.

19. Williams, R. H. and Lucy Ozarin. *Community Mental Health: An International Perspective*. San Francisco: Jossey-Bass, Inc., Publishers, 1968.

20. Fairweather, G. W. *Methods for Experimental Social Innovation*. New York: John Wiley and Sons, Inc., 1967.

8

Helping the Student
Understand Himself

R. Wray Strowig*

The major question before us has to do with *how* one may help a counselee acquire self-understanding. This is an intriguing question, because observation of youth in their relationships with adults reveals a wide variety of helping situations in progress. The nature of the helper and the helped person, as well as the character of the environment in which the helping experience occurs, all may effect the helping process. Stated somewhat differently, before one can understand what one is really doing in helping another toward self-understanding, one should know what one means by "self" and secondly, one should specify the conditions intrinsic to and impinging upon the helping process. These are the tasks to which this chapter is addressed. Parenthetically, of course, there is what may be the most fascinating question of all— namely, *why* help a student to understand himself? However, the writer shall forego the desire to wrestle with the question of why.

THE SELF VIEWED PRAGMATICALLY

The nature of the self has received much attention. Formulations by many writers may be read, among the more prominent of which are those of Lecky, Selye, Jersild, Rogers, and Moustakas. There is also a

*Dr. R. Wray Strowig held a B.A. degree from Kansas Wesleyan University, M.A. from University of Kansas, and Ed.D. from Stanford University. Author of numerous articles on counseling, guidance, mental health, and education, Dr. Strowig also directed research on educational development and counseling. At the time of his death in 1969 he was Chairman of Guidance and Counseling Department at the University of Wisconsin.

staggering body of research that purports to deal with self, most of which has been ably analyzed by Wylie.

Three findings stand out among the ideas and research efforts on the self: First, the theories are all somewhat unique and therefore so is most of the research. No two self-theories are alike, although they share some ideas in common. Second the phenomenon of self is almost completely subjective or concerned with inner states of man. There are no known ways to cross-validate independent measures of self. Third, theory and research on the self is not really on the self. Rather it is on the ideas of self, the abstractions *from* self. This is true whether the reporter or judge is the person whose self is under study or someone else. In summary, self-theory has not helped us much. We need a different set of ideas about self.

The present writer has tried to formulate a few ideas about the self, using high school and college students as models. In doing so, it is recognized that however bright and observant we may be, we are mere onlookers, standing outside of the student and trying to see all of him. That is, we are always liable to be at least partly wrong in our ideas about someone else's self. His experience is not ours, and we can therefore never hope to view his self as he perceives it. Consequently, the concepts of the self that the writer describes very briefly must be taken as abstractions only, although it is hoped they approximate the genuine article.

The Self as Objective and Subjective

To begin with, it is useful, for those of us who wish to help youth, to think of a person's self as being both subjective and objective. One might speak of his self both by mentioning his feelings, attitudes, and values and by pointing to his body and his deeds. We might abstract his description by stating that one's self extends from inner states of being through awareness of physique and acting out in behavior. In brief, the writer is suggesting that we regard the self as both, "I think; therefore, I am," and "I exist because I act." Thus the self involves reflection and feeling about one's life as well as the acting out of thoughts and feelings. To illustrate:

> Carl was a student at Harvard College. The admissions data had predicted success for him to the extent of A's and B's. To a considerable extent, the prediction was supported by his performance. Yet, he came to see the counselor with the thought of quitting school. These excerpts from Carl's words in the interview illustrate the inseparability of thought and action in the self.
> "I sure ought to be disgusted," Carl said, and grimaced. "I don't know. I was never like this before. Even my clothes—." He gestured at his dirty jeans. "Beatnik yet—the pillar of my high school class." He

looked out the window, and I was glad he did not bother to smile. "I've been a model for six years, and thought I liked it and was settled into it. Head of the family and all. Hell, I did like it, or at least I liked all the honor and respect I got. ... Boy, if they knew I gamble every night —and win!" He glanced at me with a grin, and color showed under his stubble. "Pretty reprehensible! Well, it is, really, that's the trouble— and the worst of it is that though I pretend not to, I suspect I feel proud of it ... somewhere." ["A Reporter at Large: A Problem of Identity," *The New Yorker,* Dec. 1, 1962]

Carl is a good example of the inseparable continuity between one's physical and behaving attributes and his cognitive and affective reactions, all wrapped up in one identity.

The Self as Consciousness

Counselors and others who work with youth sometimes forget that unconscious forces affect the person and his conception of himself. At least it seems necessary to use the concept of the unconscious to explain the moving forces underlying the otherwise unexplainable behavior. There is much that a person cannot report about himself, let alone understand it. He is not even aware of it. Since this chapter is devoted to working on a conception of self that corresponds somewhat to the individual's ideas of self, it is necessary to describe the self as conscious. In doing this, however, the writer is fairly sure that there is much about the person that is not included.

The material of self that counselor and client discuss will be derived from the latter's conscious awareness. The counselor in Carl's case responded to Carl in various ways attending to objective and subjective features of Carl's self, but always reacting to Carl's verbal and nonverbal behavior that seemed at least dimly in Carl's conscious awareness. This response to consciousness made it easier for Carl to react naturally and with growing realization of the meaning of his reactions. These insights may help the client to understand himself. Consciously speaking, the need of the self is for clearer identification of its features and tightening the organization of its structure. In Erikson's terms, "The overriding meaning of it all is the creation of a sense of sameness, a unity of personality now felt by the individual and recognized by others as having consistency in time—of being, as it were, an irreversible fact."

The Self as Historical

The self also has historical character. The historical facet of self comes partly from the perceptions and conclusions drawn by an individual in looking back at his personal experience. As one young lady who was trying to decide on a college major some years ago heatedly told this writer:

> I can see it now—I've *always* been a mama's girl. Ever since I can remember she has told me what to do and when and how to do it. Honestly, I don't think I've ever made up my own mind about anything at all important. . . . So you see, that's why I am *not* going to be the actress she wants me to be, no matter how I turn out!

For years, educators have been in the habit of gathering billions of facts about the growth and experience of students. We gather test scores, teacher marks, and biographies with religious zeal. A smallish portion of the data may be of value in predicting future performance. However, the only part of personal history that is relevant to understanding the self is the part that has had the impact of cognitive or affective meaning to the student. Therefore, the historical facet of self can be understood best by helping the client get acquainted with and sort out the facts about his past that are relevant to *him*.

This process is important, because it should help the person develop a sense of "having been" and "now becoming"—Erikson's "consistency in time—of being, as it were, an historical fact." While the need to establish a sense of history with regard to self reaches its peak in adolescence, the process has been going on through childhood and, hopefully, will continue to be refined throughout life. The connections between events in a personal history are intimate and they stretch far. Autobiographical data from former graduate students in counseling suggest a relationship between counseling career choices and people with whom they had identified in childhood who actively helped others.

The historical character of self also comes partly from the future. The future is a projection of self beyond the present, and as self-understanding grows the person begins to develop a sense of "becoming." In adolescence the future does not seem that real and there is little sense of intimate relationship to personal history-making. Rather, the future takes the form of wishes to be or do something, or expectations of how one is likely to turn out. Small wonder, then, that counseling with high school and college youth about their vocational aspirations is often not fruitful. Follow-up studies have shown that most of the relationships between wish and fact have been tenuous. Nonetheless, it should be stressed that, however "unrealistic" students' vocational choices may be, they are partially representative of the selves of these students at that time. Perhaps seemingly unrealistic choices would be more reasonable if they were studied in relation to the history of the students rather than their futures.

The Immediacy of Self

The self in the present tense must be viewed somewhat differently. Suppose a person impulsively decides that he does not want to control his behavior, that he is not—momentarily at least—at all interested in anticipating probable long-range consequences. While one may argue that such apparently irrational behavior theoretically could be predicted if one knew enough about the individual's history, it seems far more likely that behavior of this sort is typically unpredictable. In fact, uniqueness and improbability are hallmarks of such behavior. It seems, therefore, that we must include a facet of pure immediacy of experience in a conception of the self.

We may use Korzybski's terms to describe the immediate character of the self, calling it "first-order" experience, or "unspeakable" experience, that is unmediated by thought of the experiencing person. Such experiencing is deemed to be a distinctive and important facet of self. It is not abstracted experience and it is not time-bound. To illustrate by means of contrast: When a counselee is trying to *explain* to you how he feels, he is not relating to you the experience of feeling itself but rather his perceptions and ideas about the feeling. However, if he expresses immediately his feelings with tears, joy, or anger, in the reporting process he is experiencing directly. Too little counseling for self-understanding involves sharing and responding to the immediacy of the self. Too much counseling deals with discussions *about* the self and never really affects the self of a student.

As far as is known, there is no way that understanding of "unspeakable" direct experience can be obtained through cognitive symbolic means. Perhaps that is one reason why in our culture adults pay so little attention, other than personal embarrassment, to direct experiencing as a facet of the self. Children, especially the younger ones, possess an abundant awareness of self in the sense of immediacy, but in our society the training for the cognitive life and for social conventions seems to nearly eliminate it from awareness. However, the sense of immediacy in self is never destroyed entirely. It is evident in many of us through such experiences as the aroma of early morning coffee, the sight of a lovely sunset, and the sound of a beautiful symphony. Is this quality of self worth preserving and nourishing? This writer thinks so. In the midst of the controlled cacaphony of machines, and organization, and regimentation of today, the capacity for direct esthetic experience and what Cantril calls "value-inquiry" may be one of man's few remaining weapons for preserving his sense of identity and autonomy.

The Self as Public and Private

The last attribute of the self which is believed to be important to a useful description of the self in self-understanding is the self's public and private character. There is a parallel between the public-private features of self and the objective-subjective facet which was described earlier. However, the objective-subjective nature of self refers to the variation in concreteness or tangibility of the self, whereas the public-private aspect of self alludes to the affective, cognitive, and conative impulses of the person in giving expression to himself.

It is a mistake to view the self as wholly internal and private to the person. Ask a student to tell you who he is. After he has recovered from the shock, he may say something like this. "Why, I am John Jones. I am a student, and a son, and a brother, and Suzie Smith's 'steady.' And someday I will be a nuclear physicist, if I can just get admitted to The University !" The point of this example is that an individual does think of himself in a number of public ways. Therefore, one's own conception of the self must include some means of expanding the inner nature of self into interactions with environment.

The concept of roles is a useful concept for the counselor. It is important to know which roles the individual uses, whether voluntarily or not, and how he interprets various roles in actual expressions of self. Although we may describe a person from the viewpoint of expectations and prescriptions that derive from a culture and from other persons in a social system, the proposition involved here is that roles, as they are *adopted and adapted by the person,* are extensions of the self. Thus there is a continuum from private to public character of the self.

The self's private nature is partially derived from its public nature, in the form of perceptions that the individual has of himself in different roles, as well as his awareness of the perceptions that others have of him. Actually, private and public facets of self interact reciprocally and tend to modify each other within a striving for consistency. Tell a student often enough that he is a poor college prospect and he may begin to believe you; or he may feel so angry (his private self speaking) that he later strives mightily to prove you a liar. Some of the most surprising achievements come about because there is an incongruence between private and public facets of self. Being blissfully congruent is not always the most desirable state of existence.

It appears the private character of self has different levels of consciousness. It can be suggested that the self of a person consists in part of features that are close to the surface of expression through roles, and in part of features to which no other human being is privy. This *most-private* character of self is inviolable except through access allowed by the individual.

In this writer's opinion, it is unethical for an influential adult, whether counselor, teacher, or parent, to manipulate a child or adult, however directively or nondirectively, in order to induce him to bare facets of his most-private self. The reasoning behind this is the value judgment that privacy of self is a necessary condition of respect for persons. This is the position taken in the writer's counseling work, despite the realization that this policy may hinder helping a client understand himself. Such a policy is derived from the premise that man's individuality shades imperceptibly into his aloneness. There are both practical and philosophical limits to the helping relationship.

Summary of Self

Up to this point the subject of this chapter has been the self of the individual. A few conceptual dimensions of self have been suggested that should have practical consequences for those who wish to help others understand themselves. The dimensions or facts of self have been identified as objective-subjective, historical, futuristic, immediate, public-private and conscious. Unconscious and most-private features of student self have been ruled out for counselors, teachers, and other adults.

The writer wants to make quite clear that he does not believe that he has identified the actual stuff of self. He does hope he has indicated the great complexity of the problem of acquiring self-understanding. Personally, the writer believes that self-understanding is a lifetime goal and process. Probably, one cannot do much more than help a person early to add a cubit to the stature of his self-understanding. However, if the effort is successful even to that small degree, the result should be a deeper personal meaning to that person's life. Meanwhile, however, there is the important matter of conditions in the student's life that nourish self-understanding, to which the writer would like to turn.

THE CONDITIONS OF AIDING STUDENT SELF-UNDERSTANDING

There are five conditions which can be identified that are conducive to helping a student understand himself. They are tentatively named.

1. Openness to experiencing
2. Building a personal history
3. The search for personal challenge
4. Confrontation with decision making
5. The self-understanding helper

It should come as no surprise that these conditions have been derived mainly out of reflection on experience as a counselor and teacher. The real source of these conditions, however, is the foregoing analysis of the features of the self. And that is as it should be; for the conditions of learning that are to be created should be revealed through an adequate understanding of the nature of the learner and the nature of the subject matter.

Before describing the five conditions briefly, it is important to note that any experience of a person potentially can contribute to his self-understanding. These experiences are not found exclusively in one area of a student's life, nor are experiences with people who are specialists, such as physicians, clergymen, counselors, or social workers, the only ones that may be conducive to aiding self-understanding.

Openness to Experience

The first condition that is essential to self-understanding is openness to the stuff of experience itself. This condition is mentioned first because it is the primary process, both chronologically and qualitatively, upon which self-understanding is based. As Cantril says, "Understanding the process of living must start from naive experience in the phenomenal area."

Now it is obvious that the quality of openness resides in the student, not in his environment, although the experience itself is an interaction between self and environment. Openness to immediate experience is a characteristic of self in early childhood. It is precognitive at the time that the experience occurs. When cognition comes into play in an attempt to describe and abstract the meaning of experience, the qualities of selectivity and order or pattern are involved, and openness is gone. This is why there is little hope of changing a student's goals by giving him a straightforward rational explanation of why he can't succeed at Miracle Tech.

Openness to experience can be encouraged by providing the counselee with a wide variety of cues in a given situation. What this writer chooses to call a cue must furnish a stimulus that can be associated with the client's prior experience. Hence, a further qualification in providing cues is that they must be within the student's frame of reference. In brief, the trick is to provide as many cues as possible for the client that are within the range of what he consciously deems important. Therefore, an informal rambling but purposeful dialogue with that Miracle Tech applicant in which he can feel as well as think, and in which you react to both feeling and thought, is a much better approach to helping him understand himself. Of course, this takes time.

In discussing how people make value judgments, Cantril states that "The reliability of the directives reached through value inquiry is directly related to the adequacy of the cues taken into account." Too little of the schooling of children and youth is devoted to the satisfaction of curiosity through precognitive mental and physical immersion in great varieties of immediate experiencing. Too much emphasis on having a student acquire information *about* something is probably inimical to both his understanding of the subject and himself. Likewise, too rigid expectations from adults about what is considered "proper" behavior in reacting to experiences diminishes the likelihood of self-understanding. Our stereotypes of what sort of student is good college material are one example. We should strive for a *better balance* in school between role-taking and impulsive behavior of students.

Personal History Building

A second condition that is helpful in improving a client's self-understanding is to spend time with him in developing his personal history. This condition is directly related to both the historical and objective facets of self. The writer prefers to regard this process as history building rather than "analysis of the individual," as it is called in guidance circles, because the proper emphasis of studying and discussing data about one's self should be on a self that has existed in the past and exists now, and that is growing and changing through time—all of which helps to establish ego identity.

Apropos of the goal of self-understanding, the best use that can be made of facts about a counselee is to get him acquainted with these facts. That is even more important than having teachers and counselors informed about these facts. Actually, this writer has not found it necessary to study facts about a client before discussing them with him. The real value for both of us lies in the dialogue between us that is stimulated by confronting data about the counselee in an atmosphere of mutual respect and liking. Actually, caring is a better word for the relationship than is liking. One can't like everyone, but one can care about them.

Of course, some data about a counselee are more valuable than others; and the form of the data, whether test scores, teacher marks, health information, or others, is not especially important. What is important is the interest and meaning of data in the view of the client. The most fruitful pattern of discourse about these data may often seem illogical and unsystematic. But what is psychologically relevant for the counselee is not always logical for the counselor. Hence it is good for the client to take the lead.

The Search for Personal Challenge

The building of a personal history is easiest to encourage in a one-to-one relationship between counselor and client, whereas openness to experiencing can happen anywhere. Similarly, the search for personal challenge can occur in a counseling office, the classroom, the laboratory, or some social club. The particular setting is probably related to the kind of challenge, of which there may be a very few or a great many.

In helping the person search for personal challenge, it is important that counselors search out the compelling power of different features of an individual's environment. That is, what is needed is a considerable degree of insight into what stimulates and excites different people, what encourages them to move toward the objects in their environment.

As teachers learn to understand their subject matter from this viewpoint, there remains the creation of situations that confront a student with the challenge to inquire. One cannot advocate complete manipulation of stimulating situations by adults; this is too similar to the relations between experimenter and rats in a maze. Students should not be deprived of the excitement of discovering for themselves what really interests them. Perhaps a teacher's best role is to provide situations conducive to self-discovery.

The search for personal challenge is an aid to self-understanding because it encourages openness to experiencing, and because it stimulates the person to use his abilities in new ways that demonstrate the expanding character of the self.

Confrontation with Decision Making

Until recently this writer had always regarded the experience of decision making as a necessary prelude to embarking on some goal-directed activity. Making decisions was important primarily because that is how goals and means to the achievement of goals are arrived at. The idea that decision-making experience could be a help to self-understanding was rather novel.

The writer's first inkling of the value of decision making to self-understanding came some time ago while attending a lecture by Bruno Bettelheim at The University of Wisconsin. In the questioning that followed, one young lady said, "Dr. Bettelheim, as college students it seems that we are expected to make more and more decisions and choices. Soon there are so many that they don't mean anything to us anymore. They don't seem to add up to anything important. Why is this?" Mr. Bettelheim's answer is long forgotten because the writer was engrossed in his own reaction, which went somewhat as follows:

If a person has all of the important decisions made for him by others, there will be little opportunity for self-understanding. However, if a person is directly engaged in decision making that is important to him, the opportunity for self-understanding is present, since crucial decisions should involve considering one's own nature as well as factors in one's situation. Therefore, it should be helpful to a counselee's self-understanding if counselors (1) encourage clients to make decisions for themselves, and (2) help them to consider not only the facts in the problematic situation, but especially what it is about their own natures that helps create a choice-point and disposes them toward or away from one route or another.

To the writer's way of thinking, it is quite unfortunate that so much important decision making about whether or not to go to college, where to go, and why, is done by parents rather than the student. Parents should have their say, but the decision should be the student's. It is also sad that so often these decisions are made in the waning hours of the junior and senior years, since much more leisure is needed to take advantage of decision making as an aid to self-understanding.

Self-Understanding of the Helper

The final condition to be discussed seemingly moves away from the consistent focus that has been maintained on the self of the client. This condition is that helping a client to understand himself is enhanced partially by how well the helping person understands himself. However, the focus on the counselee really remains, since the counselor's person is a very important component of the situation or experience which is in the client's awareness.

The self-understanding of the counselor is crucial to the helping relationship for the following reasons. Self-understanding presumably adds to one's sense of identity and purpose in life. Without identity and purpose, the individual is prone to confusion and diffusion as to his own nature and movement in the stream of living. A likely consequence is anxiety with regard to self. It seems axiomatic that anxiety about one's self will inhibit one's capacity to concentrate on any other person, except in self-referent terms. The qualities of relationship that a counselor should communicate to a client are to perceive his world and his self as he perceives it, and to accept him with respect and caring. These qualities are not very likely to be present if the helping person does not understand and accept himself.

Even counselors and other adults who understand themselves have their bad moments. It is frighteningly easy to tell a student that you don't think he ought to go to college because he would probably fail, without realizing that your own fears are projected; or that you think he should go to college, not being aware that your own values are showing. It is also entirely too simple to limit counselees to fifteen-minute interviews on the rationalization that you don't have time for any more; or to cut them off short on the grounds that his air of wonderment at a new experience is just childish fancy. No—even when we understand ourselves pretty well, it is still very hard to help a client to understand himself.

Being involved in a successful counseling relationship tends to inculcate more self-understanding on the part of the counselor as well as the client. But if the writer is correct in proposing that successful help-ing requires self-understanding on the part of the counselor, then it seems likely that someone else might well help that counselor toward self-understanding. Broadly speaking, then, in order to help clients understand themselves the community should become a complete net-work of helping relationships that involve each of us at different times in the role of helper and the helped. The writer would like to think that people are moving, however slowly and awkwardly, toward such a community of personal relationships. As the poet said, "No man is an island . . ."

CONCLUSION

As a concluding comment, one cannot resist writing of self-under-standing as an objective of education. Frankly, the writer does not know of any other objective that is more important. It has always been impor-tant, but it seems more so than ever nowadays. Perhaps we don't get along with our neighbors in Cuba and Chicago because we don't under-stand them; and we don't understand ourselves. Moreover, although a lot of people are decrying the lag between our knowledge of ourselves as compared to our technology and science, there is precious little progress at closing the gap. In the schools we do not make much pro-gress on self-understanding even though there are quite a few areas of the school curriculum that deal with studies about man. The reason for our lag is plain: when the objective is self-understanding the student is both subject and learner, but he is always treated only as learner—learner of something outside of himself. Therefore there is ample justifi-cation in schools and colleges for providing counseling and other ap-proaches to helping the student study himself, which is the only road known to self-understanding.

REFERENCES

Cantril, Hadley. "Toward a Humanistic Psychology," *ETC: A Review of General Semantics*, 12 (1955), pp. 278-298.
Erikson, E. H. *Childhood and Society.* 2d ed. New York: W. W. Norton & Company, Inc., 1963.
Jersild, Arthur T. *The Psychology of Adolescence.* New York: The Macmillan Company, 1957.
———. *When Teachers Face Themselves.* New York: Bureau of Publications, Teachers College, Columbia University, 1957.
Lecky, Prescott. *Self-consistency: A Theory of Personality.* Fort Myers Beach, Fla.: Island Press, 1945.
———. *Self-consistency: A Theory of Personality.* Edited and interpreted by

Frederick C. Thorne. Hamden, Conn.: The Shoe String Press, Inc., 1961.
Moustakas, Clark E. *The Self: Exploration in Personal Growth.* With assistance
    in editing Indian progress by Sita Ram Jayaswal. New York: Harper &
    Row, Publishers, 1956.
Rogers, Carl R. "The Necessary and Sufficient Conditions of Therapeutic Per-
    sonality Change," *J. Consult. Psychol.*, 21 (1957) pp. 95-103.
Selye, Hans. *The Stress of Life.* New York: McGraw-Hill Book Company, 1956.
Wylie, Ruth C. *The Self Concept: A Critical Survey of Pertinent Research Litera-
    ture.* Lincoln: University of Nebraska Press, 1961.

9

The Behavior Therapies: Alternatives and Additions to Traditional Counseling Approaches

Milton Wolpin
C. Eugene Walker *

The past ten years have been among the most fruitful and exciting in regard to developments in psychotherapy. We appear to be on the verge—in some ways in the midst—of rather dramatic payoffs and applications of the long labors of general and experimental psychology. Some examples of clinical applications may illustrate.

Silverman and Geer [16] report the case of a 19-year-old female undergraduate with a long standing fear of crossing bridges who also had, over a period of four years, a frequently occurring nightmare which involved this same fear. After treating her for ten sessions with systematic desensitization, one of the recently developed behavior therapy techniques, both her fear of crossing bridges and the related nightmares were gone, neither of which recurred on six months follow-up.

Resnick [14] reports that six out of eight subjects who were treated for one week with "stimulus satiation" (in this instance, a marked increase in the number of cigarettes smoked per day) stopped smoking and had not resumed on a four month follow-up. Actual therapy time with each subject was one-half hour, during which the experimenter

*Dr. Milton Wolpin holds a B.A. from Brooklyn College, M.S. and Ph.D. from the University of Pittsburgh. Dr. Wolpin is currently an Associate Professor of Psychology at the University of Southern California and a consultant for the Veteran's Administration. His varied and sophisticated articles in medical and psychological journals have made significant contributions in the area of psychological counseling. Dr. Wolpin is listed in American Men of Science. Dr. C. Eugene Walker holds a B.S. degree from Geneva College, M.S. and Ph.D. from Purdue University. Currently Dr. Walker is a consultant for the Veteran's Hospital and the Head Start Program, Waco, Texas and Assistant Professor of Psychology at Baylor University. Dr. Walker's extensive publications in the fields of higher education, counseling and psychology have been widely received and highly acclaimed.

gathered data regarding prior smoking behavior and outlined the principles and procedures to be followed.

Davison [2] reports the case of a 21-year-old unmarried, white, male college senior whose parents wanted help for him due to his problems of introversion, procrastination, and masochism. The young man referred to himself as a sadist and reported masturbating about five times a week while enjoying and being stimulated by fantasies of torturing women. He dated very little, was not sexually aroused when near girls, and felt that his fantasies made it "impossible to ever contemplate marriage." Davison first presented a strong case to the patient against the validity of a "disease interpretation of unusual behavior." Following this he paired strong sexual feelings with pictures and images of females in nonsadistic contexts (e.g., having the patient masturbate while viewing pictures of girls in *Playboy* magazine). In addition, the sadistic fantasies were paired with aversive stimuli (for example, he had the subject imagine torturing females while at the same time imagining that he was drinking from a large bowl of soup "composed of steaming urine with reeking fecal boli bubbling around on top." Two of the sessions were devoted to school problems making a total of eight sessions. On one month follow-up, the sadistic fantasies were reported gone, as they had been at the end of treatment. Follow-up sixteen months later revealed that these fantasies had returned for a period. However, the patient had, on his own, repeated the procedures used in treatment. At the time of interview, he reported having "no need for sadistic fantasies" being much less shy and in fact by his old standards a "regular rake."

The three cases cited above are the work of a relatively new breed of psychotherapists, the "behavior therapists." While psychotherapy currently is still dominated by numerous varieties of Freudian and Rogerian approaches, which include heavy emphasis on retrospective considerations and/or the development of insight, it appears that significant changes will take place in this in the future. According to Matarazzo [11] within the next decade behavior therapy and existentialism can be expected to dominate psychotherapeutic approaches. It is the purpose of this chapter to offer a brief, nontechnical introduction to the behavior therapies and to contrast them with more traditional procedures. The chapter will explain and illustrate the major concepts and ideas associated with behavior therapy, rather than present a carefully reasoned and fully documented defense.

Ten or fifteen years ago most individual therapeutic approaches could be categorized as a kind of dialogue between two persons in which the major consideration was how "directive" or "nondirective" the therapist should be. In one camp were the Freudians and Rogerians, who deliberately emphasized allowing the person to figure things out by himself, and deemphasized advice-giving or direct guidance. However, at the same time there existed the organic-directive approach, which not only offered specific counsel to the patient for his problems but also focused on the use of medication for symptom relief. Behavior therapy approaches combine elements of both of these approaches. The patient is permitted to set his own goals and takes primary responsibility for achieving them; however, he does so under the guidance of and with direct training and advice from the therapist. The therapist's contribution is based as much as possible on scientific evidence, especially from the area of learning theory.

Basically there are two major orientations within the field of behavior therapy. One orientation draws heavily upon the principles of classical conditioning, the other upon the principles of operant conditioning. A simple introduction to the technique based on classical conditioning may be found in a book by Wolpe and Lazarus [20]. Numerous examples of the techniques of operant conditioning therapy may be found in two books by Krasner and Ullmann [8,17].

The system of therapy developed by Joseph Wolpe provides an excellent example of the techniques of behavior therapy based on classical conditioning. Joseph Wolpe calls his psychotherapeutic system "psychotherapy by reciprocal inhibition." Early in his career Wolpe's approach to psychotherapy was mostly psychoanalytic. However, through a variety of experiences he became somewhat disenchanted with the traditional psychoanalytic approach. He was particularly impressed by Malinowski's *Sex and Repression in Savage Society* and S. W. Valentine's *Psychology of Early Childhood.* Both of these works present persuasive arguments against the universality of the Freudian Oedipus theory, a key concept in psychoanalytic therapy. Through additional reading Wolpe discovered experiments conducted by numerous psychologists on conditioning and learning. After thoroughly familiarizing himself with this research and conducting some experiments of his own, Wolpe developed a system of psychotherapy based on the discoveries of psychologists in this area. This desire to place psychotherapy on a more scientific and therefore sounder basis is characteristic of most behavior therapists.

The general rationale of Wolpe's system is that abnormal behavior is acquired rather than inherited or caught, such as a disease. If it is acquired, it is acquired primarily through learning and life experiences. Given that abnormal behavior is learned, attempts to modify it may also profitably be based on learning theory. Parenthetically it should be mentioned that Wolpe feels that his system of therapy applies only to neurotic behavior because he considers psychoses to be organic diseases. However, this is a debatable point and many people have applied his techniques successfully to psychotic individuals.

A basic assumption of Wolpe's is that neurotic behavior consists of maladaptive responses which have been learned or conditioned to various inappropriate and irrelevant stimuli.

A brief review of classical conditioning might be in order here. The classic experiment by Pavlov [12], frequently cited, illustrates the principles of classical conditioning. When a bell is sounded, a dog typically participates in a number of different behaviors such as turning its head, moving, or barking. However, if the sounding of the bell is frequently followed by the presentation of food, the animal will eventually begin to produce saliva when the bell is sounded. Saliva, of course, is the normal response to food but not a normal response to the sound of a bell. Thus a bond has been formed between the bell and food resulting in a response to the sound which was originally made only to the food.

Wolpe assumes that the behavior of the neurotic is conditioned in the person by certain cues in times of stress[19]. Thus, very early in the individual's life, certain cues which were present during these times often became associated with the state of stress or anxiety. While these cues are not logically related to the state of anxiety, they have become associated with it through conditioning in the experience of the patient. When the person later encounters these stimuli or cues, he reacts with anxiety and performs various behavior that would be the normal or typical response to anxiety. The puzzling thing to those around the neurotic is that they do not recognize that there are any relevant cues for anxiety in the situation. The person is thus responding with an anxiety or panic response in what appears to be a nonthreatening situation to the objective observer. However, due to the subject's previous conditioning, this situation is anything but nonthreatening. For example, suppose the individual had a very stern, forbidding, and anxiety-provoking mother. He might then develop, in response to the presence of a female, numerous behaviors characteristic of a person in a state of anxiety and confusion. As a result, in relating to a female clerk in a store, a waitress, or his wife this individual might show considerable inappropriate behavior, fear, discomfort, and inability to relate to these individuals in a meaningful and sensible way. To others this behavior would seem ridiculous. But to the individual who has been conditioned to respond to a female figure with anxiety, any situation involving a female is indeed threatening.

The way to change this behavior, then, is to remove the anxiety, thus making the anxiety response and the behavior associated with it no longer necessary. The way Wolpe attempts to remove anxiety is by a process which he calls *reciprocal inhibition* which is a physiological term [15]. A more psychological expression of the same idea might refer to it as *counterconditioning.* The basic idea is to introduce a response which is incompatible with the anxiety response. The new response interrupts the conditioned reaction and does not permit the anxiety reponse to occur. According to the basic principles of learning, if a stimulus which has been conditioned to a certain response is presented repeatedly and the response prevented from occurring, the end result will be that the bond will be broken. Through counterconditioning a new response is attached to the old cues. This response then replaces the old anxiety response and prevents it from occurring.

Wolpe typically uses three sets of responses to interfere with anxiety responses. One category of responses that he uses are *assertive responses*—that is, he teaches the individual to assert himself and to cope with a given problem in a positive and agressive manner (in the good sense of the term). Secondly, he uses relaxation responses under the rationale that if a person can consciously, purposely relax he will not experience anxiety for a brief period. Wolpe uses a modified version of differential relaxation originally proposed by Jacobson [4] as well as a technique called *systematic desensitization* which he himself has developed. In systematic desensitization the person prepares a list of threatening situations dealing with a certain topic and arranges them in order from the most threatening to the least threatening. This list is presented to the therapist who begins by having the person relax completely (often with the aid of hypnosis). The therapist then goes over the list item by item, beginning with the least threatening situation. He describes the situation to the person in great detail. The patient is instructed to visualize the situation as clearly and intensely as he can but to remain relaxed during the entire procedure. If at any time the person begins to feel anxiety or fear he is instructed to raise his finger indicating to the therapist that anxiety has begun to develop. At this point, the therapist instructs the patient to forget about that situation and erase it from his mind and to continue to relax. With repeated presentation it is possible to desensitize a person to the extent that he can think about situations which were very frightening and threatening to him without becoming anxious. Sometimes simply being able to think about them without becoming fearful is sufficient and this generalizes to actual behavior. However, it is also often very helpful to give the patient assignments to go out and experience these situations in real life while attempting to relax, thereby making the anxiety removal complete. The person thus becomes able to accomplish previously feared activities without any sign of discomfort.

The third category of response used by Wolpe in his therapeutic work is sexual responses. For people having sexual difficulties Wolpe uses normal sexual motivation to overcome the problems which the person has encountered. This typically involves having the person engage in sexual activity in a carefully prescribed manner. The patient is instructed to proceed during sexual relations only until anxiety begins to be experienced, immediately ceasing at that point. Given a cooperative partner and this kind of gradual approach, sexual anxieties and disabilities have been rapidly removed.

A few case examples will be cited at this point to illustrate the principles outlined above. In a classic case reported by Watson and Rayner [18], Albert, a young child, was conditioned to respond with fear to a white rat which he previously enjoyed playing with, by presenting the rat to him and then making a loud sound (banging a steel bar with a hammer) behind his head while he was responding to the animal. Eventually Albert began to respond with extreme fear and crying in response to the rat. A fear of white rats was then conditioned. This crying response and fear generalized to other furry objects (e.g., rabbits, fur coats, hair). One can only speculate about the psychodynamics that might be attributed to such a form of behavior were he taken to a traditional psychotherapist. Certainly it is highly unlikely that any psychological test report would read, "This child fears furry objects and similar objects due to the fact that somebody made a loud sound behind his head while he was playing with a white rat during his early childhood." And yet that is exactly what had happened. This illustrates the manner in which conditioning experiences can produce fears which may also superficially lend themselves to other interpretations. A sequel to this case was the case of Peter [15]. In reporting this case, Jones goes into some detail about the relative effectiveness of different approaches to therapy for this type of fear. Procedures based on learning theory were found most effective.

The authors of this chapter have used behavior therapy techniques for a number of years. One case treated by the second author involved a classical hand-washing compulsion. The patient feared that he would develop a terrible disease which would result in his death if he touched anything that had to do with animals. This man feared that he would pick up germs from doorknobs, light switches, and other common objects encountered daily. At home he had closets full of clothes that he was unable to wear because he felt that in the process of wearing them they may have become contaminated and he would be in danger of contracting a disease from them. Since the clothes or shoes were still in perfectly good condition, he was not able to throw them away but placed them in a closet and refused to wear them. The patient had been this way for some seventeen years and had gotten to the point where his fear and difficulty in this area were so intense that he was considering committing suicide. However, he felt before he took that step he should make some effort to see if the problem could be resolved through psychotherapy.

The patient came to our attention under these circumstances. He was helped to construct a list of situations that produced anxiety. The situations were ranked from those that produced less anxiety to those that produced the most. Two of the least anxiety-provoking situations for this man were turning on light switches and opening doors. Typically in his home he used a piece of tissue paper to accomplish this task, threw the tissue paper away, and washed his hands. It was decided to begin at this point. The patient was instructed to approach a doorknob or light switch in his home and to relax completely. After taking a deep breath and making sure he was completely relaxed, he was to assert himself in a forceful manner by reaching out and turning on the switch or turning the doorknob and then to again relax completely and refuse to wash his hands. He was given the assignment of practicing this during the week and then reporting to the therapist the following week. In the following session the patient remarked that at first it was very difficult to accomplish this but that he had made an effort and it had become easier each time. The therapist went over with the patient the fact that there was actually no danger whatever of catching a disease from such activities. The patient commented that he had always wanted a psychologist to tell him point-blank that there was no danger, but that none of them ever seemed to be willing to do this.

He continued to work on his project. Within two weeks he could turn on lights and open doors with no difficulty whatever. At the far end of the hierarchy, some of the most threatening things to the patient were putting on the clothes he had been wearing when a dog had jumped on him or a cat had sat near him. As therapy progressed the patient was systematically desensitized to all the items of the hierarchy, and as a final test he was instructed to wear all of the clothes and shoes from this "forbidden" closet and to wear different ones each time he came to therapy sessions. The patient taught himself to do this gradually and before long was able to wear all of the "contaminated" clothes. About a year later the author received a letter from this patient saying that his problem had completely vanished, his depression had lifted, and he now felt better than he had in twenty years. As far as is known, the problem never recurred. Although it would have been quite easy to make various psychodynamic interpretations about the nature and source of this patient's fears, no such thing was attempted. Instead techniques of behavior therapy based on learning principles were systematically employed.

One final example may be helpful. A colleague of one of the authors treated a patient who originally complained of feelings of failure, frustration, and depression. She felt unloved and unwanted. The patient said that her life was meaningless and worthless. She was considering suicide. While on the surface this might seem like a traditional existential problem to be dealt with by insight therapy, careful interviewing and discussion revealed that the source of many of her feelings stemmed from her parents' attitudes. It developed that her parents held extremely negative attitudes toward her, frequently criticized her, and kept her in a continual state of anxiety and depression about having to please them. The therapist discussed with her the fact that her parents' attitudes probably stemmed from their own problems and were not objective evaluations of her. He discussed the fact that not everyone can have good parents, and that sometimes people have parents who are inadequate and unable to love them. It was pointed out to her that this appeared to be the case with her and that she would have to face it. She would simply have to realize that her parents were inadequate and she would have to sever herself from their influence and stand on her own feet. It was further explained to her that she should use the techniques of assertion to prevent anxiety from being aroused by her parents. She was given support and help by the therapist in carrying out these plans.

For example, when the girl bought a new dress and took it home, typically her family would berate her, indicate that it was not stylish, that it did not suit her, or that nobody would like her if she wore it. On the next occasion when the patient did this her parents' response was as predicted. She simply said to them, "Well, you two are just old-fashioned and unaware of current styles. I happen to like this dress and my friends think it's nice too." When the patient did this her parents were at first shocked, but rather quickly resigned themselves to the fact that their daughter was beginning to assert herself as an adult. The patient reported that she felt much better, and through a systematic procedure of asserting herself and expressing herself to her parents over a period of time, she moved from the point of despair and suicide to a happy, well-adjusted life.

The central elements of this type of behavior therapy, as can be seen from these examples, are counterconditioning with the appropriate response, systematic extinction of anxiety and reconditioning.

The second type of behavior therapy subsumed under the broad general category of learning theory or behavioral therapy is an orientation based on the principles of *operant conditioning,* sometimes referred to as *instrumental conditioning.* The essence of this system may be thought of as the fact that people tend to repeat actions that they find rewarding or pleasurable. It is thus based on an age-old principle but applies this principle in a systematic and scientific manner.

The simplest example of operant conditioning is the case of teaching a dog a trick. Suppose for example, you want your dog to turn around in a circle and sit up and beg for his food. In order to teach him this by the technique of operant conditioning, one would first wait until the dog was hungry and motivated to perform for food. He would then sit down with the animal and a supply of food and begin to systematically reinforce or reward the kind of behavior that he wanted the dog to perform. He might first give the dog bits of food just to get his attention. He would then give the dog bits of food only as he turned his body or head a little to the right. He would then reward the dog only when he turned his head and body significantly to the right and over a number of trials the dog could be taught to turn around in a complete circle and then sit up. Each phase would have been successively conditioned by approximations and by rewarding the dog for completing a little more of the task each time before the reward was given. The technique of successive approximations is a vital concept in this approach.

Procedures similar to these have been used successfully to teach mentally retarded children to dress and care for themselves or to perform simple activities. They have also been used in a number of other ways, such as teaching mute children to talk or inducing autistic children to interact with other people. The books mentioned earlier by Ullmann and Krasner [8,17] contain a large number of examples of these kinds of procedures and they will not be greatly elaborated in this chapter.

However, a typical example might be teaching a mute child to speak. Following an examination indicating that he is physically capable of making sounds, the therapist would have the child skip his breakfast or lunch and meet with him at a time when he was hungry and receptive to reinforcement by food (or he might use candy or some other item that is reinforcing to the child). He would begin by sitting with the child and attempting to elicit vocalization from the child, reinforcing each time a sound of any sort was made by giving him a bit of food or a piece of candy. After the child was taken to the point where he made frequent vocalizations, the therapist would begin to reward the child only when the vocalizations were the type that sounded like a certain word. At first the word might be unintelligible and rewards would be given for a sound that came close; then after a period of time a closer and closer approximation of the exact sound of the word would be required before a reward would be given. Eventually with proper training of this sort some mute children can be taught to speak. If it were found that the child was only mimicking the sounds with little understanding of the meaning of the words, the meaning and connotations of the words would also be taught by use of conditioning principles and reward.

These relatively new approaches may in some respects appear quite similar to procedures used for some time. Some of them resemble supportive therapy or didactic teaching. It is important to note, however, that they tend to be much more systematic and heavily based in theories and data generated in the laboratory rather than on intuitive guesswork.

There are a number of advantages that can be cited for these approaches, when compared with more orthodox procedures: (a) they tend to be considerably less time-consuming, (b) they often can be applied without years of extensive training, (c) they appear to be effective in a higher percentage of cases, (d) the patient can change therapists with little if any loss in effectiveness, and (e) often with brief instructions and minimal training they can be self-administered.

Let us now elaborate on each of these considerations:

(a) Behavior therapies tend to be considerably less time consuming. There is a host of case reports, especially in the new journal *Behavior Research and Therapy* detailing the many instances in which troubled behavior was changed in a few sessions e.g., from one to fifteen [3, 7, 9, 13]. Similar reports appear in other journals, including the *Journal of Abnormal Psychology* and the *Journal of Applied Behavior Analysis.* Wolpe [19] reviews his own cases, which included severe neurotics, in which the average number of sessions was about twenty.

(b) They can often be applied without years of extensive training. The first author has worked with undergraduates for the past several years, in both clinical and academic settings. His students have included both those majoring in psychology and young men and women with little or no background in psychology. Typically, with but a few lectures regarding the theory and implementation of the technique followed by careful supervision, these young and inexperienced undergraduates have begun work on modifying a variety of fears—of snakes, heights, darkness, authority, men, spiders. The results have been very positive. There is no evidence that anyone has been harmed by these procedures as employed even by inexperienced therapists. There is no doubt that clinical acumen is important, and good training as a psychologist is not being discounted. However, the point is that given careful supervision, these techniques can be readily implemented by people of minimal training. This fact may serve as a partial solution to the mental-health–manpower problem that has severly hampered treatment of the mentally ill for so long[1].

(c) That behavior therapy may be effective in a higher percentage of cases. Wolpe reports that in his work he averages improvement in about 90 percent of the cases [19] and reports from other workers in the area support the conclusion that the success rate for behavior therapy is generally higher than other approaches.

It is important to keep in mind that any new technique practiced by enthusiastic adherents typically yields dramatic results and high improvement rates at first, but that when the first blush of newness disappears, sometimes the dramatic results do also. Obviously, further careful study is needed.

(d) Patients changing therapists while therapy is in process. Routinely one of the major concerns in traditional therapy is the relationship between the patient and the therapist. Much serious thought is given to the consequences of transferring the patient to someone else or allowing another person to intervene as a parallel therapist (seeing the patient over the same period of time). Probably the data here are least definitive in suggesting any advantage for the behavior therapies; they are, however, suggestive. It has been our experience in supervising undergraduates practicing desensitization on one another that a supervisor stepping in, making suggestions and even occasionally directly taking over and demonstrating a more efficient approach, in no way interferes with the therapy. The relationship between therapist and patient in behavior therapy is much less colored by mystery, and generally lacks some of the intensity and dangerousness that characterizes more traditional therapy.

A variation tried by the first author of this chapter demonstrates something of the hardiness of the procedures and indicates how some of the rules of more traditional therapy do not apply. A classroom full of college students was divided into pairs. The pairs then scattered about the room so as to distract each other as little as possible. Each member of a given pair was made responsible for desensitizing the other member to a fear that he had. Each person took the role of therapist and patient in turn with his partner.

It should be emphasized that care was taken to avoid untoward consequences. The students were encouraged to work on minor fears—fears of bugs or fear of the dark. More central and serious problems were deliberately avoided because the students were inexperienced and supervision was minimal. In addition, the object was not primarily to provide help with personal problems, but rather to demonstrate the effectiveness of the procedures involved. However, even in a simple situation such as this, one-half of the students obtained positive results.

(e) The possibility of self-administration with brief instructions. A recent report by Kahn and Baker [6] indicates that desensitization may be implemented with a "do-it-yourself" kit and some weekly phone calls for progress checks. This innovation is still in the pilot phase of development, but the results nonetheless seem promising. So far nobody got worse and five out of six patients employing this procedure were either "cured" or "much improved."

Most of the foregoing would seem to place behavior therapy in opposition to more traditional approaches. Clearly this is not the case. Many currently practicing "behavior therapists" combine some forms of traditional therapy with behavior therapy. For example, Leventhal [10] reports using desensitization and operant conditioning while at the same time continuing to employ some of the more usual types of dialogue and interaction. In addition, behavior therapy techniques themselves often demand a close personal relationship and opportunity for some understanding to develop about what one is doing. Catharsis is a common occurence, and support and reassurance are commonly used. These are all, of course, standard therapeutic vehicles. Thus the dichotomy is in some regards artificial. This is not to say it is of no value, especially for heuristic purposes. The point is, however, that one does not have to swear allegiance to any one specific approach or procedure nor see them as necessarily incompatible.

It might be appropriate at this point to specify some of the features that further characterize behavior therapists. The focus in behavior therapy is on the actions or the behavior that the person engages in. Retrospective analysis and concern with one's history is typically kept to a minimum. The present and the immediate future are considered most relevant. The way in which the person can or cannot function is crucial, as contrasted to his insight or understanding. Ways of directly changing performance in relevant situations are sought and used. Very often variations of approaches to the new, more desirable behavior, are practiced in the therapist's office. For example, role playing is often used. Suggestions may be offered as to how to handle or deal with various problems. Specific factual information may be given. Often what a person is in need of is direct advice regarding things to say or do that he simply has not thought of with regard to certain problems. It frequently is true that "Two heads are better than one." In this regard, the argument is routinely raised by traditional therapists that people may become dependent and less capable if one assists them too much. This is true if too much help or direction are given. However, the essence of behavior therapy is to help the person learn to do for himself. Patients develop a broader repertoire of approaches, have better relationships with others, and tend to become less rather than more dependent on the therapist. This is the essence of behavior therapy.

REFERENCES

1. Albee, G. W. "The Manpower Crisis in Mental Health," *American J. Pub. Health,* 50 (1960), pp. 1895–1900.
2. Davison, G. C. "Elimination of a Sadistic Fantasy by a Client-Controlled

Counter-Conditioning Technique: a Case Study," *J. Abnormal Psychol.* 73 (1968), pp. 84-90.

3. Haslam, M. T. "The Treatment of an Obsessional Patient by Reciprocal Inhibition," *Beh. Res. & Ther.*, 2 (1965), pp. 213-216.

4. Jacobson E. *Progressive Relaxation.* Chicago, Ill: University of Chicago Press, 1938.

5. Jones, M. C. "The Elimination of Children's Fears," *J. Exp. Psychol.*, 7 (1924), pp. 383-390.

6. Kahn M., and B. Baker. "Desensitization with Minimal Therapist Contact, *J. Abnormal Psychol.*, 73 (1968), pp. 198-200.

7. Keehn, J. D. "Brief Case-Report: Reinforcement Therapy of Incontinence," *Beh. Res. & Ther.*, 2 (1965), p. 239.

8. Krasner, L., and L. P. Ullmann, *Research in Behavior Modification.* New York: Holt, Rinehart and Winston, Inc., 1965.

9. Lazarus, A. A. "A Preliminary Report on the Use of Directed Muscular Activity in Counter-Conditioning." *Beh. Res. & Ther.*, 2 (1965), pp. 301-304.

10. Leventhal, A. M. "Use of a Behavioral Approach Within a Traditional Psychotherapeutic Context: a Case Study," *J. Abnormal Psychol.*, 73 (1968), pp. 178-182.

11. Matarazzo, J. D. "Psychotherapeutic Processes," *Annual Rev. of Psychol.*, 16 (1965), pp. 181-224.

12. Pavlov, I. P. *Conditioned Reflexes: An investigation of the Psysiological Activity of the Cerebral Cortex.* Trans. F. C. Amep. New York: Oxford University Press, 1927.

13. Ramsey. R. W., J. Barends, J. Breuher, and A. Kuiseman. "Massed versus Spaced Desensitization of Fear," *Beh. Res. & Ther.* 4 (1966), pp. 205-208.

14. Resnick, J. H. "The Control of Smoking Behavior by Stimulus Satiation," *Beh. Res and Ther.*, 6 (1968), pp. 113-114.

15. Sherrington, C. S. *Integrative Actions of the Nervous System.* New Haven: Yale University Press, 1906.

16. Silverman, I., and J. H. Gerr. "The Elimination of a Recurrent Nightmare by Desensitization of a Related Phobia," *Beh. Res. and Ther.*, 6 (1968), pp. 109-112.

17. Ullmann, L. P., and L. Krasner. *Case Studies in Behavior Modification.* New York: Holt, Rinehart and Winston, 1965.

18. Watson, J. B., and Rosalie Rayner. "Conditioned Emotional Reactions," *J. Exper. Psychol.*, 3 (1920), pp. 1-14.

19. Wolpe, J. *Psychotherapy by Recriprocal Inhibition.* Stanford, Calif.: Stanford University Press, 1958.

20. Wolpe J. and A. A. Lazarus, *Behavior Therapy Techniques,* New York: Pergamon Press, 1966.

10

Student Personnel Administrators and the Campus Ministry
Wayne W. Hoffmann*

HOW DOES THE STUDENT PERSONNEL ADMINISTRATOR LOOK AT THE CAMPUS MINISTRY?

Symbols of the church's presence at the university manifest themselves in many forms. It is the physical form which usually catches the layman's eye. The student personnel administrator, from counselor to vice-president, may only see the buildings which fringe or dot the college campus. Let's look a little further than the physical and explore the given and the possibilities regarding one's relationship with the church's formal representation to higher education, the campus ministry.

Several factors must be considered as we concern ourselves with the campus ministry. First, let us recognize the nature of the campus ministry. It is as pluralistic as the denominations of our country. Where there is a strong element of a particular denomination in a geographical region, that sect will be represented at the college by both students and professional personnel. Where there are few of a denomination in a region, the presence of a professional representative may not be seen. To illustrate this, in the Deep South there are few Lutheran campus ministries. In the East there are few Southern Baptist student unions.

A second consideration of the nature of campus ministry concerns

---

*Wayne W. Hoffmann holds the B.A. from Wheaton College, Wheaton, Illinois and the M.A. from the University of Mississippi and the B.D. from Columbia Theological Seminary. Mr. Hoffmann has served as a campus minister, a U.S. Army Chaplain, a residence hall director and presently serves as Associate Head Counselor at Indiana University where he is completing his doctorate in higher education.

its self-understanding. In many denominations the rationale for a professional student worker or clergyman to be at a university is to be the pastor or shepherd of the denominational students. To complicate the matter, many denominations have no philosophy which directs action on state or local levels. Although national offices suggest, most local ministries are free to accept or reject accordingly. A danger here can be reversion to individualist concerns pointing toward provincialism. A benefit is each ministry can be tailored to its context.

In many instances the administrator is engaged in a relationship with a campus ministry which has hidden agenda from the ecclesiastical end. In some instances, the campus ministry is *primarily* concerned for the conversion of the godless university; in others, the sharing of common concerns; in still others, the outright disruption of and destruction of the university as it exists in that particular community.

To further complicate the matter, the campus ministry is likely to be patterned after the personality of the professional worker or minister. If he is strong in counseling, the university need not fear subterfuge; if he is strong on civil rights, he may not be around campus very often; if he is strong in teaching, he may want on the payroll; and if he is a gladhander, the university might want him for public relations.

To further understand the nature of campus ministry as we see it emerging into the 1970's, let us briefly look at the revolutions within the church itself. We are given a status quo condition of the institutional *Church* against which a few clergymen and laymen are reacting and rebelling. Essentially this is a theological revolution. This revolution can be described with a term, "incarnational theology," which suggests the making manifest the action of God in the flesh: "doing your thing now." The call is for action—now: in the arena of this world, and not some heavenly realm. The call is for action to counteract apathy, action for justice to correct injustice, action for peace where there is violence and war.

Many clergymen find freedom as campus ministers to say certain things and to take certain stands they feel they could otherwise not say or do in a pastorate. Consequently, campus ministers tend to be a rare breed among clergymen. They are almost outcasts from the established Church, having little identity within it except as they identify with certain people and groups of like mind. They can be, like the prophet crying in the wilderness. Sometimes they are heard by the Church or the university. But the peculiarity of the matter is that they feel they are not considered a part of the university or the church by either institution. There may be some argument from board officials, but a good sampling of campus ministers leads us to this assertion.

There is a paradox here that might help. While feeling little or no identity with either Church or university, most professional campus ministers cherish this freedom and lack of identity. This occasions stirring the tempest from time to time with appeal to an ideal or moral value that transcends church dicta and university regulations.

The traditional functions of the ministry, such as a pastor, teacher, and preacher are still important. But for the revolutionist, these functions can be too mundane and oriented to functions that either the local church or the university can carry on. Many perform these tasks, and well. But many others forsake them for more "action-oriented" considerations.

This new style of commitment is somehow rooted in a theology which is "now" oriented. The past is history, the future must be built, now is the time for action.

THE STRUCTURE OF CAMPUS MINISTRY

Campus ministry appears at the university through three general approaches. First there is the denominational ministry; second an ecumenical thrust; and third, the interdenominational or nondenominational.

Denominational ministry is concerned with an expression of care for denominational students. This is especially true in areas where denominationalism is stressed. The denomination is concerned with maintaining a student's relationship with his church. This is dependent upon cultural and sociological factors, such as the role of the Church in the community, the strength of the particular denomination, and the ethos of the college community concerning religion.

While the campus minister if given pastoral charge over his denominational students on that campus, most often his work is done across denominational lines. Where there are professional men or women assigned by a denomination to work with denominational students (a passing tradition, by the way), the outreach and contact of the campus minister to "his flock" is limited, and really best handled by the local congregation of that denomination. At this point the philosophy of campus ministry shifts into what is emerging today. We call this the *ecumenical* campus ministry.

To best consider this style we prescind from the problems of the denominational ministry charged with limited tasks and come at the same situations from the stance of an ecumenical ministry, calling them *opportunities* and *possibilities.* For instance, where a minister was caught in tension as to ministering to denominational students or others, he is now freed to minister to students, period. He is usually employed by several denominations and cut free to be the Church's professional representative at the university, distinguishable by clerical collar or style of life.

This ecumenical form of ministry is rooted in a decade or more of cooperative ministry by several denominations. Where there had been several student religious organizations on campus, now in many places one smaller or larger group has taken the place of the many. For the most part initials like UCCF or UCM are seen instead of Westminster Foundation or Wesley Foundation. Many changes have taken place on the heirarchical level of denominational campus ministry boards, slowly filtering down and affecting change on local level. For example, representatives of some denominational boards are presently operating out of united ministries in higher education, with a corporate philosophy and corporate manpower pool for assignment to colleges and universities around the country.

This can change the self-understanding of the campus ministry. No longer would the campus minister operate from a limited power base and self-image, but from one deepened and broadened, based on manifold relationships at the hierarchical level.

Presently there is a movement within campus ministry which redefines ecumenical to mean task- and issue-oriented on a given issue at a given time. This was manifest in the University Christian Movement which has recently decided to disband as an organization and maintain its concerns through local involvement. This movement reflects the revolution within the Church as it does not emerge in any unified way in any given place. Yet that is the value of its understanding of both itself and the university. It exists to confront the needs and the problems of the university and bring about reformulation, one end being a university-servant-of-the-people concept. Although this concept is written into the philosophies of thousands of universities, the UCM-type ask to see this manifested concretely. There is some similarity of concern of the movement types with the "new left" students. Another structural representation is the United Campus Christian Fellowship. It is the manifestation on local campuses of interdenominational cooperation. This organization, run by laymen from several local churches, usually hires one clergyman or layman to represent their churches to the campus.

This brings us to the interdenominational or nondenominational expressions of the Church's mission at the university. Most common are Inter-Varsity and Campus Crusade for Christ. Inter-Varsity Fellowship has been on the campus scene for almost a quarter of a century. It has moved from a very evangelical-conversion-oriented stance versus the Godless university to a moderate conservative position with some emphasis on social action. Campus Crusade, for the most part, aiming at the leaders of the Pan-Hellenic organizations and athletes, seeking to "bring them to Christ" and have them in turn lead others. Both groups are concerned more with individual's relationship with God than they are with changing structures or reformulating the university. Their task is to bring God to the university and to convert individuals within the structure.

As one quickly notes the nature of these three basic movements on campus, all rooted in the Christian faith, one sees they have definite and distinct manifestations. The student personnel administrator can better relate to these groups as he has some general understanding as to their mission and how they see themselves and their mission.

HOW CAMPUS MINISTRY VIEWS THE UNIVERSITY

Given the pluralistic nature of the campus ministry, we can assume pluralistic views. There is no way of categorizing these views into the areas mentioned earlier. These viewpoints are general in nature and not typed according to denominationalism, ecumenicism or interdenominationalism.

One way campus ministry views the university is as a mission field, ripe unto harvest and ready for the workers to reap thereunto. This is rooted in a theology of individual salvation. The university is not viewed corporately but comprised of thousands of individuals. Usually the goals of the university are not considered by this evangelical approach. This expression is not out to subvert the university but to convert individuals, to Christianize the university.

Another view of the university proceeds from an institutional self-understanding vis-à-vis another institution. This view is strong in the ecclesiastically oriented denominations such as Roman Catholicism and Episcopalianism. In this view the university is considered a part of the parish of the institutional church, and the members which are university people are shepherded, challenged, accepted. There is little or no proselytizing from this stance. The university is viewed institutionally and collectively, yet being comprised of individuals who are members of another institution, namely, the Church.

A third view stems from the main-line churches whose self-understanding include being an institution, yet one which is not in competition but in cooperation with the university. Here the idealistic goals of both education and Christianity overlap. The pursual of truth, the dispensing of truth, the serving of the community, these and others are seen as joint goals. The university is seen as partner in the process. Occasionally there are prophets within this stream who call the university into question as to whether or not they are fulfilling this responsibility.

A fourth views the university as protector and guardian of the status quo, even more so than the Church. It is from this viewpoint the support for reformulation and radical change of the practices of the university are advocated. Here such issues as government contracts prostituting the academic freedom of the university are raised. The campus ministry which views the university in this way considers itself to be engaged in a "lover's quarrel" with the university. They are not out to destroy the university, but to change it and its entangling alliances. Their struggle is a power struggle, operating essentially from a powerless base.

Another views the university as a sellout institution engaged in self-perpetuation and self-service, cranking out products like an assembly line which in turn feeds back into the process more potential products. Here the issue of dehumanization is strongly confronted. Here also is the question of whether or not higher education is engaged in training or education for adjustment.

As one gathers from this sketch, there can be no comprehensive presentation of the views of the campus ministry without going into great detail. What we have tried to do is give a general picture of the views of some of the major manifestations of campus ministry.

THE STUDENT AND THE CAMPUS MINISTRY

Relationships of students with campus ministry are for the most part passing and superficial. The campus ministry represents a reminder of back-home going-to-churchness which most students are trying to forget. Now is the time to make the break with the old ways and forge out the ways of freedom from what he had to do. Church ties get cut fast and frequently.

With some communions, however, a strong tie is maintained by the students with their clerical representative. This is especially true in the lives of Roman Catholic students. Yet the precentage of relationship is low even where tradition and Church canon are in sway.

The relationship of the student with the campus ministry is very much an individual situation. One might gravitate to a student religious center for lack of anything else to do. As one recent ad for student participation put it, "If you don't fit in anywhere else, you might fit in here." This has led to labeling many campus religious groups as misfit clubs. Although this has some validity, there is need for someone to accept and challenge those who sense rejection elsewhere.

Most of the students see the campus ministry as peripheral to the university, if they are aware of it at all. In some instances there is question whether or not the Church should waste its money on paying a professional to minister to twenty or thirty students.

In other instances where the campus ministry is involved in the life and heartbeat of the university, functioning within yet questioning and challenging, students may identify with campus ministry as an afterthought. An example of this is the action-oriented ministries that have sprung up on campus after campus. Many of these ministries make no outward identification with the Church, yet students know that the Church sponsors them, and feel free to identify with this kind of manifestation. Students are freer to express their religious questions in the secular atmopshere than in the churchy structures passed on by the forefathers. In these cases some relationships are deeper and more penetrating, although they may not last any longer than those conceived from traditional roles.

Some students see campus ministry as square or for squares. Others see it as something with which only the goody-goody types relate. It is to these students that communication of a fresh and creative nature is needed and being tried. Here it is mainly a matter of communicating what the Church is all about. At this point it is divergent and different depending upon the campus minister and the student.

In summary, most students don't have anything to do with campus ministry or the Church. Some relate for short periods of time, until their immediate needs are met; others hang on until cut loose by the minister or finally break loose themselves from the symbolical cord. Then again, others have deep and lasting relationships with the campus ministry, which affect their lives demonstrably.

Response of the Student Personnel Administrator to the Campus Ministry

One of the first responsibilities of the student personnel administrator is becoming familiar with the campus ministry. This can be done, in addition to reading, by inviting the various representatives of campus ministry to engage in conversation regarding their understanding of the university, their mission, and how the student personnel administrator can facilitate common expressions of concern. While the campus minister may know much about theology and social problems, the student personnel administrator ought not to take it for granted that he knows higher education, its structure, its complex nature, and its essential goals and objectives.

This leads to a second responsibility or opportunity presented to the student personnel administrator. If one sees the campus minister as an addition to the campus scene because of his concern for people, then the university has the opportunity to involve the campus minister in achieving some common concerns. For instance, at some universities campus ministers are adjunct to the counseling staff performing counseling services for the university within the structures of the institution. In other cases campus ministers are included in student personnel staff meetings, their qualifications being professional training in human relations and their continuous contacts with students.

A third factor one might consider is the given human need of the student for relating to values. Central to these values is the person himself. The campus minister should be concerned with the individual and what affects the individual. Because of this concern he can be of value in terms of advice and counsel. Administrators must be aware that the nature of their own job can be depersonalizing and dehumanizing. People from outside the immediate structure in which one finds himself can aid in seeing certain areas of neglect or acts of injustice which one cannot see himself.

Finally, the campus minister can be one who is refreshing and reassuring. He is out of the pecking order, and can listen to the administrator with little or no risk to the administrator. His freedom from certain hierarchal restraints can be infectious and give new verve to the student personnel administrators concern for the *people* in higher education.

11

Living and Learning Centers*

Donald V. Adams†

It is unfortunate that this chapter will be read by most people seeking answers for *large* institutions of higher education. Somehow we have allowed ourselves the luxury of believing that only the large colleges and universities need to integrate the classroom with the residence hall. The myth continues to be perpetuated that once we have

*Throughout this chapter certain terminology is used to distinguish different types of campus plans at Michigan State University to incorporate the resident life of the student with the academic mission of the University. For definition purposes the terms most frequently used are listed as follows.

Living-Learning Residence Hall. Living-learning residence hall is the name given to a coeducational residence hall, with an instructional program for the students living in that residence hall and taught by instructors who have their offices in the residence hall. Students who reside in a living-learning residence hall usually take two courses in that particular residence hall. These courses are from a core of four required courses that each student is required to take before he graduates. Usually these courses are completed during the students first two years at the university.

Academic Program in Residence Hall. A department or faculty members of a department or college who have offices and office space in a coeducational residence hall. The instructional program relates to a small percentage or none of the students residing in the residence hall. Instructors teaching in the hall may or may not have their offices in the hall. Basically the teaching program is to provide an academic atmosphere and the facilities provides needed office space and classrooms.

Residential College. A smaller residential college community within the larger university. A residentially based four year program for undergraduates. Full-time faculty is small; usually faculty appointments are jointly appointed from a number of related disciplines from within departments of the larger university. Integration between curricular and cocurricular aspects of student experience is facilitated by housing classrooms, residence hall cultural programs, faculty offices, students, and administrative staff in a single residential college setting. A residential college remains an autonomous college as any other college within the university with its own curriculum and graduation requirements.

†Dr. Donald L. Adams holds his B.A. from University of Northern Iowa in Cedar Falls,

reduced the physical distance between residence, classroom, and library we have solved the problem of personal interaction between faculty, staff, and students.

Ills of higher education are within the ranks of large and small institutions of higher education. Visiting with colleagues and students on small campuses has reinforced the readings and research that suggest new models are needed for all academic communities.

Ideas and innovations that will serve as the foundation for these new models will probably emerge from the present campus problems that are recurring with increasing frequency. Since these problems are not visible to each member of the university community, the faculty, students, and administration must identify for each other what each is seeing.

Often in an organization the issues that will become paramount *obstacles* to excellence and normal functioning of the institution are often seen by only a few people or a small segment of the institution when the problems first appear. As the problems persist and become familiar to everyone in the organization, everyone becomes involved.

To evaluate present problems that seem to be recurring with increasing frequency, all students, faculty, and administrators must be aware of the purpose, perspective, and objectives of their institution. A perspective requires a breadth of viewpoint about the institution that only combined thinking can bring. One individual—whether he is the president, student leader, dean of students, residence hall director, director of housing, or trustee—regardless of how strong his leadership qualities may be, cannot foresee and appreciate any problem in its entirety. This is why sound and creative administration requires exploration of issues by all members of the university community while they are still manageable. This is not to presuppose that all problems viewed by community members are going to become unsurmountable obstacles to excellence. Quite the contrary; the administration must lead, and have the moral and ethical fiber to give leadership to the divergent ideas and opinions as they arise. The administrator must be reminded that all change is not progress, and changes probably should not be made unless reasonable chances for success will bring about a higher standard of educational excellence for the institution.

A central dilemma of organization life is that in order to get some things done you have to organize others to do them. As soon as you

Iowa and his M.A. and Ph.D. from Michigan State University in East Lansing. He currently is Vice-President for Student Life at Drake University and is the former Director of Residence Halls at Michigan State University. Dr. Adams was instrumental in the design of living and learning centers. The unique programs he created in residential living were utilized as focal points of discussion at many educational conventions.

organize others to do them they want to get into the act of deciding what is done and how it is done. It has become increasingly evident throughout the literature of administration that the more physically decentralized the organization, with administrative autonomy given to each unit, many differing points of view will emerge within the organization. It is also clear that these differing points of view will be more tolerated in a decentralized administrative structure and thus increase the effectiveness of the organization. In other words, the act of physically decentralizing an organization will not be a panacea for all problems and questions. There must be confidence and faith in staff, student and faculty in the decentralized organization. In a decentralized organization, the lower units, or the units that have become more autonomous should and will get increased visibility with the higher echelons of the organization. When this visibility is achieved by the lower autonomous units, the members will identify more closely with that organization. The autonomy for the decentralized unit should allow the staff, faculty, and students at the grass-roots level to have more prestige, more visibility to the top echelon of the organization; this involvement will increase effectiveness and satisfaction with the organization.

The efficiency of a large or small formal organization is sizably enhanced when its own chain of command or decision-making apparatus is tied into the informal network of groups within the organization. This allows the network of informal groups to be used to support the organization's goals and objectives. The informal network of groups is the groups formed within any organization that carry certain types of prestige or certain rewards for membership but are usually not a part of the formal organization. The extent to which an administrator can identify and tie himself into this informal network of groups is a measure of how far that network can be used to support the organizational goals of the institution rather than detracting from it. One example of the above is that many student and faculty ad hoc groups are formed to solve a particular problem and then disappear when the issue or problem is resolved.

Basically, an attitude for creative administration should allow an individual staff member's feeling to become an effective contact with an agent of the organization that brings about change. The feeling that this is possible is highly desirable. Sometimes it is indispensable from the standpoint of both the individual and the organization. The individual's own morale and the bearing that this morale plays in his performance and identity with the organization are crucial concerns for colleges and universities.

Utilizing this model for decentralized administration, living-learning residence halls are essential to the present and future campus scene.

It is the purpose of these residence halls to take fullest advantage of the student peer group influence to establish an environment or cultural influence that is conductive to the aims of the university. The living and learning program provides a student community engaged in similar curricular offerings, thereby giving the students a commonality of attitudes and interests. In essence, smaller academic communities are built within the campus. Each of these smaller academic communities is established around the needs of the students who live in a residence hall that would hopefully serve students who live or attend classes in that residence hall.

Concerning the educational value of such an academic community, Burton Clark and Martin Trow have written:

> It is worth re-emphasizing that the organization of the college as a community has profound effects on student life in ways that have been given too little consideration by administrators and too little study by scholars. The *effective* size of an institution can be reduced even without a reduction of its absolute enrollment by creating what are in effect distinctive smaller communities within the larger organization. These communities include both students and faculty, a community with a sense of identity and above all else whose members share interest and commitments which can be supported and furthered rather than diluted and discouraged through the ordinary ongoing relations of the members of that community. Such communities cannot be called into being by proclamation. They must have insulation against distracting and competitive interests and appeals. In short, these have to be genuine, intellectual communities embedded in residence halls and groups of academic departments.[1]

Clark and Trow have suggested that the organization of the college in ways that enhance a community concept will achieve the aims and goals that all members of the community are striving for. Basically, the participants in a university community are students, faculty and administrators. There is little reason why a campus must be physically constituted to accentuate the mutually exclusiveness of these three groups. Residence halls planned with faculty offices, classrooms, libraries, recreation facilities, dining rooms, sleeping quarters, learning resource laboratories, and instructional media centers become living educational centers. Frequency of contact by the members of these communities in many behavioral roles will dictate shared experiences.

Sanford has presented similar evidence to Clark and Trow regarding the effective size of an institution. Sanford says: "The point is that

---

[1] Burton Clark and Martin Trow, "The Campus Viewed As a Culture," in Hall T. Sprague (ed.), *Research on College Students* (Boulder, Colo.: Western Institute Commission for Higher Education; Berkeley, Calif.: Center for the Study of Higher Education, 1968) p. 122.

coherence depends not on size alone, but on leadership, internal structure and the educational style of the college."[2]

Essentially this is what Clark and Trow suggest as a "reduction of absolute enrollment by creating what are in effect distinctive smaller communities." These communities must have their own identity, including students, faculty, and administrators with the responsibility of solving the problems of the smaller communities, all members sharing in the daily, ongoing relations within the community. These communities may have common interests in curricular offerings, class standing, culturally deprived students, or various other criteria. But most important, they must be genuine communities, interdisciplinary in approach with enough autonomy to serve its membership well within the guidelines of the larger institution.

Many behavioral scientists are suggesting that what students learn in college is a product of what they learn from each other. Sanford suggests "that what students learn in college is determined in large measure by their fellow students, or more precisely, by the norms of behavior, attitudes, and values that prevail in the peer groups to which they belong."[3] These statements are compatible with Newcomb's postulates regarding peer group influence and educational objectives. He has provided a schematic drawing which illustrates the importance of other students in the final characteristics of the graduates of institutions of higher education.[4]

From the accompanying diagram it is evident that the final characteristics of the students at any given university or college are a combina-

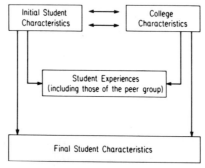

tion of initial student characteristics and college characteristics interacting with the total experiences of students. Newcomb has ex-

---

[2] Nevitt Sanford, *Where Colleges Fail* (San Francisco, Calif.: Jossey-Bass, Inc., p. 175.
[3] *Ibid.*, p. 148.
[4] Theodore Newcomb, "Student Peer-Group Influences," in Sanford Nevitt (ed.), *The American College* (New York: John Wiley and Sons, Inc., 1962), pp. 469-488.

pressed that little effort has been made by most colleges and universities to utilize the student culture or to channel students into the areas that seem most likely to encourage growth and productivity, rather than failure and departure. Thus it is that the kind of experiences that the college student assimilates depends heavily upon the social organization of that college. This social organization demands collective responses to problems commonly encountered. It makes good sense to have faculty and administrators sharing equally with students in solving common problems.

LIVING AND LEARNING AT MICHIGAN STATE UNIVERSITY

The living-learning residence halls are an attempt to relate peer group influence to educational excellence. Michigan State University has been one of the pioneers in this venture.

In the first living-learning residence halls at Michigan State University, courses in the residence halls were limited to the population of the halls. Students were somewhat homogeneous, since they were predominantly freshmen and completing courses in the University College.

The importance of limiting the courses in the residence halls to the population of that residence hall was extremely important. Each residence hall has a population of 1,000–1,200 students, equally divided by sex. Since the size of one residence hall is as large as most smaller colleges, a diversity of interest and values was evident in the student population. Since the students had the opportunity to know each other from the living-group experiences as well as the classroom exposure, there was more of an opportunity to integrate both experiences to their personal growth. Newcomb has summarized the importance of size and contact in the following:

> The formal group should be large enough to provide a range of selectivity based upon individual preferences for companionship but not so large that it will be improbable that most individuals will at least recognize each other. It is important, second, to take advantage of the fact that students' living arrangements provide the major, single source of daily contact. Peer group influence is most certain to be enhanced for better or worse if there is a considerable overlap between membership in formal college units and in living units.[5]

In the living-learning residence halls, students have an opportunity to recognize each other both in their living arrangement and college classroom. This overlap of contact should reinforce the learning and impact of the peer group. With faculty and other adult models involved

[5] *Ibid.*, p. 486.

with students where their teaching is taking place, the possibility for educational excellence is enhanced.

Another important objective of the living-learning residence hall was recognized by Benson and Augustine. They report:

> That one of the necessary objectives of the living-learning program is the building or maintaining an esprit de corps within the student body. The alienation caused from an impersonal and nonresponsive academic community can be avoided by the overlap of the classroom and residence population.[6]

Harold Taylor has stated that "the relationships among students in the residences are the greatest factors in their general attitude toward the college and toward themselves."[7]

In these days of student unrest, findings of this nature must be probed for answers to questions being asked on all campuses. To reduce alienation and increase the student's attitude toward himself and the college are worthy goals to be achieved.

After the initial living-learning residence hall which provided for a basic curriculum of course offering from the University College, Michigan State University embarked on a new idea which presented living units with academic facilities, but serving a predominantly nonresidence hall population. To implement this plan, the College of Arts and Letters and the College of Social Science instituted a teaching program for two residence halls. In these units the College of Arts and Letters housed a faculty member from each department within the College and the department of religion. The College of Social Science experimented with graduate students, living in the houses with the students, serving as the academic advisors for the Social Science majors living in the other residence hall. The undergraduate advisement center of the College of Social Science office was also in this residence hall. This allows for all undergraduate advising of Social Science majors to be done in this office. An Assistant Dean of the College of Social Science is responsible for the operation.

The College of Natural Science and the College of Education's Math-Science Teaching Program were the next planned program. This program was supervised by the Director of the Math-Science Teaching Institute and the Director of Residential Instruction for the College of Natural Science. Also, in the fall of 1965 a group of residence halls, previously all conventional residence halls with no living-learning facili-

---

[6] August G. Benson and Roger D. Augustine, "A Survey of the Living-Learning Program at Michigan State University," unpublished mimeograph report for Michigan State University, June 3, 1963.

[7] Harold Taylor, "Freedom and Authority on the Campus," in Nevitt Sanford (ed.), *The American College* (New York: John Wiley and Sons, Inc., 1962).

ties, were completely remodeled to provide for classroom facilities, faculty offices, counseling center offices, auditorium, three natural-science labs, and an undergraduate academic advising center for the academic advising of University College students. The courses for this group of residence halls were limited to the residents of the residence halls.

For the fall of 1966 a new thirteen-story high-rise residence hall was opened and complemented the existing academic programs by adding another University College teaching facility.

Michigan State University's first residential college was initiated during the 1965 fall term. This college has a major in the liberal arts with an emphasis in international understanding. The emphasis on international understanding is complemented by an intensive foreign language requirement. It is important to note that the Dean and faculty are all officed in one residence hall and most classes are taught in the residence hall. In the 1967 fall term two new residential colleges were added. These residential colleges have liberal art curricula with specific emphasis on the policy sciences and science. All of the residential colleges were planned for existing residence hall facilities and a minimum of remodeling was necessary.

This review of one university is to provide perspective and scope on the possibilities for the living and learning concept as a model for older institutions of higher education as well as new colleges and universities.

It is still too early to determine the total evaluation of the different opportunities for education in the living-learning residence halls and residential colleges at Michigan State University. The increasing demand for these facilities by upperclass students, the success evidenced by the involvement of the total community in decision making and planning for these units, a more effective community student government, involving academic, managerial, and student personnel staff all seem to have been positive by-products from this venture.

THE ROLE OF THE STUDENT PERSONNEL WORKER IN LIVING-LEARNING RESIDENCE HALLS

When the learning environment of the classroom is expected in its daily operation to reinforce the living environment of the residence hall, the student personnel worker truly becomes an equal partner with his academic counterpart in the venture of education. The curriculum becomes a strategy to increase the productivity of the peer group. The peer group becomes an integral part of reinforcing the learnings of the classroom. The student personnel worker must give leadership and direction to the integration of the curriculum and student culture. In short, the work of the student personnel staff must facilitate the learnings of the student culture, faculty culture and institutional environment.

Speaking to the importance of this environmentalist role Edward Eddy in his classical study of the College Influence on Student Character concludes:

> Parts of the environment may be positive, some neutral, and some obviously negative. We believe it is within the control of the colleges which shall be which. And we believe further that the environment will never truly have a full impact on character growth until all of its components, large and small, important and relatively unimportant reinforce the best which the college has to offer.[8]

Thus, if we are seriously to consider the conclusions by Eddy we must admit ". . . it is within the control of the college which shall be which . . . that the environment will never truly have a full impact until all of its components, large and small, important and relatively unimportant reinforce the best which the college has to offer." At times, residence hall student personnel workers have difficulty in contributing as important members to the academic community, in determining if they are a large or small component, important or relatively unimportant category. But it is obvious that Eddy says *"all must reinforce each other if we are going to produce the best the college has to offer."*

In all of the living and learning arrangements, the residence hall personnel staff work closely with the assistant dean for the teaching program, the counseling center personnel who have offices in the residence hall and business management personnel. Each of the departments determine policy and the implementation of that policy in the residence hall they represent. All of the above offices need to be decentralized so that decision making affecting the student population in each residence may be carried out at the residence level. Remembering Trow and Clark's statement regarding the decentralization of a university, it is imperative the smaller communities remain autonomous and assume responsibility for the decisions that affect this smaller academic community.

The impact of the student personnel worker or more specifically the residence hall advisory staff is often negated by one of the ills in the student personnel profession—that most staff members are pursuing the position of Dean. Most staff members are not adequately rewarded for their competencies. The "Dean's position" carries most of the fulfill-

[8] Edward D. Eddy, Jr., *The College Influence on Student Character* (Washington, D.C.: American Council on Education, 1959), p. 165.

ment. The residence hall staff are unnecessarily burdened with "super-visory" responsibilities; are viewed as "junior" staff; are inadequately trained and have the least amount of experience of other members in the smaller academic community. Too often student personnel deans view "assistant deans" as being more important and thus refuse to allow decisions to be made by the residence hall staff.

Too often young, inexperienced student personnel staff believe they can become "educators" by acquiring the symbols of the academic world; e.g., faculty rank or academic title. Many times student personnel deans are unwilling to place staff of true academic competence at the residence level. The residence hall staff will gain legitimacy within the academic community in direct proportion to the staff's competency in understanding and discovering knowledge of individuals, groups, and organizations.

The study and research of academic environment on house and residence hall student populations, the free-university concept, imple-menting the successful "off-campus" continuing and adult education concept to the "on-campus" student population are all important con-cepts for review and mastery of a residence hall staff.

Specifically in the living and learning residences or residential col-lege the residence hall staff should share in the recruitment of students, college student government, academic advising, research, studying the effects of student peer group influence, and serving on joint staff-stu-dent and faculty committees. The selection, training, and evaluation of the student residence staff and recommending the selection, promotion and retention of the faculty are also integral aspects of the residence hall staff.

Basically, the residence hall staff must be chosen, retained, and evaluated primarily for their contributions to student development and their contributions to the smaller academic community. A systematic method of planning for the "ideal" student, staff member, and commu-nity growth would be the model relationship. The student personnel staff becomes the catalyst for defining and teaching the ingredients of the climate for learning.

SUMMARY

Basically, the living-learning model for education takes full advan-tage of the residence experience which provides the major, single source of daily contact for students. The effect of students on other students is enhanced by the overlap between membership in the class-rooms and living units.

Decentralization of the university decision-making process is a necessary ingredient in the initial stages of planning.

To create an administrative superstructure to supercede the traditional lines of responsibility in the total university administration would negate expertise of knowledge from each participant. Each of the participants—students, staff, and faculty—has a body of knowledge that all participants need to share. The faculty brings subject matter, the business manager brings a good food service, well-maintained facilities, and efficient business knowledge, and the student personnel staff has a perspective on the college student in higher education which encompasses the students membership in the residence and academic community. Thus the learning environment and living environment are expected to reinforce each other. Evaluation of staff and faculty must evidence this expectation.

Money, research, technology, experience, and expertise do not seem to be limiting factors in the decade ahead; decision making for quality undergraduate education must reflect attitudinal priorities. Will our educatonal leaders promote the system of rewards to fulfill this committment? This is the answer we are seeking.

12

Information Systems in Student Personnel Administration

William R. Osmon*

INTRODUCTION

It would be difficult to contemplate what the future holds for student personnel administration in higher education without including a discussion of how the information proliferation and the techniques to master it will alter the role of student personnel administrators. Information is a term now being applied to all those elements of data that are related to the performance of a function. The development of an all-encompassing idea of information systems has or will cause a reconceptualization of the work of the student personnel specialist most closely associated with the information system. In addition, student personnel administrators responsible for overall student affairs will find their professional lives altered when information system concepts are introduced to their campuses. The changes in roles and the new titles that will result will be much more than a mere enlargement of current job descriptions. New positions will develop and new skills must be provided.

The information explosion and the demand for information systems have been aided by the development of the computer. But it should be

*Dr. William R. Osmon holds the B.S. from Indiana State University, M.Ed. from the University of Florida, and the Ed.D. from Indiana University. Prior to assuming his present position, he was on the faculty of the School of Education at Indiana University and was the Director of Institutional Research and Testing at Indiana State University. Dr. Osmon is currently Dean of Student Administrative Services and Associate Professor of Education and Psychology at Indiana State University, Terre Haute, Indiana.

noted here that computers are not necessary requisites to the advent of information systems, nor are they responsible for the production of the elements included in a system. With the electronic computer now firmly established as a necessary tool of higher education administration, it is apparent that an increased understanding of the potential of information processing is imperative. However, with computers, new concepts of management in higher education are possible because of the availability of information in different forms.

WHAT IS AN INFORMATION SYSTEM?

Several definitions of an information system would be possible, depending upon the needs to be served by the system. A production manager may define it as a means to measure production against expected output. A trucking-terminal dispatcher may conceive of an information system as the tool for planning the most efficient loading and equipment routing. A registrar would probably use the system to register and maintain records for students. For purposes of discussion in this paper, an information system will be defined as matrices of elements standing in interaction. There are general concepts holding for all systems regardless of the configuration of the elements and the extent, quality, and nature of their interaction. Basically, however, any information system should be thought of as a rigidly planned technique for assembling data elements and transforming them into useful management reports.

Elements of information are unique bits of data in their most simple forms. These bits of data serve as the building blocks for the information base of a system. For example, in a student personnel information system, these would include name, address, sex, age, term of enrollment, test scores, demographic data, grades, academic action, major, minor, honors, etc. All colleges and universities collect and store these data and many have been analyzing them in relation to each other. The basic goal of an information system is not the identification or collection of the elements of the system, but the adequate conceptualization of their interaction and interdependencies.

An information system will not be the mere enlargement of current activities, nor will it mean the transferral of current activities to a machine. For example, an information system could be thought of as a clerical replacement for current data-handling processes, or it could be planned to provide quicker response to data-handling requirements. A system must be capable of defining all of the intricate interrelationships of information exchange required in managing an enterprise of the size and complexity of a university student personnel area. To define the nuances of interaction between the information elements is a most difficult task. To implement methods of achieving the desired interchanges with creditable and reliable data and in time to formulate wise decisions is even harder.

The Systems Approach

The task of initiating an information system must not be left to chance. Careful and long-range planning are requisites even to the most simple of systems. In industry and more recently in higher education, a speciality role, the *systems analyst,* has developed to insure that adequate planning is effected. His technique of problem solving is called the *systems approach.* Stated another way, it is the application of rigidly defined activities by specialists to describe the interaction of information and process elements within a given problem area. The results of such carefully formulated study should be a comprehensive plan for the solution or for the lessening of the demands formerly placed upon the people and machine performing the operational tasks. In essence it is a team activity that has been conducted by many for decades as a logical way for solving problems. The term *system analyst* was coined by computer professionals to describe the activity of a *computer* specialist who could conceive of problems in such a way that some of the components of the solution could be assigned to a computer function. Computers, by design, demand that any problem to be computerized must be systematically divided into its logical parts. The role definition of a systems analyst now has generally taken on an additional dimension—professional training in a specific professional operational discipline. Witness Ph.D. programs that accept computer proficiency in lieu of a foreign language.

A student personnel administrator assigned to the student affairs administrative staff whose task of organizing a set of procedures to follow in dealing within the area does not by necessity require the individual to be a computer specialist. The first requisite is a person who understands and can identify problems within the area. His basic responsibility is to help the administrators responsible for the area make decisions. A working knowledge of computer applications is required if the time from inquiry to decision is to be kept to a minimum.

The basic tasks of the educational systems analyst as a member of the personnel staff is to examine the business of education, identify the procedural and operational problem areas, and help design solutions that enhance operations. When computer applications are possible, computer specialists are added to existing student personnel speciality teams. Often there is a tendency for the newcomer to student personnel problems—as well as the existing student personnel specialists—to look to the computer as the solver of problems rather than as one solution to some problems. Unions of computer-oriented systems analysts and non-computer-oriented operational specialists have been unhappy marriages. You need only scan a little of the literature available on the resulting chaos in many organizations to understand the reluctance of university administrators to make the commitment to information systems.

Response Time

The choice to adopt computer techniques in the management of universities is no longer an alternative for most as it was a decade ago. Enrollment increases have forced most colleges and universities to install data-processing departments. The climates of most campuses are now analogous to a rocket in flight. Constant and immediate corrections to their directions are imperative for survival. A technician does not have the time to look to his slide rule for correction of the flight path. Since an immediate response is required, a computer constantly monitors rockets in flight. This situation is said to be *real-time*—that is, each inquiry from the rocket for flight instructions must be responded to within thousandths of a second. A university president does not have a direct wire to a computer for his corrections of course, but he must have available *information* that will allow him to make decisions within minutes rather than days. It becomes quickly apparent to a university administrator responsible for tens of thousands of students and millions of dollars of physical plant that his decisions must be based upon quickly accessible, creditable, and reliable management reports. Conscious that current procedures will not effectively handle current information demands, many university administrators are beginning to ask why their heavily financed computer centers do not provide avenues for efficient information flow.

The response time of the personnel administrator represents an area of great concern. How does he contend with demonstrations? How does he react to riots? How does he control violence and prevent property damage? Does he usually have a week or two to ponder over his decisions as he once did, or must he react to a critical situation in a minimum of time? Do his old reports still serve his needs or has he found that reports for the most part are one of a kind—each one in response to an operational situation not anticipated? Are his reports out of date and of little use when he receives them? "Yes" answers to the above questions illustrate the environment of real time or shortened response time that personnel administrators are faced with. Information must be available at the time of inquiry or only serve to support success or help understand failures in decisions.

Role of the Computer

The role of the computer in the development of an information system is more easily understood when one considers the definition of a system as one in which matrices of data elements are standing in interaction. If two matrices contained four elements each, there would be a possibility of 28 combinations of elements considering two at a time. Four matrices containing 50 elements would provide a possibility of 19,900 combinations taken two at a time. Without the data-handling techniques of a computer, only the more obvious and critical comparisons can be made. But the subtle interactions of the information elements are those which more often than not provide the real insights into the most critical of the decisions that must be made. An information base that is computer-resident would allow the personnel administrator to search the data for the nuances of interdependencies that provide answer to the strategic situations.

How much will a personnel administrator need to know about computers? It should first be assumed that he has on his staff the educational systems analyst who was described earlier. Without the systems analyst available to study carefully the situation, the personnel administrator would have little time to devote to the problems of day-to-day management. However, the personnel administrator should take the necessary steps to acquaint himself with the basic principles of data processing and more importantly information processing, a discipline that joined us with the development of the latest data-processing equipment.

It is outside the scope of this chapter to acquaint fully the reader with the essentials of data processing or information processing. Three generations of computers for general use have been introduced within the last two decades. Each generation has transcended the previous generation to the point that a person proficient in the use of the previous generation must unlearn many of the concepts that were his faithful servants for many years. Detailed and careful study of data- and information-processing applications available to the third-generation users will warrant the attention of all personnel administrators.

It would seem that student personnel information-system planning without extensive involvement of the chief personnel administrator would leave unanswered many of the critical questions of management. One of the greatest challenges likely to occur is the extent to which operational area administrators responsible for the design and maintenance of an information system can serve the needs of complex multiversity of the next decade. With expanding budgets careful and detailed analysis of all operations will be commonplace. The administrators without a carefully planned and efficiently managed information base will find it difficult if not impossible to answer the probing questions of trustees, legislators, alumnae, and most importantly—involved students.

What Information Will Be Collected?

It would be easy to be seduced into thinking that with the storage capacities of modern computers it would be most wise to collect and maintain all information that is available. Early in the data-processing evolvement it was commonplace for another punched card to be added to a student's pile of cards when new or additional information was required. We have all been a participant in the results of such actions. Think back to your last university enrollment and the number of cards that were required for a simple registration. Information collected and maintained represents an allocation of university resources both in staff and dollars.

The systems-analysis process of designing an information system will be of invaluable assistance in the decision to include or exclude data in the information base. The student personnel systems analyst will help other staff examine the appropriateness of each of the information elements that would be available and help them estimate the cost in both staff time and financial resources that would be allocated to the system. To collect thirty information elements concerning a topic that will involve only 300 students out of 20,000 may seem less important when it costs 25 cents per student to collect it. It may be more efficient to collect information at the time it is used. Duplicate files may seem unnecessary after careful study of the uniqueness of each file. It should be added, however, that anticipation of future needs is a much more difficult effort than the continuance of past procedures.

There is no simple answer to what information should be collected. Information needs are as changing as university environments. A sensitivity to change is the most important factor in determining information needs. The professional student personnel administrator must provide this sensitivity.

How Will a Computer Resident Information System Affect the People Who Use It?

If it can be assumed that an efficient student personnel information system has been designed and implemented, what is most likely to be the effects on the staff and the sequence of events related to the effects. First, the professional staff will look to the information system as a clerical replacement. Numerous useless and untimely report summaries will be generated. Conflicts with fellow staff members will result unless there is a clear understanding that the information base is for all to use and to *maintain.* Many will assume that use is a right, but maintenance of information base is best left to clerical personnel. Nothing will cause an information system to fail more quickly than for the professional staff to assume an attitude of use without the accompanying responsibility of constant editing and maintenance. Information elements change frequently on university campuses; insensitivity to the problems of invalid data will not be an uncommon occurrence during the early phases of an information system.

Secondly, people's jobs will change and the change will be dramatic and perhaps traumatic for some. Jobs are defined by the information people use in performing them. An information system will change both the content and syntax of the information elements. With all relevant data available in the information base, the chief administrators will often make changes in organizational flow without being aware of it. When it is no longer necessary to ask for certain data from a certain person, that person's job has been jeopardized. Changing job specifications will be a difficult adjustment for many.

Since information flow dictates organizational structures in institutions, the way personnel administrators administer a college or university will change. For many the buffer of information preparation will be gone when upper-level administrators have direct access to the information base. The importance of some staff functions will be enhanced, others will lessen. The position a person occupies in the information system will reflect the importance of his role in the organizational hierarchy.

Finally, personnel administrators will be forced to learn in great detail how their work affects others. It will quickly become apparent in an information system if one individual is not meeting his responsibilities to the system. Others dependent upon him from the collection of information crucial to the performance of their task will quickly point to the deficiency. This is perhaps one of the greatest pitfalls to beware of in the continued performance of an information system. If one person fails to meet his responsibility in either collection or maintenance, it will not be long before others will return to old methods of collecting and maintaining everything they need for the conduct of their job. In addition, the trust that is initially generated will be directly related to the credability of the information in the system. Why should a person give up their reliable file in their desk drawer when the data from the system are frequently in error? The strictist adherence to sound information collection and maintenance techniques are imperative.

How Will An Information System Be Used?

An information system will provide a quick response to frequent but unique inquiries. Traditional reports will be generated for the day-to-day operations of the student personnel offices. But providing comprehensive and complex operational data without expending excessive staff and financial resources will be the hallmark of information systems.

Applications not within the capacities of present systems and techniques will provide the greatest impetus for the evolvement of information systems. One such application will be simulation. *Experimentation without risk* is perhaps the best definition of simulation. Proposed changes can be tested through the information system rather than in real life. Simulated results are measured against anticipated outcomes. A myriad of variations of treatments will be possible without the commitment of resources. Optimizing decisions is the criterion of performance for simulation exercises. Examples of applications include (1) the effects of several unique allocations of resources, (2) determining the effects of changing housing policies, (3) and the effects of more stringent admission standards. Simulation is a task that computers will handle with ease. It is the conceptualization of the simulation model that requires the major effort. The parameters of the model must meet rigid empirical and intuitive tests of validity criteria.

Other applications will include forecasting, trend analyses, model building, and *linear* analyses. Leadership in the design and implementing of an information system will be crucial. Expertise to realize the full potential of a system will come with experience and experimentation.

A PROPOSED STUDENT RESEARCH INFORMATION SYSTEM (SRIS)

The remainder of the chapter describes in outline form a proposed Student Research Information System (SRIS) for student personnel areas. Most universities regardless of their organizational structure may be divided into four operational units: (1) academic affairs, (2) business affairs, (3) student affairs, and (4) public and developmental affairs. The following discussion will refer specifically to the student affairs area. Each segment of the university will have an operating system within the area in addition to interaction with each of the other units. An information system that would bring together all systems could be an Integrated University Information System. While it would be desirable to think in terms of a total system, it appears that for most colleges and universities it would be difficult to implement such a project without first developing an operating system within each of the areas. Careful planning and modular design will allow the interface of numerous systems at a later date.

STUDENT RESEARCH INFORMATION SYSTEM (SRIS)

A student research information system should serve two purposes. First it should serve the day-to-day operational needs, and secondly it should provide an information base suitable for research. It was indicated earlier that organizational structures often are dictated by the flow of information within them. If it could be assumed that a SRIS should be the student information base of a university, it would seem appropriate for certain university offices to be associated administratively. These would include:

1. Admissions and High School Relations Office
2. Registration Office
3. Testing Office
4. Financial Aids Office
5. Student Research Office
6. Student Life and Activities
7. Residence Hall Programs Office

For purposes of discussion of the Student Research Information System, it is more convenient to group the above categories into four groups. The accompanying diagram illustrates the grouping.

Admissions and Related Divisions

The data categories are arranged in chronological order of collection of information from top to bottom. Within the admissions division, data categories that should be included are:

1. High school data
2. Demographic data

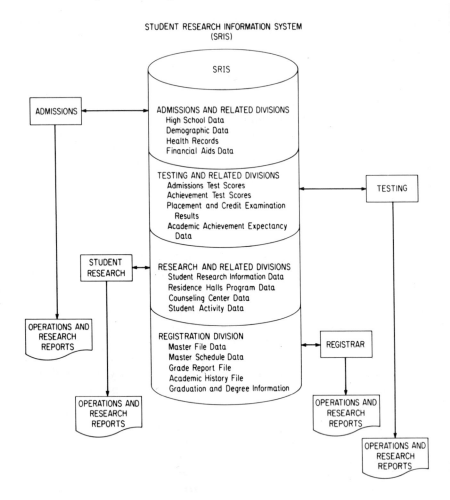

STUDENT RESEARCH INFORMATION SYSTEM
(SRIS)

3. Health clearance records
4. Financial aid data

Testing and Related Divisions

For some universities this would not represent an administrative unit, but in institutions of at least ten thousand students it is a common office. Data collected within this unit would include:

1. Admissions test scores
2. Achievement test scores
3. Placement and credit examination results
4. Academic achievement expectancy data

Research and Related Divisions

This grouping includes data which are used less in the operational functions of the student personnel area, but more in the research and planning functions of the unit. Some operational categories are included; residence hall programs, counseling center, and student activities. These areas require a minimum of operational support, but include information of a strategic nature vital to research. Also included is student research information data (other than psychological and demographical data).

Registration Division

Data categories generally found within a registrar's office are included:

1. Master file data
2. Master schedule file
3. Grade report file
4. Academic history file
5. Graduation and degree information

Physical File or Logical Files

The SRIS is illustrated as one file containing all information necessary for operational, strategic, and research functions. Computer storage capacity and file-design philosophy will dictate the number and size of files. Modularity of files is more important than file size and design. When an SRIS is established it will probably be done in stages. It is difficult if not impossible to anticipate all information that would be included in the entire system at the time of implementing one phase of the system. For this reason each section of the file should be conceived of as a building block that must fit within a total configuration. With this as the criterion of design, each new phase will add a module that is easily interfaced with the previous. At times it will be necessary to consolidate modules for convenience and efficiency, but these again must be modular in nature or the next phase of development. Physical files requirements should never force abandonment of the logical file concept.

RESEARCH AND OPERATIONS APPLICATIONS

Admissions

Admissions offices serve one basic purpose—the recruitment and selection of prospective students. For most schools this is a time-consuming, competitive, and difficult task. Communications to prospective high school students usually are channeled through the guidance counselor. An information system should serve the operational needs related to communications and also provide means for evaluating the efforts expended. Each communication project should be designed so that data are gathered and stored within the admissions file for evaluation at the termination of the project.

One criterion measure should be kept in mind for most admissions research—how well does the effort or treatment serve to assist in the recruitment and selection of students? Admissions programs are intended to provide each university community with the type of students that will allow the objectives of the institution to be met. The organization of the SRIS reflects this dimension, since the admissions staff has access to *all* student data through graduation. Admissions research begins with the basic information that is collected at the time of admissions and continues through a student's academic tenure.

Admissions research reports to the high schools should serve two purposes. First, they should describe in detail the academic performance of the student from a given high school. Secondly, the reports should describe the achievement characteristics of the total student body so that comparisons are possible. Both purposes may be performed within one research effort as illustrated in the accompanying chart. Within a single document a high school counselor finds the performance of each of his students, the composite achievement of all students for that high school, the academic potential of students from that high school and composite achievement of all freshmen in the university, and composite information for academic potential and achivement. An information system that provides a quick and efficient interface with registrar data makes this type of report possible within reasonable financial and time limits. A report for every high school within a given state could be prepared in less than two hours.

A myriad of research reports to the university community is also possible with the advent of an information system. For example, the university community should be kept aware of the changing characteristics of the prospective students since response time within the academic setting is often slow. A recruitment effort aimed at increasing the number of urban poverty students would probably fail the second year if the admissions office failed to advise the academic community of the impending arrival of the students the previous year.

Analysis and projection of potential freshmen should also occupy a priority role in the admissions research program. Too many or too few

STUDENT INFORMATION FORM
5 / 68

NAME __NEFF JUDY__   SEX __FEMALE__   S S NO. __304-50-7645__   MAJOR __HISTORY__

CAMPUS ADDRESS __RHODES HALL__   ZIP _____   SCHOOL __ARTS AND SCIENCE__

HOME ADDRESS __351 CHURCHMAN__, __BEECH GROVE IND__   ZIP __46107__   CLASSIFICATION __1ST SEM FRESHMAN__

BEGINNING FRESHMAN __XX__ YES __XX__ TRANSFER STUDENT _____   DATE OF ADMISSION __01 / 24 / 68__   DATE OF BIRTH __08 / 06 / 49__

HIGH SCHOOL __BEECH GROVE HIGH SCHOOL__   COUNTY __MARION__   STATE __INDIANA__   DATE OF GRADUATION __JUNE 68__

OTHER COLLEGES ATTENDED __NONE__

PARENT OR SPOUSE __NEFF MR RALPH__

ADDRESS __351 CHURCHMAN__, __BEECH GROVE IND__   __46107__

S.A.T. SCORES

MATH __420__ VERBAL __433__   TOTAL __0853__

PERCENTILE NORMS

MATH __35__ VERBAL __65__   TOTAL __49__

H. S. RANK PERCENTILE __80__

CEEB ACHIEVEMENT TESTS

NAME OF TEST	SCORE	%ILES
ENGLISH COMP	397	41
MATH 1	444	35
A-HSIT/SOCST	546	89

PLACEMENT TESTS

NAME OF TEST	SCORE	CLASS PLCMENT
SPANISH	62	202
SPEECH	40	201

RANGE OF FIRST SEMESTER PREDICTED GRADE AVERAGE
CHANCES IN 100 THAT GRADE AVERAGE WILL BE EQUAL TO OR HIGHER THAN

GRADE AVERAGE	1.30	1.40	1.60	1.70	1.80	1.90	2.00	2.25	2.50	2.75	3.00	3.50
CHANCES IN 100	92	89	82	78	73	69	63	48	34	21	12	XX
	DROP			C				C+		B	DEAN'S LIST

** LESS THAN 5 CHANCES IN 100.

OFFICE OF ADMISSIONS

UNIVERSITY TESTING OFFICE

faculty, too many or too few residence-hall rooms present conditions that should be avoided on all campuses. Input from the other levels of the information system would supplement such a program with data concerning attrition rates and changing residence patterns. Each research effort can reflect the totality of information available in order to facilitate the most pertinent decision.

Testing

The testing function within the organizational structure supplements the admission procedures described above. Since information element territorial boundaries have been broken with the information system, cooperation seems assured between units of the university. A testing office would add to the admissions test data the information obtained in the placement and credit examination program. Many costly duplications of efforts can be avoided by the availability of both admissions and university-level achievement data at the time placement and credit examination programs are initiated. Often placement and credit data are two or three years old before they can be translated into operational policies. Semester-by-semester analyses are provided through the use of an information system that is current at *all* times. The real-time dimension described earlier becomes more practical and useful when viewed in this context.

Academic prediction data are natural byproducts of a research program that analyzes test data on a semester-by-semester basis. See the accompanying example of aid to university advisors. It was generated by an admissions and testing office with academic advisors' needs in mind. On one document is found a summary of numerous research efforts to translate test score data into useful decision-making aids. The expectancy table at the bottom of the report is revised yearly using data from the immediate preceding freshman class. Through simulation, other academic curriculum-model expectancy tables can be used to supplement the general model found on the document.

Multivariate-analysis test-related research is facilitated, since all classes of information are available for each student. A scan of the file interfaced with statistical computer routines allows a student personnel administrator to actually generate research potentials that are not possible when the data are viewed separately. Relationships not anticipated are identifiable through scanning of the information system with standard statistical routines. Random-sample generators provide instant study groups for graduate students assigned to the student affairs area. The applications are limited only by the imagination of the user.

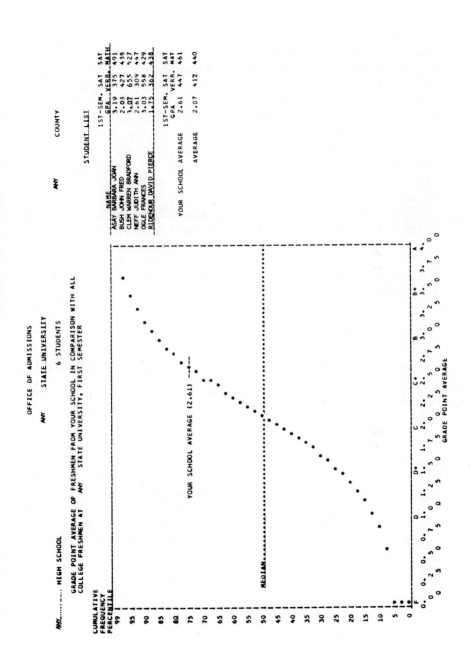

Other Functions

The major operational function that the SRIS can provide deans of students, counseling centers, registrars are those described as inquiry-oriented. Why should each operational unit of a university have in file drawers parts of the information found in the SRIS? A more logical system would make the information available from a central file to each administrative office. Computer technology is developed to the point where this is not only possible but practical. Display stations are available that will allow an inquiry into an information base to be answered in seconds. Many universities are now using this system to supply advisors and student personnel administrators with information needed to do an effective job.

Research activities of an institutional nature are another dimension of university administration that will be facilitated by the advent of a SRIS. Descriptive analyses of the university environment, socially and academically, are limited only by the information available. University environmental studies will provide input to admissions efforts and to long-range planning.

Registration Functions

A Student Research Information System would be of little impact without a creditable and reliable data base. While it is true that other administrative units will be responsible for initiating a student record, it will be the role of a registrar's office to collect the majority of the information. In addition, the all-important task of maintenance of the system must be effected by registration-related functions. The maintenance function is as critical to continued research efforts as is the collection function.

Operational applications of the SRIS to a registrar are as numerous as the function that he must perform. Efficient registration, scheduling, and grade-reporting procedures will evolve since only a numeric address key is needed for transaction with a student record. Cumbersome and expensive procedures should be replaced early in the development of an information system.

SUMMARY

It can be stated with confidence that use and expansion of a Student Research Information System will prevail only where the needs of both operations and research are served. However, if rigid research capacity criteria are met, sophisticated modern managerial operations procedures will also be possible. The student personnel administrator who can combine research activities and modern higher-education managerial concepts will provide invaluable leadership for the profession.

13

Dropouts: Recent Studies— Implications and Observations

William Hannah*

It is not strange that the concern about the dropout problem in the United States today has developed to such enormous proportions. As one looks at recent history and the increasing demands of society, with its concomitant pressures on students, one can well wonder why attrition has not grown at a considerably faster rate than existing research portrays. We can recognize that the current and growing "philosophy of uncertainty" influences, indeed even permeates, the entire area of higher education if we consider that present student unrest is saying anything to us. (It might be saying that there is a decreasing fit between students and colleges, caused by this evident student anxiety.) And although we must admit that uncertainty is undeniable, without doubt it carries along a burden in the student of nondirection and consequent loss of commitment to specific tasks and to definite decisions concerning life's goals, values and objectives. Pervin (1965) points out that students leaving Princeton report that problems of motivation consistently are noted as contributing to withdrawal, and that uncertainty about what to study is the reason most frequently given for dropping out of college.

Surely such ambiguity affects attrition. More research studies than ever before are attempting to identify the more serious and subtle

*Dr. William Hannah holds a B.S. from Rider College, Lawrenceville, New Jersey, M.A. from Columbia University, Teachers College, New York and his Ed.D. from the University of Southern California, Los Angeles. Dr. Hannah has led a distinguished career in research, teaching and administration. Formerly Research Coordinator for Project on Student Development in Selected Small Colleges at Plainfield, Vermont, he now serves as Director, Financial Affairs, Westmont College, Santa Barbara, California.

causes of withdrawal relating to reasons other than the more obvious ones usually spelled out so succinctly in the findings of individual colleges and universities.

This chapter assesses the more recent studies found in journals of research and books which deal with college attrition. It also discusses the implications of these findings and then suggests some new directions and attitudes in personnel administration which may help to modify the anxieties among college administrators that tend to disrupt efforts in understanding this phenomenon.

STUDIES ON COLLEGE ATTRITION

The extensive literature on college dropouts dates back at least forty years and includes hundreds of studies providing insight into reasons why students fail to persist in the academic community. Correspondingly, the task of total review becomes almost insurmountable if one decides to examine all the literature available. Consequently a sampling of these studies and reviews was chosen, deriving mainly from publications of recent years. However, some attention is given to older studies for the perspective they provide for more recent books and articles. The listed references give credence to the amount of time spent in trying to resolve this problem which college and university people have felt is a reflection on their institutions' academic efficiency. This list contains more than thirty-five studies across a wide range of research design and type.

To begin with, this writer does not necessarily agree with the common assumption in our society that value accrues to all young people from participation in higher education in the United States. These analyses will consider the possibility that preparation for life, and meeting the challenges and opportunities which the society has to offer, may well be served by other directions and other approaches. But we recognize that student personnel administrators may well take the opposite view.

The literature gives broad insight into this almost exclusively American area of concern. On occasion one comes across references to attrition in other countries and is left with the idea that dropping out of college elsewhere in the world is not of particular concern to societies where it is an accepted pattern of life, or where, because of the sense of responsibility of the educational institutions of a nation, it is almost not allowed. In Europe, dropping out apparently is acceptable, probably because of the system of education which relegates the average and poorer student automatically to a vocational education and thus a less professional type of occupation, and which places a high premium on academic proficiency and persistence. In Japan, attrition in college is not even considered because dropping out by the student reflects a failure on the part of the institution in its responsibility to educate successfully all students enrolled.

In the United States, our concern dates to the early part of this century, and culminated in the 1930's with McNeeley's (1937) study under the auspices of the Department of Education, which considered attrition among over 15,000 students who entered 25 universities in 1931 and 1932. McNeeley discovered that over 62 percent of this number withdrew during the next four years. Previous to this, many studies in the 1920's and 1930's reflected the growing concern and, no doubt, gave impetus to the government's decision to examine the issue. In this large analysis of dropouts, the author concluded that, excluding transfers from the 62 percent already noted, over 45 percent of those entering were lost to higher education.

During the 1940's, again, many studies from colleges, universities, and educational agencies indicated the deepening interest in the problem of college attrition, probably more because of practical administrative concerns than from concern over student or college weaknesses. During the war years fewer studies appeared; interest was sustained, but with the influx of veterans a somewhat smaller amount of research was published.

However, in 1950 the Office of Education, under again increasing interest, instituted a monumental study [Iffert, 1957] based upon a sampling of approximately 13,000 men and women who had enrolled in colleges and universities in the fall of that year. All types of institutions (147) were represented: universities, technical institutes, liberal arts colleges, teachers colleges, and junior colleges. The study showed that slightly less than 40 percent of the freshmen class remained at the institution of first enrollment to graduate four years later. An additional 20 percent graduated later from the first college, or graduated from another institution in four years. Therefore about 60 percent of entering freshmen eventually received degrees. This study, which has stood as a landmark ever since, dealt mainly with reported reasons for leaving, but also elicited impressions of students concerning other aspects of the college organization, services, and climate. One of the main findings, dealt with the fact that the first year of college is the most critical period for dropouts, showing that fully 28 percent of entering students leave during this time. In many ways the findings of this study supported the earlier research by McNeely.

These two large national studies spelled out the problem and give a fairly clear picture of its size for the nation as a whole. This was necessary, for it is against such a background that individual colleges in some measure can assess their own performance and seek to identify their particular problems, relating their attrition rates to a national norm. However, such averages never can solve the problems of individual institutions, because there are as many variations in problems as there are institutions; and local and institutional factors always seem to affect a particular rate of attrition. This is clearly pointed out in a study made recently [Nelson, 1966] in which it was shown that as many as fifteen college and community variables can affect the attrition rates of institutions without any consideration being given to student input or output variables.

In Summerskill's (1962) review of the literature the following facts about attrition were discussed. He states that "age of the student per se does not affect attrition although older graduates may encounter more obstacles to graduation." (p. 631)   He also indicates that there is little sex difference in terms of the rates of attrition; however, the reasons for withdrawal are different for men and women. He found that socioeconomic background does affect the adjustment to the college environment and consequently is a factor in affecting attrition rates.

Farnsworth (1955) showed that success in college was related to the educational level and the parental attitude toward intellectual matters, by giving evidence that where parents prize education, everything else being equal, the students also will value academic achievement. This is supported by a recent study of engineering students where interest or disinterest of parents in the student's study affected the leaving rate [Greenfield, 1964]. It is suspected that Jewish families are particularly conscious of educational advancement, as Summerskill (1955) points out in his study; therefore there may be ethnic influences which also encourage persistence in the academic endeavor.

The cultural and educational climate of the hometowns of students have been studied in many instances in an attempt to identify reasons why certain students fail to persist. Results of these studies seem to show that the level of educational opportunity and the interest in cultural advancement in these communities, in some fashion, relate to college success. It has been seen by one study in particular [Strang, 1937] that students from rural homes show a higher attrition rate than those from more cosmopolitan areas. These are difficult variables to isolate, however, and do not allow for much assurance that indeed the condition is directly responsible for attrition. But they may be a factor. Socioeconomic factors have been examined extensively in terms of the search for reasons of nonpersistence.

These factors have been second in number only to the examination of academic achievement in all the studies examined. On the local and national level many studies have delved into the problems of student achievement in an effort to arrive at some method of prediction of college success. There is a consensus among the writers that high school grades are definitely related to college attrition. Where it has been shown that students were successful on the secondary level, the pattern of success tends to be continued on into the higher educational environment. Of course, exceptions do occur, and later in this chapter this will be discussed by examining other factors which seem to work against the success of those who, previous to their college experience, were adequate students. Summerskill (1962) in quoting Iffert states:

> It is possible substantially to reduce high attrition rates by simply raising college admissions requirements with respect to secondary school grades. Iffert found that the attrition rate for men attending twenty colleges and universities would have been reduced from 61.2% to 43.9% if admissions had been confined to the top fifteenth of high school graduating classes.   (p. 634)

He also concluded that

> The percentages ... seem to show that standing in high school graduating class was a much better indicator of the probability of graduation than standing in the placement tests.   (p. 634)

Abel (1966), in discussing the student in college who is certain of his vocational and academic goals, implies that most certainty comes from previous successes related to academic achievement; therefore when a student is certain of what he wishes to do, and whose grade-point average is above 2.0, he is more likely to persist in college. On the other hand, a student who is also certain but who is performing below a 2.0 average will withdraw at a rate twice that of the higher achieving student. The findings of Gadzella and Bentall (1967) reveal that high school grade-point average was the only single variable that indicated a significant mean difference between the college graduate and the college dropout, whether male or female. They state clearly that this is the best single source of data which is predictive.

Little (1953) found that, in terms of high school rank, 78 percent of dropouts ranked in the lowest 30 percent of their high school graduating class as compared with 37 percent of dropouts recorded as being in the highest 30 percent. He also found a proportionately higher number of dropouts ranking in the lower third of mental tests.

Therefore the evidence mounts that at the present time the only real predictor of college success rests upon our knowledge of past performance. We can lament this paucity of information because we have the uneasy feeling that many more factors are involved; one thing we can be certain of is that other factors are indeed an influence. The confusion of students and their grasping at reasons for leaving college can be recognized readily, and from this, as many writers indicate, multicausality is the obvious conclusion. Without recognizing the other significant factors about college attrition we cannot rightly prescribe remedies. The outward manifestation of weakness in our system, or in the low achievement of some students, cannot be used solely to solve our problems; and really does not advance us much beyond the old methods of European educational processes. Although our point of departure in cutting off students from educational opportunities is different, for many able nonachieving students in America our system results in the same disappointments, frustrations and despair (maybe for fewer students, but nevertheless for some). Such "apparent" weaknesses may or may not be weaknesses at all, but simply may derive from a condition either within or outside the student which is tied to his own development involving identity, integrity, and independence. All these traits militate against the solidifying of internal motivations which is so necessary to success in the academic environment. In other countries the achievers persist and the nonachievers fail, failure in that one opportunity affects the accomplishments of a lifetime. The best we can say in the United States is that at least second chances are available to many who ultimately can succeed—may it always be so. The present system may be the best we can maintain under the circumstances. Nevertheless, conscious consideration of the process of maturation and of the forces in the institution causing confusion are necessary.

Again, Summerskill (1962) discovered that fully 33 percent of college dropouts are due to poor grades and academic failure. He cites twenty-three studies of which the above percentage is an average. Again and again studies show the college GPA as a factor in withdrawal [Barger and Hall, 1964; Carlson and Wegner, 1965, Forrest, 1967; Weintraub and Salley, 1945], and suggest that not only poorer achievement is the cause, but that other factors, especially among high-ability students, are additional causes of attrition. However sizable the academic problem is, Summerskill suggests that "motivational and adjustment problems may be ascribed to an even larger number" (p. 643) and quotes Farnsworth (1959) who says, "no reliable statistics are available as to how many of those who leave college do so because of emotional difficulties or conflicts. However, we have good reason to believe that in some institutions the proportion is considerably more than half." (p. 643) From his analysis, "10% to 15% of dropouts report that personal adjustment problems are involved in their leaving school." (p. 644) Nevertheless, there may be a difference between self-report and actual cause and he implies that the percentage may be much higher. Consequently, more effort should be exerted, and more subtle approaches must be sought in order to ascertain the influence on attrition of these more obscure forces in the students.

To this point an attempt has been made to show the present state of college attrition, and to identify the main variables associated with nonpersistence in college. Now a look at those areas which are now eliciting more interest than heretofore; the areas of student personality and college characteristics.

In this investigation some studies have thrown new light on the personality characteristics of college withdrawees and, although not conclusive, they direct one's attention to certain peculiarities in students which seem to mitigate against college persistence. One such study [Suczek and Alfert, 1966] carried on at Berkeley supported by the Office of Education (DHEW), examined 1,621 entering freshmen. It compared all dropouts with stay-ins and the authors found that male leavers when compared with male persisters were seen as more independent and rebellious, while male stay-ins were more cautious and dutiful. Among females, dropouts were more impulsive, while stay-ins were more conforming. Failing male dropouts were compared with male dropouts in good academic standing, and it was evident that male failures were less controlled and rigid, while the failing female dropout category contained the least mature of all groups studied and showed the least developed personality. Female leavers in good standing had the highest impulse level, were the most complex individuals of all groups tested, and were more controlled and flexible. The authors, examining transfers, nontransfer dropouts, and returnees, found that transfers are much like stay-ins, showing less maturity than either the nontransfer dropouts or the returnees; they are more conservative, conventional, compliant to authority, are task-oriented and ambitious. The nontransfer dropouts were seen as valuing sensations more, enjoying fantasy and imagination, and motivated by rebelliousness. The returnees were seen as the most mature of all groups tested. They were complex, flexible, realistic, tolerant, adventurous, imaginative, and valued intellectual and esthetic pursuits. This last observation brings to mind a statement by one researcher who after much study on leavers suggested that possibly leaving college was not the horrible tragedy often described. He [Dalrymple, 1967] said education is a preparation for life, yes; but life should be a preparation for education, agreeing with Kubie (1966) who presents the same idea. The implication is that maybe the returnee has, outside the educational institution, found some maturing influences which make him more ready and mature, willing to accept what the college or university has to offer. Professional school transfers from Berkeley [Suczek and Alfert, 1966] were described as inhibited, dependent on authority and convention, and intolerant of differences and ambiguities; implying that narrowness or the desire for narrowness in education has a stultifying effect upon personality. According to this study, the general results of the college experience are limited by the frequent conflicts involving establishment of autonomy in the student. Dropping out, especially, is a frequent result of this stress. The authors further implied that rebelliousness against externally imposed values was a factor in withdrawal involving the need to provide a time, away from campus, for reassessment of directions and values.

Other studies consider some of the same and other variables, with the resulting development of patterns relating to personality characteristics. Aiken (1964) discovered that aptitude scores, when related to leavers and stayers did not discriminate between them; while from biographical data he concluded that lack of motivation for academic matters was the main reason. In a study involving the Minnesota Multiphasic Personality Inventory (MMPI), Barger and Hall (1964) found that higher scores on the masculinity scale identified both men and women who left college. These leavers were seen as rebellious, nonconformist, and high-activity-oriented persons; indicating that motivational elements were active here. With these orientations, the trait of quiet, scholarly study was missing, implying lack of motivation and inability to solve academic problems. In using the Minnesota Counseling Inventory (MCI), Brown (1960) discovered that women dropouts were withdrawn, introverted, depressed, and tended toward social isolation; while men dropouts tended to be irresponsible and nonconforming. Dalrymple (1967) further states

> Psychological factors which cause students to lose motivation, quarrel with teachers or contemporaries, or crack up, usually afflict students who have also suffered personal dissatisfactions, academic difficulties, physical symptoms, disciplinary problems, or some combination of these.

Using the Gordon Personal Profile (GPP) and the Gordon Personality Inventory (GPI), Daniel (1967) found that persisters were more trustful and tolerant, persevering, inquiring, energetic, vigorous, calm and collected, and cautious. In this same study, leavers were seen as less persevering and inquiring. Grace (1957) discovered from his investigation that withdrawers were dependent and irresponsible; disagreeing with others who, as previously stated, saw independence as a prime trait in dropouts. Heilbrun, University of Iowa (1965) found that in high-ability groups for both men and women, dropping out was associated with more assertive, less passive social behavior. He states that persistence relates to students in this ability group who are more passive and task-oriented and are influenced by conformity to institutional values. Those leaving students above, described as more assertive and less task-oriented, encounter greater difficulty in value conformance, and are more likely to leave college prior to the second year. The author further explains,

> The greater academic and social regimentation imposed upon incoming students of large universities is a greater source of frustration to the bright student than to those of lesser ability, and involves rewarding of intellectual pursuits (at lower levels).

Heilbrun in a study of female freshmen (1962) using the Adjective Check List Need Scales (ACL), suggests that it is the relative absence or denial of certain needs that is crucial in implementing or deterring the female student's continuation in school. He describes these students as higher on heterosexuality and change, and lower on achievement, order, and endurance.

Another study involving high aptitude students [Hill, 1966] which, in part deals with personality traits; divided the sample into three groups; graduates (G), voluntary withdrawals (VW), and enforced withdrawals (EW), which were examined for differences in psychometric information. He found that creative ability was lowest in the VW group, highest among the G group, strangely the EW group rated higher in creativity than did the VW's. In personality, the only significant differences found were that G males were greater socializers, and that females of the G group were highest in achievement via independence. A significant feature of this study was expressed by the author: "Among the better predictors of withdrawal, simply asking the student about his chances of graduation was highly significant."

Marks (1967) suggests the same idea, "simply ask him." The figures in Hill's study showed that the VW group were much less certain of graduation than were either the G's or the EW's.

A study, [Jensen, 1958] again using the MMPI, indicated that nonachieving students consistently differed from students of high ability on 6 of the 11 scales. It was seen that generally low-scholastic-ability nonachievers encountered more adjustment problems, than other students. Gifted students expressed themselves as having fewer adjustment problems; this shows that greater scholastic ability favors adjustment while low ability obstructs it, which has implications in terms of personal adjustment and withdrawal. This of course ties with Terman's study of the gifted.

In a study using the Omnibus Personality Inventory (OPI) made by Rose and Elton (1966) dropouts were clearly seen as distinct in personality traits from other groups. The authors discovered that leavers were the most maladjusted, had least interest in literature, art, and philosophy, were illogical, irrational, uncritical, and disliked reflective and abstract thought.

One study which the present writer [Hannah, 1967] completed using the OPI involving freshman dropouts, revealed that traits such as greater estheticism (interest in artistic matters), less maturity (anxiety, hostility, and aggression), greater independence and irresponsibility militate against persistence in the college environment.

These studies reflect the state of research efforts in the understanding of personality differentials of college withdrawees at the present time. It is evident that much disarray exists, and much must be done in order to sort out the various forces working against college persistence. Realizing that no one study can adequately satisfy that understanding, these many efforts are seen as a start at bringing into focus the more subtle forces in the student which tend to move him toward his decision to leave the academic community for, what appears to him, better and greener fields elsewhere. It is implied from these studies that the students are confused and, in many cases, unaware of the forces within themselves. They have perception and understanding, and use external reasons for their decision, but how many indeed are aware of the internal pressures and subconscious elements of their natures which drive them to seek satisfaction away from the influence of academic striving? It is also evident that the clarity we need is not in evidence, however, a beginning in understanding has been made and hopefully, with additional effort, more clarification will emerge in the very near future.

"Boiling down" these various findings is difficult. Some findings conflict with others and we are perplexed by this, and by the varied nature and amount of the data available. The dropout's personality traits vary with the forces at work at a certain time, and at a certain institution. However, three major rubrics derive from the foregoing findings.

1. Generally stated, the *real dropout* is independent, rebellious, impulsive, unmotivated by college, irresponsible, nonpersevering, immature and uncertain of his direction.
2. The *transferring dropout* is merely moving elsewhere and does not differ appreciably from his persisting peer, if anything, he is much like his persisting peer—cautious and dutiful.
3. The *returning dropout* is the most mature; he is flexible, realistic, tolerant, adventurous, and valuing of intellectual pursuits.

Is this an oversimplification? Probably. Any generalizations about all dropouts are precariously founded, but we need to see these findings in their simplest terms if they are to be meaningful to us, and if we are to use them in our endeavor to help students now. There is no doubt that subcategories of dropouts exist, for Suczek has shown us this; any effort to make generalizations about all dropouts causes anxiety and necessarily leaves us with some of the same uneasiness that existed before.

But the data available should be used and converted to something understandable for use today. Let us use these in that context until we know more. We are being told by the findings, that dropping out is a function of uncertainty and nondirection, because of forces within the student which he may or may not be able to control. We are told that mobility between institutions is not a serious problem and is simply the exchanging of one environment for another, which may be more compatible with the individual, whatever the reasons might be. We are told that the dropout who returns does so in a more mature state. His experiences generally have been good, his interest has been sparked, and his internal motivations have been enhanced.

One additional area of study with which this review is concerned is that of college characteristics. Farnsworth (1955) states: "The entire college atmosphere, both intellectual and social, is different on a campus where almost the entire student body will graduate, from that on a campus where only a minority of students will graduate." This has a great implication, especially for those colleges with large attrition rates. A transiency—and more serious, a sense of transiency—in a group generates instability and uncertainty affecting both those who persist and those who do not. Sanford (1956) further emphasized this when he said

> [Research] might obtain evidence that the phenomenon had less to do with factors in the student than with a certain condition in the college itself, and this condition might immediately assume greater practical importance than withdrawal, because it was now perceived as something that affected all the students.

Nelson's study (1966), already cited, was instituted as a response to Sanford's statement. He selected 100 four-year institutions with very low freshman dropout rates, and compared them with a comparable group of colleges and universities that had attrition rates which were much higher, using 22 selected variables—some personal and some nonpersonal—relating to the institutions. It was found that colleges with low freshman dropout rates did differ significantly from the comparison group on 15 of the 22 characteristics. Nelson points to four general statements resulting from his study:

1. The higher the proportion of men in the institution, the greater the possibility that the institution will have a higher dropout rate or be classified among the higher freshman attrition category.
2. The more selective the college is, the more likely it is that the institution will fall in the low freshman attrition category.
3. The smaller the size of the institution and the smaller the community is in which it is located, the lower the freshman attrition rate will be.

4. Institutions with low freshman attrition rates are more likely to be affluent than those with higher rates of attrition among freshmen.

Although this study dealt with rather obvious factors; studying things such as the library, faculty, size of college, size of local community, selectivity and affluence, it indicates that the characteristics of any college tend to influence retention rates. The general conclusion presented was that administrators who seek to understand and to cope with the freshman dropout problem must take into consideration both personal and nonpersonal factors associated with the phenomenon of freshman attrition.

Administrators in colleges have generally assumed that the climate within a college could affect changes in students, and could influence them in positive directions; college public relations departments have propagandized these assumptions. The question might be asked, "If there are positive effects, is it not possible that unknowingly, we might be fostering negative effects as well?" It would seem that this is true, as Dalrymple (1967) notes:

> Colleges differ in their characteristics just as individuals do. Some are authoritarian, others permissive; some specific in their pedagogical approach, others abstract; some overly paternalistic, others excessively impersonal; some sectarian, others secular. Under these circumstances, the student will either fit or not fit the college or a particular part of it. He may be stimulated, lulled, bored, frustrated, angered, or nurtured by the environment he finds and by its interaction with his personality and talents.

A few studies have attempted to assess these factors, but very few. Already cited is Heilbrun's study (1965) in which he speaks of regimentation and rigidity fostering dropout in the high ability group of students. Iffert (1957) has noted that counseling and guidance services for most students are unproductive in value to the student. Holmes (1959) states that criticism by students of the counseling services was second only to criticism of food on campus. The writer [Hannah, 1968] in studying attitudes among members of the sophomore class who were classified as potential dropouts, discovered minimal participation between potential leavers and college personnel, coupled with low value ratings of the college counseling programs in terms of decisions to withdraw. In this same study it was seen that restrictive rules and regulations and unstimulating activities such as religious services were high on the list of criticisms. "As students leave, to whom do they go for advice?" The writer discovered that first, friends are contacted and discussions ensue between both friends of the same and opposite sex; secondly, students discuss with and listen to parents; finally, almost after the decision has been solidified, the college personnel are contacted—possibly only as a formality—before the final exit comes. Harsh as this may sound, little value seems to derive from these college counseling systems. Johnson (1954) observes that proper counseling could remedy the attrition problem, and by implication we could comment, "if it were only examined thoroughly and instituted adequately." Panos and Astin (1967) suggest that

> Students are more likely to complete four years if they attend colleges where student peer relationships are characterized by friendliness, cooperativeness, and independence; where the students frequently can participate in college activities, where there is a high level of involvement with, and concern for the individual student, and where administrative policies concerning student aggression are relatively permissive. (p. ii. Abstract)

Chickering (1966) has defined well the relationship between institutional differences and characteristics of students at small colleges. He states that students who fit one pattern of operation in one college may well feel out of place at an institution where another pattern was dominant. He states that major questions are raised about the development of mental health of students in small colleges in both practice and behavior, when there is compatibility or noncompatibility of students to institutions. It may be further stated that the diversity of practices and behavior in large universities may raise larger and more difficult kinds of problems and questions in terms of stress to the student when considering their affect on withdrawal. The question of homogeneous college populations and resultant benefit is still an open one. No available data have measured whether "oneness of mind" in certain groupings is better than "differences of opinion" when the consideration is college attrition. We suspect that a balance between the two is desirable, but what that balance should contain in terms of these two elements is yet unknown.

That more needs to be known about the students' dispositions, personality characteristics, and influence of college characteristics goes without saying. The foregoing studies of these variables reveal an added interest in the students' influence in the academic setting, and the colleges' responsibility in providing a proper climate in which successful achievement can be made, both in terms of quantity and quality. The question posed here is, "Is it reasonable to suggest that students be fitted to the proper environment in order to maximize the benefit they are to receive from their experience in college, and will such "fitting" indeed benefit them in terms of total development and the minimizing of attrition?" This we do not know. Pervin (1967) maintains that his "data do not suggest that homogeniety of colleges and homogeniety of students within college is best. Rather they suggest that there is an optimum fit between student and college, the qualities of which will vary for different students and different colleges."

But what do dropouts say about their withdrawal after a time away from college? One study carried on by the writer [Hannah, 1968] revealed some very significant attitudes. Typical of these feelings were responses to a question asking whether the decision was wise or unwise. Consistently, the leavers responded by referring to subjects involving uncertainty, independence, and need for time for a reassessment of their lives. Here are some respondent's remarks taken at random from among four hundred dropouts. Each quote is that of a different person.

Uncertainty

"I want to say this very much; when I left college I was lost. I had no place to go. I was down and no one was there to help me—I remain bitter."

"At college I felt I had no direction, and was very indecisive."

"I wasn't interested ... it was horrible."

"I felt I was a machine [in college]."

"It [college], for the most part, was just sort of a vacuum, most of the time I was bored."

"I have lost interest in everything. I feel as though I have accomplished nothing, and I feel that it will be a while before I ever accomplish anything."

"I am definitely disillusioned, the aims and goals institutions pay lip service to, in practice, are impractical idealisms."

"It seems the less direction students are afforded the more confused they become until they are striking out in all directions at once in an attempt to find some guidance."

Independence

"Finally, I am able to do what I want."

"I am free to do anything I want without breaking college rules."

"I felt forced to do many things I didn't want to do. I am on my own and feel free to develop as a person."

"The college was my parents' choice—now I am shaping my own future instead of my parents shaping it for me."

"I am free to be me."

"I am happier in my new found freedom and independence than I was in the strict confines of college; independence also brings obligations and responsibilities."

Reassessment

"I needed to grow up and I did. I discovered that I hadn't been ready for college."

"I am happier, less nervous, and have learned more about life in general from my experiences than any book could have taught me. Colleges are useful for some people. My temperament and attitudes were not suitable to the college environment. College is not for everyone, no matter what the faculties say."

"I now know where I am headed and have chosen my profession."

"I have become more certain of my future plans. It has given me the time away from college that I needed."

"It [withdrawal] has brought some of life's rich rewards to me."

Return to College

"It helped me to realize the importance of college and how very much I wanted to go. Now I am ready to go back."

"It was wise to withdraw and wise to return. A year away from school helped me discover that even if it was hard work, it was a lot better than anything else I could do. I know now that I can do college work; I think I was just not ready for it before."

"I continually understand more of the expectations of a college and how they coincide with my own expectations, and I have a chance to experiment with different jobs. I will return."

"My temporary withdrawal, through travel and life abroad, I developed an enthusiasm for learning about places and people. Confidence in myself has increased."

"I feel I have matured, and will be a better person to continue my education at a later date."

"I matured and fortunately had the opportunity to go to another college."

"I plan to go back to college because I realize my potential and what I am and ought to do with it. I now enjoy my work, but realize its limitations. I hope this period of adjustment will better prepare me for my future education that I am sure I now must have."

"I found ideals, beliefs which I wanted, plus goals for college. Going to college will now be more relevant and meaningful. . . . I could not see these when I was there."

These are the expressions of those who find the academic atmosphere unpleasant and confusing. They are seeking other directions, other meanings, other experiences. As the educator considers these, there is the nagging sense of not meeting the need, not seeing the reality as dropouts do. These thoughts bring to mind the statement of

Chuang-tse, the Chinese teacher, who having considered problems of understanding and being understood said, "How shall I talk of the sea to the frog, if he has never left his pond? How shall I talk of frost to the bird of the summer land, if it has never left the land of its birth?" Understanding and direction comes from knowing, and knowing derives from the process of learning involving meanings related to life and its experiences. Dalrymple (1967) further states:

> We should recognize that for some students, at some point in their careers, dropping out of college can be more educational than remaining in college. This knowledge should be kept in mind by every secondary guidance counselor and passed along to college-bound students from time to time.

Some Observations

Apart from many specific questions which derive from the review of the literature just presented, two overriding questions may be asked.

1. What are the implications presented by these data in approaching solutions to college attrition?

2. What do these data say to us in terms of student personnel administration?

First, it is obviously necessary to be aware of trends and tendencies in college attrition in order to be an effective student personnel administrator. Understanding of the causes of attrition allows for sensitivity to student attrition before the fact. The myriad duties of the people in student personnel militates against proper and adequate functioning in all areas, but without the knowledge of causes and influences relating to withdrawal the administrator is often caught unawares by, and held responsible for, large and unnecessary attrition rates.

To be aware of the experiences of potential withdrawees is not only necessary for efficiency, but allows conscious consideration of possible predictions and solutions. The stress to the student of his own internal uncertainties, the responsibilities of external pressures causing emotional turmoil, anxiety, nondirection, and even confusion are all in evidence whether they be of academic or a more subtle nature. Often, the concern for the continuing student is placed in a category of importance above that of the noncontinuing student, but the complete understanding of the forces affecting the performance of the whole college program also depends upon knowing the characteristics of both those who persist and those who are interrupting their formal education. Both persisters and nonpersisters are in an important developmental stage. The forces which affect one also affect the other, therefore, to consider the dropout apart, as one who has failed, is not necessarily within the realm of adequate analysis, nor considerate of all who attend college. Current thinking is more and more emphasizing a need for accommodation to those who, for whatever reason, decide to leave the academic community. These data discussed suggest the need for a new concept, a new outlook, a new approach to our normal judgments depreciating withdrawal; one which allows room to fail, time for students to assess themselves, and space for growing autonomy apart from academia.

Second, these data reemphasize the fact that our only real predictor of success in college is found in the previous performance of the entering student. Those students who have a background of success in academic achievement bring the attitude of success, and its corresponding motivation, with them to the institution. Where this experience and the positive and supportive attitudes of parents are prevalent, successful achievement is continued. Where students themselves are uncertain of their academic abilities, aims, and goals, and where parents are indifferent or uninvolved with, or opposed to, the students plans, the rate of attrition increases considerably.

Third, the most critical period in terms of withdrawal is the initial year in college. Adjustment to a new environment is difficult for most entering college students—new experiences cause excitement, new associations cause personal stress, new dependencies create anxieties and guilt. These data seem to suggest that higher attrition rates prevail when students come from more provincial areas involving smaller schools and smaller communities. Students who enter college having graduated from more cosmopolitan schools and communities have higher persistence records. This suggests that the underlying philosophies of rural homes, schools, and communities may in fact have weaknesses in terms of ability to sustain its product in a more sophisticated life and under new and strange modes of living. Persistence in these data is seen as most successful when the college climate emphasizes good community spirit, friendliness, active student participation, and rapport among the various segments of the college or university.

Fourth, the most recent understandings and considerations are with the differences in personality characteristics and motivational aspects of students who decide to withdraw as compared with those who do not. These understandings may have greater implications for the colleges and for the administration of student personnel centers than other factors, because the present student unrest is bringing to light emerging forces which are developing and which tend to influence the internal programs of colleges. Consequently, all students will be affected, and will tend to create new student attitudes, values and goals. These data reflect some common understandings about dropouts among the researchers: that developing autonomy, greater discontinuity from family, rebellion, impulsivity, irresponsibility, appear in those who decide to leave. These traits are reflected in more assertive and aggressive, less passive roles, less controlled, less conforming, less persevering, more irrational, and less mature patterns of behavior.

These variables lead to a consideration of those students who are variously described as alienated, liberated, or uncommited, who have been so well explained by Kenniston (1960) and Flack (1967). These authors show the alienated as going through a process of development of autonomy with its concomitant rebellion, uncertainty, lack of value conformance, lack of scholarly pursuit, social isolation and nonperseverence. In effect, the dropouts here are of a more serious type, for in fact dropout is seen as total—dropout from college and from society.

Kenniston (1967) makes a distinction between the alienated and the activist. His description is worthy of note because he points out that common stereotyped views are:

> ... incorrect in a variety of ways. They confuse two varieties of student dissent, equally important they fuse dissent with maladjustment. . . . Student dissenters generally fall somewhere along a continuum that runs between two ideal types—first, the political activist or protester, and the second, the withdrawn, culturally alienated student. [The activist] participates in a student demonstration or group activity that concerns itself with some matter of general political, social, or ethical principle. . . . Whatever the issue, the protester rarely demonstrates because his own interests are jeopardized, but rather demonstrates because he perceives injustices being done to others less fortunate than himself. He is politically optimistic.
>
> The culturally alienated student is far too pessimistic and too firmly opposed to "the System" to wish to demonstrate his disapproval in any organized way. . . . Alienated students are more likely to be disturbed psychologically, and although they are often highly talented and artistically gifted, they are less committed to academic values and intellectual achievement. [They] believe in inter-racial living and emphasize immediacy, love, and turning-on. (pp. 110-114)

Some of these students may not drop out, but their whole tendency is to withdraw, whether in overt or covert ways. The activist tends to remain in college, performing the necessary requirements of the academic program, but at the same time resisting the values of a society which he has decided to try to change; he withdraws in more covert ways. The alienated tends to withdraw directly, both from school and from any participation in a society he feels is not worth saving.

The great emphasis among these types is their opposition to "the System," which by implication goes beyond the system of the small college community or large university with which they themselves are concerned. Because of this extension to the larger society, the uncertainty, already stated many times, develops questions as to the value of the academic endeavor; its validity, its relevance, and its practical usefulness in their lives. Obviously such questions are being asked, and student personnel people have the responsibility to ask similar questions as to what policies and practices in the personnel program are indeed relevant to these dropouts and which are not.

Apart from the consideration of programs, personnel people should again be reminded that dropping out, for not only the alienated but for many others who decide to leave, may be the means by which leavers gain better and more mature understanding of their own personal weaknesses in relation to society. Administrators should be willing even to suggest withdrawal, if this seems to be a reasonable solution to seeming insurmountable difficulty, and at the same time resist feelings of disloyalty to the institution when such advice is given. If indeed concern for the student exists, it should exist even at the expense of the college and university involved. The author in some instances has seen change take place in dropouts' attitudes concerning what are the purposes of education as the former student has experienced association with the real world. Idealogical and psychological distortions are often modified as experiences in real life are seen apart from the abstract. The development of independence generally accelerates when experience is generated outside of the restrictive requirements of academia, and the limiting regulation of structure adult-directed institutions. As this independence increases, so also does certainty in many cases. As one gains his little successes in relation to the world, his directions become more sure and his own values develop; therefore his personal decision-making powers increase and his willingness to listen and ask advice may be enhanced. It is possible to clarify ambivalences about college, as one girl leaver said to the writer, "I no longer find myself limited by the lack of a college degree—my work has given me satisfaction." The point is that maybe, for some, more satisfying directions can be found in noncontinuance in college. Student personnel administrators should always stand ready to advise in directions other than persistence if he really believes that life can prepare one for learning. This may mean advice contrary to that societal value which emphasizes that a college education is a necessity for all.

Fifth, the literature as related here suggests that counseling in the college framework is not being done well. For all the claims presented in the literature, represented by college bulletins, college counseling programs (if one considers students' responses) is of poor quality. The main theme of these studies, when counseling is considered, is that little particular value derives from opportunities students have in this area. The question is not, "Who is to blame?" but "Why are these services not used by those who need them most?" One hardly needs to speak to the implication. The ongoing counseling program either has not been structured well, or the student, implicitly, through his experiences on the campus, suggests that he has not sensed the concern of those who could benefit him most.

Finally, the scientific approach to knowing the problem of attrition, seen in the collection of data, the discovery of findings, the description of results, and the inferences drawn are necessary, but one has the uneasy feeling that this is somehow remote from the real reactions and attitudes of those who decide to separate themselves from intellectual pursuits. What do these dropouts say about their withdrawal experience? What are their feelings about college personnel, college climate, and activities? How do they express themselves about the wisdom of their decision to leave college? The foregoing data indicate an unease with the tensions and pressures of academic life among many of those who withdraw. Some require a time away, some are seeking independence, others are looking for real experiences, many do not see the need for college, a few are concerned about what the college requires, and many recognize the advantage of associations in the real world, and a need of developing influences in working for tangible things. Mainly though, withdrawal reflects a need to reassert one's directions—to get one's bearings—in short, there seems to be a need to separate from the world of confusing ideas and to reestablish some certainty and continuity with reality.

SUMMARY

A combination of factors have been presented here with reference to underlying reasons for withdrawal. Surface reasons are readily available to all dropouts, and these are used by them to describe their withdrawal. At the same time a great deal of uncertainty is in evidence —uncertainty about themselves, uncertainty about life, and uncertainty about directions. The desire for independence is strong not only independence from parents, but from instutitions as well. Their desire to develop apart from structured influences is seen by their own statements. We should recognize this and be willing to accept this desire for autonomy if indeed we wish to help them through this time of confusion. Their own insights about themselves are noteworthy and necessary for clarity. Possibly the college setting for some is not the place to gain these insights, because they may perceive the setting in terms of unreality.

We close this chapter with a student comment that is very significant and suggests a need for a new approach by those who administer student programs [Cartwright, 1967]:

I loathe the notion America is promoting that one has to go to college in order to "make it." How about those who don't want to? Those who have a couple of dreams of their own that they'd like to try out? When a notion like that becomes an unwritten law, a matter of course, then we defeat ourselves: we end up forcing pure character and imagination—our only chance for health and future—into systems of education that return to us a beast who is intelligent only because he has finally been trained to answer with the acceptable notions of our times. (p. 16)

REFERENCES

Abel, W. H. "Attrition and the Student Who Is Certain," *Personnel and Guidance J.,* 44 (June 1966), pp. 1042-1045.

Aiken, Lewis R. "The Prediction of Academic Success and Early Attrition by Means of a Multiple-Choice Biographical Inventory," *American Educ. Res. J.,* 2 (1964), pp. 127-135.

Barger, B., and E. Hall. "Personality Patterns and Achievement in College," *Educ. and Psychol. Meas.* 24 (2) (Summer 1964), pp. 339-346.

Brown, Frederick G. "Identifying College Dropouts with the Minnesota Counseling Inventory," *Personnel and Guidance J.,* 39 (December 1960), pp. 280-282.

Carlson, S. J., and K. W. Wegner. "College Dropouts," *Phi Delta Kappan,* 46 (March 1965), pp. 325-327.

Cartwright, L. W. "The New Hero," in Otto Butz (ed.), *To Make a Difference.* New York: Harper & Row, Publishers, 1967.

Chickering, A. W. "Institutional Differences and Student Characteristics," *J. Amer. College Health Assoc.* (December 1966), pp. 168-181.

Dalrymple, W. "The College Dropout Phenomenon," *NEA Journal,* 56 (April 1967), pp. 11-13.

Daniel, Kathryn B. "A Study of College Dropouts with Respect to Academic and Personality Variables," *J. of Educ. Res.,* 60 (January 1967), pp. 230-235.

Farnsworth, D. S. "We Are Wasting Brain Power," *J. Nat. Educ. Assoc.,* 1959.

Farnsworth, D. S. "Some Non-Academic Causes of Success and Failure in College Students," *College Admissions* 2 (1955) pp. 72-78.

Flack, R. W. "The Liberated Generation: An Exploration of the Roots of Student Protest," *J. Soc. Issues,* 23 (July 1967), pp. 52-75.

Forrest, D. V. "High School Underachievers in College," *J. Educ. Res.,* 61 (December 1962), pp. 147-150.

Gadzella, B. M., and G. Bentall. "Differences in High School Academic Achievements and Mental Abilities of College Graduates and College Dropouts," *College and University,* 42 (Spring 1967), pp. 351-356.

Grace, Harry. "Personality Factors and College Attrition," *Peabody J. of Educ.,* 35 (June 1957), pp. 36-40.

Greenfield, Lois B. "Attrition Among First-Semester Engineering Freshmen," *Personnel and Guidance J.,* 52 (June 1964), pp. 1003-1010.

Hannah, W. "Freshman Leavers and Stayers." Unpublished paper, presented at the 19th Annual Meeting of the Vermont Psychological Association, April 1968, Bolton, Vermont.

———. "Withdrawal from College," *J. College Student Personnel*, 10 (6) (November 1969), pp. 397-402.

Heilbrun, A. B., Jr. "Prediction of First Year College Dropout, Using ACL Need Scales," *J. Counseling Psychol.*, 9 (Spring 1962), pp. 58-63.

Heilbrun, A. B., Jr. "Personality Factors in College Dropout," *J. Appl. Psychol.* 49 (February 1965), pp. 1-7.

Hill, A. H. "A Longitudinal Study of Attrition Among High-Aptitude College Students," *J. Educ. Res.*, 60 (December 1966), pp. 166-173.

Holmes, C. H. "Why They Left College," *College and University*, 34 (Spring 1959), pp. 295-300.

Iffert, R. E. "Retention and Withdrawal of College Students," *Office of Education Bulletin*. No. 1. Washington, D.C.: Government Printing Office, 1958, p. 177.

Jensen, V. H. "Influence of Personality Traits on Academic Success," *Personnel and Guidance J.*, 36 (March 1958) pp. 497-500.

Johnson, G. B. "A Proposed Technique for Analysis of Dropouts at a State College," *J. Educ Res.*, 47 (January 1954), pp. 381-387.

Kenniston, K. "The Sources of Student Dissent," *J. Soc. Issues*, 23 (July 1967), pp. 108-137.

Kubie, L. S. "The Ontogeny of the Drop-out Problem," Paper presented at the conference on *The College Drop-out and the Utilization of Talent*, Princeton University, 1964.

Little, J. K. "The Persistence of Academically Talented Youth in University Studies," *Educ. Record*, 40 (June 1959) pp. 237-241.

Marks, Edmond. "Student Perceptions of College Persistence and Their Intellective Personality and Performance Correlates," *J. Educ. Psychol.*, 58 (4) (August 1967), pp. 210-221.

McNeely, J. H. "College Student Mortality," *U.S. Department of Interior Bulletin No. 11*, 1937.

Nelson, G. A. "College Characteristics Associated with Freshman Attrition," *Personnel and Guidance J.*, 44 (June 1966), pp. 1046-1050.

Panos, R. J., and A. W. Astin. "Attrition Among College Students," *American Council on Education Research Report*, 2 (4) (1967).

Pervin, L. A. "A New look at College Dropouts," *University, A Princeton Quarterly*, (Winter 1964-65).

Pervin, L. A. "A Follow-up of Male College Dropouts," *Cooperative Research Project No. S-029-64*, Princeton University, 1965.

Pervin, L. A. "A Twenty-College Study of Student X College Interaction Using TAPE (Transactional Analysis of Personality and Invironment): Rationale, Reliability, and Validity," *J. Educ. Psychol.*, 58 (5) (1967), pp. 290-302.

Rose, H. A., and C. F. Elton. "Another Look at the College Dropout," *J. of Counseling Educ.*, 13 (Summer 1966), pp. 242-245.

Strang, Ruth. *Behavior and Background of Students in College and Secondary School*. New York: Harper & Row, Publishers, 1937.

Suczek, R. F., and E. Alfert. "Personality Characteristics of College Dropouts." Research Report, Cooperative Research, Office of Education DHEW and University of California, Berkeley. Project #5-8232 (1966).

Summerskill, John. "Dropouts from College," in Nevitt Sanford (ed.), *The American College*. New York: John Wiley and Sons, Inc., 1962, pp. 627-657.

Weintraub, R. G., and R. E. Salley. "Graduation Prospects of an Entering Freshman," *J. of Educ. Res.*, 39 (October 1945), pp. 116-126.

14

New Dimensions in Junior College Student Personnel Administration

John R. Fawcett, Jr.
Jack E. Campbell*

INTRODUCTION

Society's need for the junior college is evident, and the stated purposes of the junior college were developed in accordance with the needs of society. Each division of a junior college designed to further one of these purposes must operate at the highest possible level of efficiency if the junior college is to be successful.

One of the primary purposes of the junior college is to provide guidance for the individual student through a program of student personnel services. This purpose was recognized early. In 1927 Frank Waters Thomas designated guidance as one of the four principal functions of the junior college. Thomas was concerned primarily with the welfare of those students who lacked the academic ability necessary for admission to a four-year college or university.[1]

*Dr. John R. Fawcett, Jr., holds the B.A. in English from The Citadel; the M.S. in Education from Miami University, Ohio; the M.A. in English from East Tennessee State University; and the Ed.D. from Florida State University where he held a Kellogg Foundation Fellowship for study in Junior College Administration. Dr. Fawcett is currently an associate professor of education and director of the doctoral program in higher education at the University of Mississippi. Dr. Jack E. Campbell holds the B.S. in Education, M.A. in Education from East Tennessee State University, M.A. in Guidance and Counseling from the University of Alabama and the Ed.D. in Student Personnel Work from the University of Mississippi. Dr. Campbell is currently the Academic Dean at John C. Calhoun Junior College and Technical School in Decatur, Alabama, where he formerly served as Dean of Students.
[1]Frank Waters Thomas, "The Functions of the Junior College," in William M. Proctor (ed.), *The Junior College* (Stanford, Calif.: Stanford University Press, 1927), p. 11.

The junior college student personnel worker of today is still concerned with the academically deficient student, but his conception of student personnel work encompasses a great deal more. Smith related student personnel work to one of education's central aims, that of democracy. He stated:

> It appears that the trend toward implementation of the broad program of student personnel services is not only the popular approach but also the one consistent with democracy in education.[2]

A broad program of student personnel services based on democratic principles depicts a concern for the total development of the individual student. This concern was emphasized by Max Raines when he asked:

> What does it profit an individual if the school is near enough to make attendance feasible and open enough to permit him to enter, if, once in, he is not helped in those many non-functional areas where help is necessary to promote his development?[3]

The challenge of providing a program of student personnel services in the junior college which will aid the individual student in his total development is compounded by the multipurpose nature of that institution, and by its diversified student body. Efforts directed toward meeting this challenge have resulted in junior college student personnel work becoming more professionalized and more respected as an integral part of the total educational program. Certain philosophies are now widely accepted. Substantial agreement now exists on the areas which should be included in a student personnel program and, although no uniform organizational structure exists, it is now possible to discuss workable patterns of organizing and administering the various student personnel services.

PHILOSOPHY UNDERLYING JUNIOR COLLEGE STUDENT PERSONNEL ADMINISTRATION

Widely accepted philosophies are indicative of the fact that student personnel work is well on its way toward being recognized as the most central entity in the junior college. The centrality of student personnel

[2]E. M. Smith, "Which Way Guidance and Personnel Program?" *Junior College Journal*, 28 (December 1957), pp. 186–189.
[3]Max Raines, "Report to the Carnegie Corporation on Appraisal and Development of Junior College Student Personnel Programs," *Junior College Student Personnel Programs Appraisal and Development* A Report to the Carnegie Corporation, November 1965, p. 8.

work in the junior college was stressed by Charles Collins when he remarked:

> The student personnel program should be the point, the hub, the core, around which the whole enterprise moves. It provides the structure and creates the pervasive atmosphere which prompts the junior college to label itself as student centered.[4]

The members of the Commission of the American Association of Junior Colleges were of the opinion that no other activity was more urgent to the life of the junior college than its student program.[5] Weatherford emphasized that the student personnel program is the very lifeline of the institution. He pointed out that "the student personnel program touches the life of every student, a claim that cannot be made by any one academic department."[6]

The student personnel program must not only touch the life of every student, but it must also be recognized as an integral part of the total education program. To be recognized as an integral part of the total education program, the student personnel program must be based on clearly defined objectives. Services functioning merely to expedite operation of the institution will no longer suffice. A considerable amount of planning, competent leadership, and a qualified staff are indispensable if the program is to be effective and respected.

The program of student personnel services should support the instructional program but should not be considered as secondary to the instructional program. Too often the student personnel program suffers because the administrators of the institution give priority to the instructional program. The fact should not be overlooked that a competent student personnel worker is just as much an educator as a classroom teacher.

AREAS OF JUNIOR COLLEGE STUDENT PERSONNEL WORK

Junior college student personnel work with all its complexities can best be described in terms of the basic areas of which it is comprised. Stemming from the basic areas of student personnel work are the many functions or services that affect the life of the student from the time he applies for admission until he graduates.

[4]Charles Collins, *Junior College Student Personnel Programs: What They Are and What They Should Be* (Washington, D.C.: American Association of Junior Colleges, 1967), p. 13.
[5]May Russ, "Commission Reports on Student Personnel Practices," *Junior College Journal*, 32 (April 1962), pp. 467-470.
[6]Sidney Weatherford, "The Status of Student Personnel Work," *Junior College Journal*, 35 (February 1965), pp. 21-23.

Admissions and Registration

Helpful programs of admissions and registration expedite the student's transition from high school to college. Basic to both programs is an adequate record system.

Functions pertaining to admissions and registration have first and perhaps the greatest impact upon the junior college student. In more instances than not, the admissions officer or registrar is that school official with whom the entering student makes his first contact. The old adage that the first impression is often a lasting impression certainly holds true for the initial contact for a young person seeking to enter college.

A well-run admissions office does more than insure that prospective students are meeting the entrance requirements. Questions about college attendance must be answered through the admissions office. Bulletins and brochures which characterize the college must be provided, and the previous course work of the student must be evaluated and communicated to the faculty. Orientation and testing activities, normally categorized under the area of guidance and counseling, must be planned and implemented as part of the admissions process.

Registration should be designed so as to enable the admitted student to enroll in the courses of his choice with as little difficulty as possible. Preregistration and registration procedures must be carefully planned and clearly interpreted to the students and faculty. Procedures for class changes and withdrawals must also be developed and implemented. Successful admissions and registration programs are contingent upon an effective system of record keeping. The available personal data pertaining to each individual student should be synthesized and developed into a system with as little duplication of information as possible. The attainability of student records must be governed by regulations which are realistic and meaningful.

Guidance and Counseling

Functions pertaining to the area of guidance and counseling permeate the entire student personnel program. Therefore, the guidance and counseling area, as a special area, is difficult to define. Thornton stated, "The purpose of guidance is to assist the student in reaching sound decisions in matters of vocational choice, educational planning, and personal concern."[7] General functions viewed by Hillway as being related to the guidance service included the dissemination of accurate

---

[7]James Thornton, *The Community Junior College* (New York: John Wiley and Sons, Inc., 1966), p. 255.

information, psychological testing, and professional counseling.[8]

Because of its relevance to other areas of student personnel work, guidance and counseling is of great importance, and calls for the utilization of all available data on the student to include his high school record, college record, and test scores. Counseling interviews must be scheduled and conducted for all students. An effective faculty-counselor referral system must be implemented. A library of educational and occupational information which depicts the various sources of occupational information and identifies the manpower needs within the community must be maintained. And finally, orientation activities to assist the individual in making a satisfactory adjustment to college must be conducted.

Student Activities

Student activities in the junior college should be encouraged. Nothing is more vital to the total development of the individual student. Yet an effective program of student activities is difficult to implement. Medsker pointed out that student activities programs were rated less favorable than other aspects of student personnel services by stating:

> Almost 40 per cent of the students said that existing programs were inadequate (or worse) in meeting their particular needs and interests.[9]

The problem which Medsker pointed out seems to stem from several factors. First, the junior college student body definitely is different from that at a four-year institution. The secure upperclassmen of the four-year institution are not available in the junior college to provide the needed leadership and stimulation. Also, a higher percentage of the student leaders in high school, upon graduation, elect to attend the four-year institution in lieu of the junior college. Thus the junior college student personnel worker is confronted with the task of training students for leadership roles. These programs must be intense and continuous as the full-time student only remains in the junior college for an average of two years.

Another factor is that the junior college student body is primarily a commuting student body which resides at home and spends a minimum amount of time on campus. A lack of identity with the junior college often exists for students attending college under these conditions. The identity of the student seems to remain with outside local agencies, particularly with the high school from which he graduated.

---

[8]Tyrus Hillway, *The American Two-Year College* (New York: Harper and Row, Publishers, 1958), p. 143.

[9]Leland Medsker, *The Junior College: Progress and Prospect* (New York: McGraw-Hill Book Company, 1960), p. 18.

The diversity of students presents an additional factor to consider in developing an activity program. The adolescent who recently graduated from high school, the veteran who has decided to resume his formal education, the housewife continuing her education, the professional man seeking a continuing education, and the elderly couple striving to remain active all have an opinion of what the student activities program should consist. Many students see little value in extraclass activities and will elect not to participate while others will overemphasize the activities in neglect of the classroom experiences.

Such factors present a tremendous and exciting challenge for the student personnel worker. Activities which are meaningful to a maximum number of students must be planned and developed. These activities must be carefully coordinated and should be relevant to the instructional program as well as to the other aspects of the student personnel program. Policies and regulations governing the student activities should stem from cooperative efforts of the administration, faculty, and students. Fordyce suggested that a climate in which policies are honest, straightforward, and conducive to the various activities is to be provided.[10] The policies and regulations should be stated in a well-prepared student handbook and should be comprehensive, relating to all activities from the student elections to the enforcement of social standards.

Discipline

The establishment of policies governing student conduct is an important aspect of the junior college program. The student personnel worker, particularly the "head" student personnel worker, is expected to recommend these policies to the chief administrator, and subsequently the student personnel worker is expected to see that students adhere to the adopted policies. The policies, once developed by the use of the democratic process, should become a part of the contractual agreement that all entering students have with the college.

Procedures for the investigation of disciplinary cases must be established so as to be in keeping with the "due process" concept. Minor infractions of rules should be handled on the level at which they occur. For instance, parking violations might well be handled by either a single individual or perhaps a student court; classroom conduct should be handled by the instructor of the class. On the other hand, in certain cases where probation or suspension might result, the accused individual is entitled to a hearing by a committee consisting of administrators,

---

[10]Joseph Fordyce, "Creating a Good Climate," *Junior College Journal,* 35 (December 1964), pp. 17–20.

instructors, and students. Prior to the hearing, the accused individual should be informed of the charges against him, and he should be allowed to seek counsel if he so desires. During the hearing he should be given every opportunity to present his side of the issue. Once the committee has reached a decision, the chairman of the committee should inform the student, face to face, of the action which the committee plans to recommend to the president of the college. The student, if found guilty, should be informed of his right to appeal and the procedures for doing so. Once the president approves the recommendation, the action becomes final.

A student personnel worker, preferably the dean of students, should provide an interpretation of the disciplinary action to the parents of the involved students.

Financial Aid and Placement

Although the junior college attracts a diversified clientele, students from low-income families make up a substantial portion of the student body. The low education cost of the junior college makes it attractive to this group.

Although the educational cost for the junior college is comparatively low, his financial need may still be great. Not only may he need assistance in paying for his education, he may need a part-time job to alleviate financial problems at home. In fact, his primary reason for electing to attend the junior college may be that he can live at home and work part-time at a local establishment.

With these thoughts in mind, the importance of an effective financial aid and placement program becomes obvious. Many students would not attend college without them, and yet, as Medsker stated, "they find it difficult to obtain information about scholarships, loan funds, and part-time employment while enrolled."[11] Reynolds also expressed concern for students. He reported that many business offices have handled this activity and, in these instances, major consideration has been given to the security of the borrower rather than to a realistic appraisal of the student's financial needs.[12]

An effective program of financial aid and placement will include means for communicating pertinent information to prospective students as well as to the students currently enrolled. Once the student applications for financial aid have been received, the financial needs

[11]Medsker, *op. cit.*, p. 18.
[12]James Reynolds, *The Junior College* (New York: Center for Applied Research in Education, 1965), p. 59.

must be determined. The various types of available assistance should be weighed against the needs of the students and awards should be made in the fairest manner possible. The awarding of a "financial aids package" where the student receives aid from a variety of sources such as loans, scholarships, work-study, and grants, seems to be the popular approach in the dissemination of available funds. The administration of a job placement program involves constant consultation with prospective employers, the purpose being to bring the employers and students together whether the concern is for a summer job or a part-time job during the academic year.

Health Program, Food Services, and Student Housing

A health program, student housing, and food services may or may not be considered a part of the student personnel program. These student services, however, have a direct bearing on the total development of the individual and thus, by the very nature of these services, become a major concern of the student personnel worker.

The "typical health program in the American junior and community college" was illustrated by Hillway as consisting of:

> (1) required medical examination chiefly for new students; (2) facilities for first aid; (3) special examinations for participants in athletic events when required by state law; and (4) a bare minimum of treatment leading to the correction of defects.[13]

The features cited by Hillway seem to be minimal. The size of the institution and amount of time students spend on campus are factors to be considered in developing additional health-care activities.

A report by Gleazer disclosed that 44 percent of the 655 junior colleges listed in the 1961–62 edition of the *American Junior Colleges* had dormitories.[14] The trend, however, seems to be away from the construction of dormitories on junior college campuses. Where dormitories do exist, an added aspect of student personnel work also exists. Hillway explained the effect that dormitories have on the student personnel program:

> While the operation and control of dormitories usually are placed in the hands of the business manager, the student personnel office should have responsibility for such matters as the assignment of rooms, the selection and supervision of dormitory supervisors and counselors, and the development of social and educational activities within the housing units.[15]

---

[13]Hillway, *op. cit.,* p. 157.

[14]Edmund Gleazer (ed.), *American Junior Colleges* (Washington, D.C.; American Council on Education, 1964).

[15]Hillway, *op. cit.,* p. 157.

Where dormitories do not exist, a list of available housing in the community should be provided in the student personnel department.

The student personnel program's influence on the operation of food services were viewed by Collins as including:

> Designing of the food services to foster student-faculty contact, to contribute to community solidarity, and to develop social skills; supervising and administering this student facility.[16]

Faculty Involvement in Student Personnel Work

An article by Donald Robinson in a 1960 issue of the *Junior College Journal* dealt with the role of the faculty in the development of student personnel services. Robinson stated, "The crucial issue in student personnel work is the development of better working relations between teachers and student personnel specialists and a clear understanding of relatedness of functions."[17]

Orientation of the faculty to the student personnel program must begin during the preschool conferences in the fall and continue throughout the school year. Faculty members need to be apprised as to the philosophy and objectives of the student personnel program, the various services provided, and the role of the faculty in the provision of the services. More specifically, a faculty member must be prepared to accept his responsibility in such functions as the registration of students, academic advising, utilization of student records, referral program, student affairs committee, student activities, and implementation of policies.

Livingston recognized the importance of accessible, accurate academic advising, but it is, he observed, "often considered both by teachers and counselors to be an extra job not entirely within the defined area of responsibility of either.[18] That it is imperative to find ways of improving the teacher's role in the academic advising program was amply substantiated by Medsker's study in which he disclosed:

> Faculty academic advising was given a negative evaluation by nearly 30 per cent of the students who felt their advisors were merely carrying out their assigned duties or were not interested at all. Twenty-two per cent of the students evaluated the asistance they received from their advisors as "of no value" or "incomplete" or "inaccurate."[19]

---

[16]Charles Collins, *Premises: Planning Student Personnel Facilities* (Washington, D.C.: American Association of Junior Colleges, 1967), p. 3.

[17]Donald Robinson, "The Role of the Faculty in the Development of Student Personnel Services," *Junior College Journal*, 31 (September 1960), pp. 15-21.

[18]Frank Livingston, "Counseling for the Entering College Student," *School and Community*, 54 (April 1968), pp. 24-25.

[19]Medsker, *op. cit.*, p. 22.

Blocker and others reflected a negative view on teachers as academic advisors when they commented:

> The concept that everyone on the faculty should be a student counselor or academic advisor is sheer nonsense. Assignment of counseling responsibilities to ineffective and untrained instructors casts serious doubts on the adequacy of the entire program.[20]

With these negative findings, what is there left for the student personnel worker to do in his attempts to involve the faculty in a program of academic advising? Obviously the faculty cannot be excluded. An ideal approach to the problem would be to select the instructors who are best qualified to be academic advisors and pay them extra compensation for the extra work. Another approach which is desirable is to reduce the teaching load of the instructors who are functioning as academic advisors. These approaches, unfortunately, cannot always be implemented. An alternative is to include the responsibility of academic advising in the instructor's job description and provide him with continuous in-service training designed toward improving his skills in this important function.

ORGANIZATION AND ADMINISTRATION

There is no uniform method of organizing and administering the various student personnel services in the junior college. This is as it should be since the operation of the student personnel services should be in keeping with the institutional philosophy.

In the early days, well-planned and coordinated programs of student personnel services were practically nonexistent. Higgins and Thurston observed that a collection of services often developed more on the basis of expediency rather than in terms of institutional philosophy.[21] What resulted was a decentralized approach to administering the student personnel services in which several persons reported directly to the president of the institution. Experience has revealed that this method is undesirable in most colleges. Speaking for the Student Personnel Commission of the American Association of Junior Colleges in 1952, Humphries pointed out that the president or his assistant tended to carry too much responsibility in student personnel programs.[22] Medsker concurred by stating:

---

[20]Clyde Blocker, Robert Plummer, and Richard Richardson, *The Two-Year College: A Social Synthesis* (Englewood Cliffs, N.J.: Prentice-Hall, Inc., 1965), p. 243.

[21]Sadie Higgins and Alice Thurston, "Challenges in Student Personnel Work," *Junior College Journal,* 34 (November 1963), pp. 24–28.

[22]Anthony Humphries, "Toward Improved Programs of Student Personnel Services," *Junior College Journal,* 22 (March 1952), pp. 382–392.

The question is not whether the person can coordinate them, but is whether he will coordinate them in view of the heavy demands on his time, even in a small institution.[23]

A few institutions, Hillway implied, may still be discovered in which a decentralized program exists but examples are becoming rare.[24] What has become more prevalent is a centralized approach to organization and administration in which central coordination of the student personnel services is the result. This centralized organizational structure includes a Division of Student Personnel Services. The division should be headed by a specially trained individual who is responsible to the president for the coordination and supervision of all student personnel services. This head of the division should be given the title of Dean of Students, Director of Student Personnel Services, or Vice President of Student Affairs.

The head of the Student Personnel Division should have a qualified staff to perform the specific functions. The desired number of staff members naturally is contingent upon the size of the institution and the scope of the student personnel program. To aid him in operating the student personnel program, the head of the division should utilize the services of a student affairs committee consisting of faculty members and students.

In many junior colleges glaring weaknesses exist in the student personnel program because its scope is not clearly defined, and thus the responsibilities of the student personnel director are not clearly delineated. In discussing a two-year study initiated in 1963 by the Committee on Appraisal and Development of Junior College Student Personnel Programs, Max Raines outlined a "Basic Student Personnel Program" which included twenty-one related functions; the functions encompassed sixty-five illustrations of related tasks.[25]

Campbell recently attempted to delineate the responsibilities of the student personnel director by conducting a study which was:

> An appraisal of the relative importance of the assigned responsibilities of the student personnel directors or comparable administrators in public junior colleges which were members of the Southern Association of Colleges and Schools. Basic to the appraisal was the identification of the frequency with which each responsibility was currently assigned to the student personnel directors in these institutions.[26]

[23]Medsker, *op. cit.,* p. 162.
[24]Hillway, *op. cit.,* p. 159.
[25]Max Raines, "The Student Personnel Situation," *Junior College Journal,* 37 (April 1967), p. 34.
[26]Jack E. Campbell, *An Analysis of Selected Responsibilities of Student Personnel*

Student personnel directors were asked to respond to a rating instrument which contained a comprehensive list of 135 selected responsibilities associated wholly or in part with the office of the student personnel director. Campbell noted:

> The student personnel director does not necessarily perform all the functions of the student personnel division himself. He is, however, considered to be personally *responsible* for seeing that certain functions are performed in a coordinated manner.

The list of responsibilities were selected from an extensive review of literature. Many of the related tasks enumerated by Raines were utilized as responsibilities in Campbell's rating instrument. In defining the three purposes of the study Campbell stated:

> One purpose of the study was to identify (1) responsibilities that are currently assigned to the student personnel directors; (2) responsibilities for which the assignment to the student personnel director is essential; (3) responsibilities for which the assignment to the student personnel director is desirable; (4) responsibilities for which the assignment to the student director is undesirable.
>
> A second purpose of the study was to determine whether there were significant differences in the ratings of the responsibilities by the student personnel directors who were currently assigned the responsibilities and the student personnel directors who were not assigned the responsibilities.
>
> A third purpose of the study was the development of a guide to be used primarily as a self-evaluation device by the student personnel directors in public junior colleges.

A relevant hypothesis which was tested in the study was:

> There will be no significant differences in the ratings of the responsibilities by the student personnel directors who are currently assigned the responsibilities and the student personnel directors who are not assigned the responsibilities.

The guide which was developed in this study is presented on pages 193-205 in the form of a summary listing of the 135 responsibilities with the indicated assignment, ratings, and acceptance or rejection of the null hypothesis. Instructions for interpreting the guide are as follows:

> ... a ✓ to the left of the responsibility designates that the responsibility was currently assigned to a majority of the student personnel directors. The values which the student personnel directors in the assigned, nonassigned and composite groups applied to the responsibilities are indicated in the following manner:

Directors in Public Junior Colleges Which Are Members of the Southern Association of Colleges and Schools (University of Mississippi, May 1969), pp. 1–186.

<u>3</u> An appraisal of essential was applied to the responsibility by the rating group.

<u>2</u> An appraisal of desirable was applied to the responsibility by the rating group.

<u>1</u> An appraisal of undesirable was applied to the responsibility by the rating group.

A letter of <u>A</u> is recorded in the appropriate column on the table if the null hypothesis was accepted for the responsibility; a letter of <u>R</u> indicates rejection of the null hypothesis.

The study produced the following conclusions:

1. The null hypothesis of no significant differences in the ratings of the responsibilities by the student personnel directors who were currently assigned the responsibilities and the student personnel directors who were not assigned the responsibilities was rejected for 124 of the 135 responsibilities. The null hypothesis was accepted for eleven of the responsibilities.

2. The assignment of responsibilities relating to admissions and registration to the student personnel director is desirable.

3. The student personnel director should be assigned the responsibility of directing and coordinating all guidance and counseling programs. Essential responsibilities of the student personnel director include the coordination of all standardized testing programs, the conducting of counseling interviews, and the direction of the student orientation program.

4. The student personnel director should be assigned the responsibility of organizing and administering all student activities, with the athletic program as a possible exception. Supervision of the athletic program, certification of athletes to athletic associations, and the selection of the athletic committee are questionable responsibilities for the student personnel director. The student personnel director should, however, be assigned the responsibility of approving the interschool and intramural athletic schedules and budgets.

5. The development and implementation of policies governing student discipline should be a responsibility of the student personnel director.

6. The student personnel director should supervise and coordinate a program of financial aid, placement, and follow-up.

7. Responsibilities relating to public relations should be assigned to the student personnel director when the responsibilities are for activities related to the basic student personnel program.

8. The student personnel director should be assigned certain responsibilities relating to the plant and student services. An essential responsibility is that of assisting in the planning of new buildings for student services. The supervision of food services is a questionable responsibility for the student personnel director. The student personnel director should not be assigned the responsibility of supervising and managing the college bookstore.

9. Orientation of the faculty to the student personnel program through the in-service program is an essential responsibility for the

student personnel director. Cooperation with the faculty in implementation of certain policies, maintenance of an open-door policy to the student personnel office, and working with the faculty in the utilization of student records are essential responsibilities of the student personnel director.

10. A student personnel director should have responsibility for planning, organizing, and supervising a central administrative unit or student personnel division. In this centralized administrative approach an essential concern of the student personnel director should be the preparation of job descriptions and organizational patterns, preparation of budgetary requests for the total program, and identification and interpretation of staffing needs. Most importantly he should integrate the student personnel services into the institution's total educational program. The student personnel director also should develop and nurture the professional growth of his staff and plan for a program of research and evaluation.

11. The student personnel director should be assigned the responsibility of representing the student personnel division on the administrative council. Staff procurement, budgeting, reporting, long-range planning, evaluation, and development of educational policies are essential responsibilities of the student personnel director as he complements the functions of the president of the college.

12. Self-improvement by the student personnel director should be an essential responsibility which encompasses frequent consultation with the president, attendance at professional meetings, professional reading, and visits to the campuses of other junior colleges. A self-evaluation of the office of the student personnel director is also an essential responsibility.

13. Substantial agreement seems to exist regarding responsibilities which should be assigned to the student personnel directors in public junior colleges which are members of the Southern Association of Colleges and Schools.

14. The student personnel directors lack a clearly defined set of assigned responsibilities.

15. Student personnel directors who are currently assigned a responsibility place a higher value on the assignment of that responsibility than the student personnel directors who are not assigned the responsibility.

A scrutiny of the guide and conclusions of Campbell's study should provide a basis on which to determine the responsibilities which should be assigned to the student personnel director. Presidents of the junior colleges should consider the use of this summary listing in the orientation of newly appointed student personnel directors who desire and need a knowledge of a body of responsibilities that may or may not be assigned to the student personnel directors. Once the description of the student personnel director's position has been determined, a better organized and supervised program of student personnel services should result.

Summary Listing of Responsibilities with Indicated Assignment, Ratings, and Acceptance or Rejection of the Null Hypothesis

Assigned to Majority	Responsibility	Rating by Assigned Group	Rating by Nonassigned Group	Rating by Composite Group	Acceptance or Rejection of Null Hypothesis
	A. Responsibilities Relating to Admissions and Registration				
✓	A-1 Supervision of all student admissions	3	2	2	R
✓	A-2 Preparation and distribution of descriptive material	2	2	2	R
✓	A-3 Evaluation of transcripts and previous course work	3	2	2	R
✓	A-4 Appointment of members admissions committee	2	2	2	R
✓	A-5 Handling of inquiries about college attendance	3	2	2	R
	A-6 Synthesis of available personal data	3	2	2	R
✓	A-7 Development of integrated record system	3	2	2	R
✓	A-8 Maintenance of policies of record accessibility	3	2	2	R
✓	A-9 Conducting of research on student characteristics	3	2	2	R
	A-10 Planning and scheduling of preregistration and registration interview	3	2	2	R
✓	A-11 Designing of forms and procedures	3	2	2	R
✓	A-12 Processing of class changes and withdrawals	3	2	2	R
	A-13 Projection of future enrollments	3	2	2	R

Summary Listing of Responsibilities (*Continued*)

Assigned to Majority	Responsibility	Rating by Assigned Group	Rating by Nonassigned Group	Rating by Composite Group	Acceptance or Rejection of Null Hypothesis
	B. Responsibilities Relating to Guidance and Counseling				
✓	B-1 Direction and coordination of all guidance and counseling programs	3	2	3	R
✓	B-2 Coordination of all standardized testing programs	3	2	3	R
✓	B-3 Selection of appropriate testing instruments	3	2	2	R
✓	B-4 Administration of tests to students	2	2	2	R
✓	B-5 Interpretation of test results	3	2	2	R
	B-6 Development of normative and predictive test data	3	2	2	R
✓	B-7 Interpretation of curricular requirements	3	2	2	R
✓	B-8 Assisting of students in their selecting of courses	3	2	2	R
✓	B-9 Conducting of program of academic advising	2	2	2	A
✓	B-10 Implementation of an effective referral program	3	2	2	R
✓	B-11 Conducting of counseling interviews	3	2	3	R
✓	B-12 Interpretation of occupational information	2	2	2	R

B-13 Identification of sources of occupational information	3	2	2	R	✓
B-14 Study of manpower needs within the community	2	2	2	R	✓
B-15 Direction of the student orientation program	3	2	3	R	✓
B-16 Conducting of orientation classes	3	2	2	R	
B-17 Teaching of effective study skills	3	2	2	R	
C. Responsibilities Relating to Student Activities					
C-1 Organization and administration of all student activities	3	2	3	R	✓
C-2 Recommending of the appointment of faculty advisors	3	2	2	R	✓
C-3 Reviews and recommendations on charters and bylaws of student organizations	3	2	3	R	✓
C-4 Control of the calendar of student activities	3	2	3	R	✓
C-5 Conducting of leadership program for students	3	2	2	R	

Summary Listing of Responsibilities (*Continued*)

Assigned to Majority		Responsibility	Rating by Assigned Group	Rating by Nonassigned Group	Rating by Composite Group	Acceptance or Rejection of Null Hypothesis
✓	C-6	Supervision of student elections	3	2	3	A
✓	C-7	Implementation of social policies	3	2	3	R
✓	C-8	Training of student guides	3	2	3	R
✓	C-9	Interpretation of student services	2	2	2	R
✓	C-10	Preparation of student handbook	3	2	3	A
✓	C-11	Analysis of needs for activities and facilities	3	2	3	R
✓	C-12	Development of informal program of student activities	3	2	3	R
✓	C-13	Supervision of the activities budget	3	2	2	R
	C-14	Supervision of athletic program	3	2	3	R
	C-15	Approval of interschool and intramural athletic schedule	2	1	2	R
	C-16	Certification of athletes to athletic associations	3	2	2	R
	C-17	Selection of athletic committee	2	1	2	R
✓	C-18	Selection of student affairs committee	2	1	2	R
✓	C-19	Assisting in graduation	3	2	2	R
			2	2	2	R

D. Responsibilities Relating to Discipline				
D-1 Development of policies governing student discipline	3	2	3	R
D-2 Investigation of disciplinary cases	3	2	2	R
D-3 Selection of discipline committee	3	2	2	R
D-4 Interpretation of disciplinary action to students	3	2	3	R
D-5 Interpretation of disciplinary action to parents	3	2	2	R
D-6 Placement of students on disciplinary probation	3	2	2	R
D-7 Suspension of students	3	2	2	R
E. Responsibilities Relating to Financial Aid, Placement, Follow-up				
E-1 Reception of student applications for financial aid	3	2	2	R
E-2 Administration of student loans	3	2	2	R
E-3 Selection of scholarship committee	2	2	2	R

Summary Listing of Responsibilities *(Continued)*

Assigned to Majority	Responsibility	Rating by Assigned Group	Rating by Nonassigned Group	Rating by Composite Group	Acceptance or Rejection of Null Hypothesis
✓	E-4 Administration of student scholarships	3	2	2	R
✓	E-5 Supervision of college work-study program	3	2	2	R
✓	E-6 Procurement of funds for grants-in-aid	3	2	2	R
✓	E-7 Analysis of financial needs of students	3	2	2	R
✓	E-8 Administration of a veterans affairs program	2	2	2	R
✓	E-9 Administration of a job placement program	3	2	2	R
✓	E-10 Maintenance of liaison with employment agencies	2	2	2	A
✓	E-11 Consultation with prospective employers	2	2	2	R
✓	E-12 Arrangement of placement interviews	3	2	2	R
✓	E-13 Conducting of program of summer employment	2	2	2	R
	E-14 Conducting of follow-up studies	3	2	2	R
	F. Responsibilities Relating to Public Relations				
✓	F-1 Maintenance of relationships with secondary schools	3	2	2	R

F-2 Provision of speakers for area and local civic organizations	2	2	2	R
F-3 Arrangement of student groups to give programs	2	2	2	R
F-4 Arrangement of staff members of render services	2	2	2	R
F-5 Maintenance of alumni list	2	2	2	R
F-6 Encouragement of the organization of alumni clubs	3	2	2	R
F-7 Supervision and solicitation of high school graduates to attend college	2	2	2	R
F-8 Writing of articles emphasizing faculty and/or student accomplishments	3	2	2	R
F-9 Provision of area news meeting with campus news	2	2	2	R
G. Responsibilities Relating to Plant and Student Services				
G-1 Assisting in planning of new buildings for student services	3	2	3	R
G-2 Supervision and management of college bookstore	2	1	1	A

Summary Listing of Responsibilities (*Continued*)

Assigned to Majority	Responsibility	Rating by Assigned Group	Rating by Nonassigned Group	Rating by Composite Group	Acceptance or Rejection of Null Hypothesis
	G-3 Development and/or maintenance of an accident insurance program	2	2	2	R
√	G-4 Recommending of policy concerning automobiles on campus	3	2	2	R
	G-5 Supervision of program of campus security	2	2	2	R
	G-6 Supervision of student housing	2	2	2	A
	G-7 Supervision of food services	2	2	2	R
	G-8 Supervision of a program of health services and facilities	3	2	2	R
	H. Responsibilities Relating to Faculty				
√	H-1 Orientation of faculty to student program through the in-service program	3	2	3	R
√	H-2 Informing the faculty as to their role in registration	3	2	2	R
√	H-3 Supervision of a program of academic advising	3	2	2	R
	H-4 Assignment of advisees to faculty	3	2	2	R
	H-5 Supervision of faculty in their academic advising and registration activities	3	2	2	R

✓	H-6 Providing for faculty to utilize student personnel records	3	2	3	R
✓	H-7 Interpretation of student personnel records to faculty	3	2	3	R
✓	H-8 Providing for faculty referrals	3	2	2	R
✓	H-9 Selection of faculty members to serve on various student affairs committees	3	2	2	R
✓	H-10 Supervision of faculty members performing specified duties in the student activity program	3	2	2	R
✓	H-11 Maintenance of an open-door to the student personnel office	3	2	2	R
✓	H-12 Cooperation with faculty in implementation of certain policies	3	2	3	R
	I. Responsibilities Relating to Central Administrative Unit (Student Personnel Division)				
✓	I-1 Preparation of job descriptions and organizational patterns	3	2	3	R

Summary Listing of Responsibilities (Continued)

Assigned to Majority	Responsibility	Rating by Assigned Group	Rating by Nonassigned Group	Rating by Composite Group	Acceptance or Rejection of Null Hypothesis
✓	I-2 Preparation of budgetary requests for total program	3	2	3	R
✓	I-3 Identification and interpretation of staffing needs	3	2	3	R
✓	I-4 Determining of the scope of the program	3	2	3	R
✓	I-5 Signification of student personnel services as an integral part of the total educational program	3	3	3	R
✓	I-6 Providing of program for research, planning, and evaluation	3	2	3	R
✓	I-7 Conducting of staff meetings	3	2	3	R
✓	I-8 Assigning of office space to staff	3	2	2	R
✓	I-9 Organization of student affairs committee	3	2	2	R
✓	I-10 Selection of members of student affairs committee	3	2	2	R
✓	I-11 Arrangement of joint meetings of staff with high school counselors	3	2	2	R
✓	I-12 Arrangement for staff participation in professional meetings	3	2	3	R

J. Responsibilities Relating to Upper-Administration				
J-1 Representing of student personnel division on administrative council	3	3	3	R
J-2 Maintaining of an organizational chart of division	3	2	3	R
J-3 Procurement of prospective staff members for division	3	2	2	R
J-4 Negotiation with prospective staff members	3	2	2	R
J-5 Recommending of prospective staff members for employment	3	2	3	R
J-6 Preparation and administration of budget for division	3	2	3	R
J-7 Presentation of annual report to president	3	2	3	R
J-8 Study and recommendation of admission policies	3	2	2	R
J-9 Presentation of long-range plans (over one year)	3	2	3	R
J-10 Representing of division at certain board meetings	3	2	2	R
J-11 Report of the results of any local research	3	2	2	R

Summary Listing of Responsibilities *(Continued)*

Assigned to Majority	Responsibility	Rating by Assigned Group	Rating by Nonassigned Group	Rating by Composite Group	Acceptance or Rejection of Null Hypothesis
✓	J-12 Direction of a self-study of the student personnel division	3	2	3	R
✓	J-13 Maintaining of an effective follow-up program of a self-study	3	2	3	R
✓	J-14 Recommending of changes to president concerning purposes of the college	3	2	2	R
✓	J-15 Recommending of changes to president concerning policies of the college	3	2	2	R
	J-16 Assistance in planning of new buildings for student personnel services	3	2	3	R
	K. Responsibilities Relating to Self-Improvement				
✓	K-1 Frequent consultation with the college president	3	3	3	A
✓	K-2 Meeting with the student personnel directors at professional meetings	3	3	3	A
✓	K-3 Visiting on campuses of other junior colleges	3	2	3	R
✓	K-4 Reading regularly a professional journal	3	3	3	A
✓	K-5 Maintaining a current professional library	3	3	3	A

	✓				
K-6 Attending formal training courses periodically	✓	3	3	3	R
K-7 Writing professional articles for publication	✓	2	2	2	R
K-8 Conducting self-evaluation of the office of the director of student personnel		3	3	3	A

Key:

✓ Assignment of responsibility to a majority of student personnel directors

3 An appraisal of essential
2 An appraisal of desirable
1 An appraisal of undesirable

A Acceptance of null hypothesis
R Rejection of null hypothesis

SUMMARY AND CONCLUSIONS

In this chapter an attempt was made to present first a philosophy underlying student personnel work based on widely accepted concepts; second, a general discussion of the major areas of junior college student personnel work; and third, trends and guidelines in the organization and administration of the various student personnel services.

The most recent studies were cited in an effort to enrich the presentation. The studies seem to be a continuation of the attempts made by the American Association of Junior Colleges in 1949 and 1962 when it conducted studies to stimulate junior colleges to develop more adequate programs of student personnel services.[27] But as Weatherford pointed out, "despite accomplishments in the profession, many junior colleges are paying only lip service to this important function."[28] the study by the Committee on Appraisal and Development of Junior College Student Personnel Programs depicted a lack of effective student personnel programs. As Collins phrased it, "Not many junior colleges have student personnel programs whose adequacy even approaches the importance of the task to be done."[29]

Hopefully the material presented in this chapter will contribute toward the student personnel worker's task of providing a better student personnel program. Society needs the junior college and the junior college needs an effective program of student personnel services. The development of the individual students is contingent upon the student personnel worker's ability and effort to provide such a program.

BIBLIOGRAPHY

Books

Blocker, Clyde E., Robert H. Plummer, and Richard C. Richardson. *The Two-Year College: A Social Synthesis.* Englewood Cliffs, N.J.: Prentice-Hall, Inc., 1965.
Collins, Charles C. *Junior College Student Personnel Programs: What They Are and What They Should Be.* Washington, D.C.: American Association of Junior Colleges, 1967.
Collins, Charles C. *Premises: Planning Student Personnel Facilities.* Washing-

[27]American Association of Junior College Committee on Student Personnel Problems, "Report to 30th Annual Meeting of the American Association of Junior Colleges," *Junior College Journal,* 20 (May 1950), p. 551. See also Russ, "Commission Reports," pp. 467–470.
[28]Weatherford, *op. cit.,* pp. 21-23.
[29]Collins, *op. cit.,* p. 41.

ton, D.C.: American Association of Junior Colleges, 1967.

Gleazer, Edmund J. Jr. (ed.). *American Junior Colleges.* 6th ed. Washington, D.C.: American Council on Education, 1964.

Hillway, Tyrus. *The American Two-Year College.* New York: Harper & Row, Publishers, 1958.

Medsker, Leland L. *The Junior College: Progress and Prospect.* New York: McGraw-Hill Book Company, 1960.

Raines, Max. "Report to the Carnegie Corporation on Appraisal and Development of Junior College Student Personnel Programs." *Junior College Student Personnel Programs Appraisal and Development.* A Report to the Carnegie Corporation, 1965.

Reynolds, James W. *The Junior College.* New York: Center for Applied Research in Education, Inc., 1965.

Thomas, Frank Waters. "The Functions of the Junior College." *The Junior College: Its Organization and Administration.* Edited by William Proctor. Stanford, Calif.: Stanford University Press, 1927.

Thornton, James W. *The Community Junior College.* New York: John Wiley and Sons, Inc., 1966.

Articles

American Association of Junior College Committee on Student Personnel Problems. "Report to 30th Annual Meeting of the American Association of Junior Colleges," *Junior College Journal,* 20 (May 1950), p. 551.

Fordyce, Joseph. "Creating a Good Climate," *Junior College Journal,* 35 (December 1964), pp. 17–20.

Higgins, Sadie, and Alice Thurston. "Challenges in Student Personnel Work." *Junior College Journal,* 34 (November 1963), pp. 24–28.

Humphries, Anthony. "Toward Improved Programs of Student Personnel Services," *Junior College Journal,* 22 (March 1952), pp. 382–392.

Livingston, Frank. "Counseling for the Entering College Student," *School and Community,* 54 (April 1968), pp. 24–25.

Raines, Max R. "The Student Personnel Situation," *Junior College Journal,* 36 (February 1966), pp. 6–8.

Robinson, Donald W. "The Role of the Faculty in the Development of Student Personnel Services," *Junior College Journal,* 31 (September 1960), pp. 15–21.

Russ, May. "Commission Reports on Student Personnel Practices," *Junior College Journal,* 32 (April 1962), pp. 467–470.

Smith, E. M. "Which Way Junior College Guidance and Personnel Programs?" *Junior College Journal,* 28 (December 1957), pp. 186–189.

Weatherford, Sidney. "The Status of Student Personnel Work," *Junior College Journal,* 35 (February 1965), pp. 21–23.

Dissertations

Campbell, Jack E. "An Analysis of Selected Responsibilities of Student Personnel Directors in Public Junior Colleges which Are Members of the Southern Association of Colleges and Schools." (University of Mississippi, May 1969), pp. 1–186.

15

In-Service Education*

John W. Truitt
Richard A. Gross†

In-service education has long been a method for the improvement of instruction in institutions of higher education. Workshops and conferences, as well as faculty and departmental meetings, have assisted those with classroom responsibilities to achieve greater teaching competence.

Although in-service education has played a significant role in academic life, student personnel work has not utilized such activities. Establishment of comprehensive programs of in-service education represents a long-neglected need of student personnel staff which can contribute effectively towards solving some of the problems facing higher education, and more particularly, the student personnel area.

*Material originally published in the monograph, *Inservice Education for College Student Personnel,* a publication of the National Association of Student Personnel Administrators, Bulletin No. 1, June 1966. Reprinted by permission.

†Dr. John W. Truitt holds the B.S. degree in Social Studies and the M.Ed. degree in Guidance Education from Mississippi State University and the Ed.D. degree in Educational and Personnel Administration from Michigan State University. Dr. Truitt is currently Vice-President for Student Affairs and Professor of Education at Indiana State University. Prior to coming to Indiana State University he was Director of the Men's Division of Student Affairs at Michigan State University. His design of an in-service education program and his organizational manuals have been widely utilized by student affairs staffs across the country. Dr. Truitt is a frequent speaker at national academic organizations and his writings have made significant contributions to student personnel work in higher education. Dr. Richard A. Gross holds a B.A. from Wheaton College, Wheaton, Illinois, M.A. and Ph.D. from Michigan State University at East Lansing. Dr. Gross is the former Dean of Students at Wheaton College, Wheaton, Illinois and is currently Vice-President and Dean of the Faculty at Gordon College in Wenham, Massachusetts. Dr. Gross has been a frequent speaker and contributor to state and national student personnel organizations.

Nature and Scope of In-Service Education

Broadly conceived, in-service education encompasses all phases of student personnel work that contribute to continuing professional development and competence. The program includes activities, planned in accordance with specific objectives, intended to enhance the professional growth and competence of a student personnel staff (both individually and collectively). Several suggested activities for an in-service education program include workshops, case studies and conferences, research, tape recordings and films, staff seminars and retreats, directed readings and discussion, visiting lecturers, interschool visitations, panels, role-playing, individual evaluation and supervision, and attendance and participation at professional meetings.

In-service education for student personnel workers should be directed toward professional upgrading of each staff member as an individual, and the increased competence of the staff as a functioning whole. In accomplishing this, a program will assist staff members to advance professionally in two ways—in a general role as a person and an educator and, in a specific role as a student personnel administrator in his own specialty.

Thus, emphases in well-conceived in-service programs include: the stimulation and promotion of professional growth to enlarge one's vision, purpose, and motivation and enable each staff member to realize higher levels of responsibility and achievement; and the development of specific techniques and procedures to assist in fulfilling more narrowly defined job responsibilities. This chapter is directed toward both emphases with selected aspects applicable to one or the other.

There is a developing emphasis upon the inclusion of student leaders in in-service education programs. Student leadership which plays a developing role within the effective student personnel program, is fostered through the establishment and upgrading of in-service education for student leaders as well as for student personnel staff. Thus the continuing development of staff responsibility and competence cannot be divorced from the development of student leadership. In this regard, in-service education provides an opportunity for student-staff relationships within the context of common objectives and effort.

Status of In-Service Education in Student Personnel Work

Critical examination of professional literature and a survey of existing programs reflects that insufficient attention has been given to the potential role of in-service education programs as a means of improving professional programs. Considerable attention is given to preservice preparation and standards for student personnel workers, yet various writers [Burnett, 1954; Hill, 1960, 1961; Kirk, 1955] highlight the paucity of literature relative to in-service education programs. Stoughton accentuates this lack by noting that "The scarcity of research on in-service training and growth should be viewed as a harsh challenge to a profession in which knowledge has increased so rapidly and in which there are known to be many workers whose professional training is, to say the least, limited." [Stoughton, 1957, p. 182] Most literature in this area deals with counseling, faculty advising, and residence hall programs.

A survey of in-service education in 100 colleges and universities holding membership in the National Association of Student Personnel Administrators indicates the current status of ongoing professional improvement activities [Gross, 1963]. Findings show that 36 percent of the institutions surveyed do not have in-service education programs for the student personnel staff; however, a significant number of the administrators reporting indicated an interest in this aspect of student personnel work and a desire for assistance in establishing a program. Responses of the remaining schools sampled indicated limited in-service activities, except a few selected institutions where concerted effort has been made to implement professional programs. The basic conclusions of the study were:

> There is little attention given in colleges and universities to the development of comprehensive in-service education programs embracing all student personnel services and workers. The programs that do exist generally lack overall planning and structure and are informal and inadequate. In-service education is a low-priority item in the professional life and practice of student personnel workers. [Gross, 1963, p. 111]
>
> A small portion of student personnel budgets is designated for professional improvement activities. (p. 112)
>
> Student personnel workers have not fully availed themselves of existing materials, resource personnel, opportunities and ideas applicable to professional growth activities. (p. 113)
>
> Chief student personnel administrators rely heavily upon professional organizations and meetings to promote the professional upgrading of student personnel workers. (p. 113)
>
> Common problems face student personnel administrators in developing and carrying on a professional betterment program. Among these are lack of time and budget, failure to recognize the importance of improvement activities, and insufficient knowledge of basic principles and techniques applicable to in-service education. (p. 112)

In-service education programs for personnel staffs and student leaders must be given increased emphasis if student personnel workers are to achieve adequate professional status and competence.

The purposes of this chapter are to

1. Communicate to student personnel workers a general concept of in-service education.
2. Challenge student personnel workers with the need for and potential of in-service education.
3. Assist student personnel workers in planning and implementation of in-service education programs.

THE NEED FOR IN-SERVICE EDUCATION IN STUDENT PERSONNEL WORK

Significant reasons necessitate the inclusion of in-service education in student personnel programs.

The inadequate or unrelated preservice education of many in student personnel work underscores the importance of in-service education. Preservice education and experience of many personnel workers is often in a field unrelated to their job responsibilities. The most logical alternative or expectation of these persons is that they develop their professional competence "on the job." Not only have many existing personnel workers entered the field with a lack of appropriate professional education, but growing demands for student personnel services in institutions of higher learning have resulted in placing in personnnel positions individuals who fall below the desired level of preservice education. Regardless of the individual's education and experience, it must be recognized that student personnel work is a dynamic and changing field of endeavor, and creative means of keeping abreast professionally must be continually sought. In-service education takes on added significance when one realistically views the evolving nature of student personnel work and the qualifications of many of those employed in this unique educational endeavor.

Continued professional growth of its members is one of the distinguishing features of a profession and can be achieved through in-service education. An emerging profession such as student personnel work is in need of a continuing consciousness of a higher level of professionalization if it is to meet the demands of the future. The lack of systematic integration of theory underlying student personnel work makes it imperative that members of the profession be vitally concerned with in-service improvement.

In-service education programs can effect change in the student personnel program. The impact of a complex society in a changing world is felt more each year on college campuses. Growth in institutions, development of new programs, and impinging policies of national organizations make it necessary to make periodic changes in administrative policy. These changes and the rationale for them must be communicated to staff and student leaders if a desirable degree of understanding and acceptence is to be achieved. In-service education is one means by which policy change can be implemented and communicated.

A structured in-service education program is necessary to provide continuity for a specialized and constantly changing staff. Student personnel programs, particularly as they exist on large campuses, may present a variety of specialists, each performing a specific function and sometimes unrelated to others. Interrelation of all student personnel functions is essential to the maintenance of maximum effectiveness of the total personnel program. In-service education programs can provide for the development of common objectives, a unifying frame of reference, a means of communication, and the improvement of functional relationships of specialists that must work cooperatively.

As a result of the rapid expansion of the college population, new student personnel positions are being constantly created at all levels. This provides opportunities for promotions within the staff and the necessity of recruiting additional personnel. For example, each year many institutions face the increasingly difficult problem of staffing residence halls. Persons recruited for residence hall work usually remain a minimum time before completing graduate work and assuming a higher-level position. However, while carrying out their responsibilities in a residence hall, they must learn to work with students at a high level of professional competence. In-service education assists greatly in providing continuity of the program for both new staff members and those who have recently been promoted.

The fact that new staff members rarely assume their initial positions at their peak effectiveness requires the establishment of in-service education programs. New workers assume assignments in student personnel work with varying experience and personal motivation. Many are direct from graduate study. The lack of quality internships in professional preparation programs adds to the necessity of providing means whereby these persons can increase their effectiveness. It is not always possible to give individual orientation and instruction to new workers; therefore, programmed in-service education provides, with a minimum time and effort, a vehicle for professionally upgrading all staff members.

In-service education programs provide excellent opportunities for each staff member to contribute to the student personnel program. Because of the diversification and changing nature of personnel work, the full potential of all workers must be utilized in the development of student life programs and the profession.

Any student personnel program depends upon contributions of the total staff, members of which vary in professional ability. The professional growth of a worker, and the contribution he can make to the program and profession, can be augmented by a program of in-service activities. Availability of professionally productive staff members in a planned give-and-take manner is a considerable asset to any personnel program. One measure of a student personnel worker's growth is whether or not he assumes greater responsibility as he acquires the ability and experience to do so. In-service education should provide methods by which the creativity of individual staff members can be integrated into the developing program.

An in-service education program provides opportunity for staff members to contribute to the total student personnel program. Through in-service education, a personnel staff can develop a common understanding of and approach to the objectives they wish to realize in student life programs. Thus, coordination of personnel activities can be achieved through in-service education programs. Personnel workers should be given preparation to carry out responsibility commensurate with their positions. Each worker should be expected to make decisions germane to his function but within the philosophy of the total student personnel program. With this as an operating frame of reference and the upgrading of each staff member's professional competence, more effective student personnel programs will emerge.

Properly planned in-service education programs enable the personnel staff to transcend the routine of daily personnel functions. Student personnel work has been criticized because most of its work is procedurally oriented and not considered to be educational in nature. Practice has exceeded a thorough understanding of theory and research applicable to personnel work. In-service education activities that emphasize the broad foundations and implications of student personnel work enables a staff to think beyond the present problems and expand professional horizons, not only affecting what is accomplished today but in the future as well.

An in-service education program assists in raising aspirations of staff members. Professionally oriented staff members are constantly challenged and motivated by their experiences to achieve more effective ways of carrying out their daily responsibilities. This motivation may come from attending national and state conferences or in-service education programs on the campus. When the student personnel worker is able to put into practice the knowledge that he has acquired, this new experience is usually accompanied by an attitude of satisfaction and accomplishment. It raises the desire of the personnel worker to improve himself. One method of increasing the aspirational level of staff members is to assign to them important roles in the in-service education program.

GENERAL PRINCIPLES OF IN-SERVICE EDUCATION PROGRAMS

Certain principles are universal in the establishment and functioning of in-service education programs. To initiate and administer a program of in-service education effectively, it is first necessary to understand the following general principles upon which such a program is based.

An in-service education program should be based upon objectives which give direction to the overall student personnel program and provide a basis for evaluation. Too often professional growth activities lack overall purposes and are unrelated to other existing aspects of the in-service program. Failure to establish and adhere to mutually understood purposes and operationally defined objectives accounts for uncoordinated, haphazard, and aimless activities often labeled as in-service education.

Each in-service education program must be planned, initiated, and perpetuated in view of individual staff and institutional goals and needs. While there are general principles which characterize all in-service programs, no one pattern or model is universally applicable to all institutions. Each program must fit the needs of a particular staff and institutions.

In-service education programs should be geared to varying levels of professional preparation and experience of individual staff members. This principle is related to the previous one and takes cognizance of differences in preservice education, experience, potential, and job responsibility of each program participant. Not only should the in-service education program include all staff members, but the content, procedures, and level of active participation should reflect their individual needs and abilities. It may be necessary, particularly for a large staff, to conduct the educational program at different levels and thus provide maximum profit for each staff member. Thus some phases of an in-service program will be applicable to an entire staff while other aspects may be appropriate only to selected staff members.

In-service education programs should involve maximum participation of the total staff in the planning and ongoing activities. Continuing support and involvement in the program are best encouraged if participants share in its formulation. Such a procedure allows the staff to express topics and activities of special interest and need while at the same time building mutual respect and support and fostering individual creativeness.

Study topics and activities for in-service education programs should reflect both immediate and long-standing issues which face the staff, institutions, and student personnel work as a profession. Immediate problems or issues serve as topics or questions that generate interest in upgrading the level of the program. Consideration of such questions improves existing staff policy and procedure. However, a student personnel staff needs to look beyond the immediate and pressing problems that are encountered daily and relate these problems to the future.

In-service education programs should utilize the knowledge and skill of the program participants as well as that of consultants and other resource personnel. The personal study and participating of individual staff members are the core of the in-service education program. In addition, the judicious use of resource persons, both on and off campus, provides not only new knowledge and skill, but also new dimension and perspective that serve to stimulate continuing interest in the program. The involvement of resource personnel not only adds a new perspective but affords these consultants an opportunity to develop a knowledge and appreciation of the role of the student personnel program on the campus. Hopefully, then, consultants will assist in interpreting to others the efforts and objectives of the student personnel staff.

Opportunity should be made to allow the application of new knowledge and increased understanding of theory and technique, which are gained through in-service education activities, to the program and services of the institution. A critical factor in realizing personal growth and increased institutional effectiveness is the transfer of learning derived from the program into the practices of the institution. This will not only improve the total student personnel program but should also provide continuing interest in and impetus to the in-service education program.

In-service education programs should be continuously planned, conducted, and maintained during a regularly designated time in the normal work schedule of the staff. In-service professional education must be a purposeful program conscientiously planned. Time for professional in-service education through reading and research is intrinsic to the job responsibilities and work schedule of teaching faculty, but this is not normally the case for student personnel workers. The nature of student personnel work with such areas as continuing administrative functions, committee meetings, and student advising does not readily provide opportunities for professional reading, discussion, research, or writing. Time for these necessary professional activities must be regularly scheduled and jealously guarded. If professional in-service education activities are planned in conjunction with regular staff meetings, it is possible that a discussion of daily or routine problems will encroach upon time planned for more generalized and long-range study and discussion. If this does happen, separate meetings should be scheduled to plan, discuss, organize, and conduct the in-service education program.

In-service education programs should be continuously evaluated with the program participants playing a major role in the evaluation. The ultimate objective of an in-service education program is greater professional skill as manifested by increased staff and institutional effectiveness in working with students. Applying the results of an in-service education program to the ongoing, daily functioning of the institution and then evaluating the outcome are essential to the successful in-service education program. Only by application can efforts of the staff be validated and effects of the program established.

Responsibility for initiating, implementing, and directing an in-service education program should rest with one individual, preferably the chief student personnel officer. Impetus for continuing staff professionalization can and should be provided by the staff director or department head who should not only "set the pace" in terms of his own professional development but should allocate funds from the budget and designate staff time so that the in-service education program is encouraged. In institutions where the in-service education program is conducted at various levels, direction for specific aspects of the program may be delegated to other members of the staff. Specific planning which is characterized by the above general principles is the province of the chief student personnel administrator who has at his disposal the means by which these principles can be implemented into a successful program.

DEVELOPMENT OF AN IN-SERVICE EDUCATION PROGRAM

Introduction

Steps to plan and develop an in-service education program represent formidable barriers to its implementation. The task is further complicated by the very problems inherent in the needs for such a program. Regardless of all other considerations, cooperation and coordination of staff and student leadership are essential to an effective program. Other essentials include techniques, procedures, principles, materials, and types of in-service education activities. Technical ability is absolutely necessary for planning, organizing, implementing, and evaluating an in-service program, but technical ability alone is not sufficient. All ingredients are needed to insure a viable program.

Program Planning

Planning is the starting point. The committee or staff approach is generally recognized as most desirable in program planning, organizing, and implementing, as it not only provides for pooling ideas but is also a positive influence in furthering staff motivation during the year. Full staff participation develops a broad understanding of the program and a strong sense of responsibility for its success. An in-service education program should be planned to develop sequentially. It is not enough to determine what activities should be included; special attention must be given to the relationship of one activity to another and the sequence in which they are presented. Information and activities related to one's specific job responsibilities are suggested as an initial consideration. Greater skill in discharging individual responsibilities reflects those aspects in which a staff member gains confidence and emotional support. Thus all other aspects of the in-service program are built upon the initial emphasis. Once the program has assisted in developing greater job competence, it is desirable to broaden the in-service emphasis to include more general study topics and activities.

Staff Motivation

As part of the planning process, factors underlying the need for a program should be thoroughly understood and communicated to each participant. One key to staff motivation and student leader cooperation lies in understanding the need and potential for such a program. This is important because many staff members view in-service education as an activity external to primary responsibilities. Constant review of the factors which underlie the need for in-service education is one of the best ways to demonstrate that staff improvement and their increasing ability to perform at a higher level is the heart of in-service education.

Determination of Objectives

When the need for an in-service education program has been established, objectives of the overall program, as well as those of each program activity, should be clearly defined. Goal definition provides direction to the general program as well as to the specific activities and procedures which constitute the total program. It is imperative that the objectives of in-service education be related to those of the total personnel program.

Programs of in-service education usually have a twofold emphasis, each intended to accomplish a particular objective. The first emphasis is general in nature and includes consideration of topics related to the overall objectives of the program and student personnel work. Study areas such as "Institutional Goals and Student Personnel Work" and "Philosophy of Student Personnel Administration" are representative of topics germane to the general emphasis of the program. These general topics are universal in nature, applicable to all participants and levels of in-service education, and valid each year. The second emphasis is more specific and includes topics related to the immediate concerns and special interests of participants. These specialized areas of study are important at given times and for selected staff members. They are not, however, universal in scope and therefore are not included for all participants year after year.

Utilizing general and specialized study topics and activities is important, since both emphases are necessary if an in-service education program is to meet the needs of diverse groups in a centralized program.

Functionally Coordinated Programming

As previously indicated, goals sought by in-service education are directly related to the goals of student personnel work and basic objectives of the institution. The "functionally coordinated programming" approach allows for practical expression and reinforcement of those overriding objectives. In addition, a centralized program of in-service activities provides effective cooperation, communication, and coordination of all phases of the program. This is essential to establish continuity of planning, implementation, evaluation, and in general more effective administration of the total program.

Common Terminology

A common terminology relative to in-service education within a given institution will provide a means of communication necessary for the full expression and understanding of all persons involved in the program. Lack of common terminology will create confusion and loss of effective communications.

Staffing

Maximum participation on the part of all staff members is basic to the realization of the goal of in-service education, increased professional growth, and competence. Although staff members will assume major responsibility for planning and participation in various in-service activities, the judicious use of resource and consulting personnel must not be overlooked. The inclusion of faculty members and administrators in the in-service education program will supply new ideas to the staff as well as an interdisciplinary emphasis to the program.

Experienced staff members are valuable assets to any in-service program. Many types of in-service activities have as their primary objective acquainting new staff members with policies, procedures, and functions of a new position. Experience has shown that whenever possible it is desirable for experienced workers to teach new staff the responsibilities of their positions. This practice not only provides orientation and in-service education to new staff but also tends to create *esprit de corps* among staff. This should be done, however, within the framework of a structured program so as to insure that in-service activity is properly related to job performance.

Resource Material

Materials play an important role in the in-service education program. Journals, textbooks, films, tapes, outlines, operating handbooks, procedural manuals, and other supplementary materials should be put to optimum use. Staff members at all levels should participate in the collection, sharing, formulation, and maintenance of materials. This is particularly important in writing handbooks and manuals applicable to the continuing operation of the personnel program in a specific institution. These materials play a large role in the communications between staff members and student leaders. In addition to providing a common understanding of goals and procedures, they assist in providing continuity to the program. Student leaders and assistants usually demonstrate the approximate amount of faith, concern, and regard for resource materials as do staff members.

Evaluation

Little has been accomplished in the evaluation of in-service activities for student personnel workers. No experimental approaches to the problem are evident in the literature.

Feedback from participants in the form of questionnaires and checklists has been the typical means of evaluation and, while admittedly limited, has proved helpful. Each participant should have an opportunity to evaluate the program's effectiveness according to his needs and experiences. To do this, a chart of the time and emphasis given to each in-service activity and topic should be made and circulated to each participant. Staff participants can assist in establishing consensus regarding the appropriate amount of time and emphasis which should be given any phase of the program. Ths method helps determine which topics and activities should be emphasized or eliminated. In addition, the typical evaluation of speakers and panels can be used. There is no question that more imaginative and refined approaches to evaluation are needed.

SELECTED IN-SERVICE EDUCATION ACTIVITIES

The purpose of this section is to present a general description of selected in-service activities in order to illustrate their nature and the principles of planning, organization, and implementation. Not all activities that may be included in a program will be described, nor will each aspect of the activity necessarily be analyzed.

Workshops have great potential for in-service education, especially in institutions having large residential student populations. Most workshops fall into three general types. The first is for student leaders who assist in some manner with incoming freshmen in the orientation process. Most of these take place on campus but others such as retreats or leadership campus occur off-campus. The second type is for a specific area such as residence halls and includes staff members, student assistants, and student government leaders. The program usually deals with the specific operation of the hall and has few topics of a broad general nature. The third is a centralized and comprehensive workshop which includes, within one framework, sessions for various groups and levels such as personnel staffs of residence halls, student leaders from the all-college student government, fraternities, sororities, interest clubs, residence halls, publications, and other student areas. The centralized workshop often encompasses all groups and topics included in the first two types mentioned.

Although workshops are useful when conducted both prior to and during the academic year, there has been an increased utilization of the precollege leadership workshop, for both staff and student leaders. This trend is directly related to the growth in the number of resident students on a college campus. Staff and student leadership is essential for the development and maintenance of educationally oriented programs in living units in order to assist their development through in-service education.

Methods of developing a preschool workshop program format within the framework of the previously mentioned types can range from talks designed to increase staff and student leader morale to formal programs with nationally known speakers presenting broad and complex topics.

It is usually best to have a precollege workshop extend over a period of time which will afford participants an opportunity not only to absorb and discuss information affecting the long-range program but also to devote the appropriate amount of time to matters which must be considered prior to the arrival of the student body. The length of the total precollege workshop, then, is predicated on a balance between the administrative functions which must be performed prior to the return of students and the information necessary for program coordination and development for the entire year. When a large amount of information is presented in a short period of time much of it is not digestible and the participants do not receive maximum benefit from the workshop.

In-service education meetings for residence personnel have great potential for individual and program development. This aspect of in-service education usually is concerned with developing the potential of staff, student assistants, and student leaders with regard to their functions in the programs and administration of living units. Some topics in these meetings will emphasize organization of living unit and responsibilities of this personnel. Others will stress the development of student programs within the living unit such as entertainment, athletics, recreation, student conduct, safety, scholarship, and others. These program areas and the accompanying in-service meetings provide opportunity for vast numbers of underclass students to obtain needed data and information before they assume leadership roles of a campus-wide nature.

In-service education meetings for student leaders in living units may be handled in several ways—one entirely within each living unit, the residence hall director and his staff being responsible for all in-service activities. Such a program is not coordinated with those of other residential units but structured according to the specific needs and program of each living unit and its staff.

Another program utilizes a general session for student program chairmen of all living units. This concentrated general session may be divided into three parts, each approximately 30 to 45 minutes in duration. One approach may consist of talk by a resource speaker to all participants regarding the educational implications of student leadership programs in the living units. The topic might not always deal specifically with the program areas but will be related to them in some manner. Part two might consist of group discussion sessions where participants are divided according to areas of responsibility. These discussions would center around the concepts presented by the speaker in the general session and the methods, techniques, and means to further development of each program area in the living unit. Part three may consist of an informal social affair for all program participants and resource persons. It is desirable for resource persons to interact informally with participants until all have had an opportunity to discuss fully their ideas, problems, and questions.

The major difference between the second and third presentation is that each individual student program area has its own general session with the full time period, as much as two hours, devoted to it. For example, if the student program areas of the living units were athletics and recreation, scholarship, activities, student conduct, and safety, the sessions for each of these student program areas would be scheduled on a different date, usually in the evening or on a Saturday morning, once a semester or quarter. One advantage is that it provides more time and more resource personnel with the total focus on a particular program area.

A combination or variation of these sessions could be used, depending upon the objectives. While the above described activities are primarily devoted to the development of student leadership, they are likewise beneficial to those who hold staff positions in the living units, particularly as staff provide leadership for and actively participate as resource personnel.

Leadership conferences for student leaders provide an excellent means of combining student responsibilities on the campus with responsible citizenship in the larger community. A leadership conference may be sponsored by the Student Government Association or the student personnel administration for officers and student leaders of student governing groups, interest clubs, and academic-related organizations. These conferences have several levels of student leaders and the program must be tailored to meet the needs of many groups. Such a conference has great potential for its broadening effect on the student leader who has had years of experience in activities and political life on the campus. The nature of the program, however, is usually dependent upon the state of development of the student leadership in-service education program. If the program is new or underdeveloped, the nature of the program usually deals with "how to do it" topics. If the program is well developed, it may consist of broad general topics. These conferences are examples of student leadership in action because they are typically formulated and implemented by a committee of students with the advice and assistance of the student personnel staff. Choice of a multitopic conference will involve more than speaker. Time devoted to speeches makes other activities of lesser importance, and student participation is kept at a minimum. If student participation is desired, the logical choice will be one with a single topic with only one speaker or resource person. Much time can then be utilized for discussion sessions with students serving as discussion leaders. This method involves preconference preparation of techniques of group discussion, often the most valuable aspect of the conference. The monotopic conference may be concluded with a short question and answer session.

Staff meetings can serve the same purposes as a workshop or professional meeting by bringing together various points of view and interests and assisting in integrating on-the-job experiences. The regular staff meeting has considerable potential for staff development if given the proper emphasis and thoughtfully planned. Too often such meetings deal only with routine matters at a surface or elementary level. The creatively conceived staff meeting can do much to increase staff competence and professional stature and should be included as part of the total in-service education program. In addition to facilitating communication of complex problems to a large number of persons, staff meetings are valuable problem-identifying and problem-solving situations and in this respect serve as the basis for creating and planning in-service education activities.

Staff meetings from an in-service education standpoint provide face-to-face communications about program planning, organization, implementation and evaluation. From these discussions come many ideas that give in-service education programs their real meaning.

Classroom education is an effective method of achieving the basic objectives of in-service education. Student personnel administrators may be involved in classroom in-service education courses in connection with leadership courses designed to broaden the perspective of student leaders regarding their roles in campus life. A second area of classroom involvement deals with those courses designed to give further instruction to staff and student assistants who are full or part-time employees of the college. These courses, often required for persons who operate the residence halls and other living units, are given for academic credit in some institutions. Personnel administrators who often teach student personnel administration or psychology are provided with an opportunity to balance theory and practice.

Professional staff seminars are based upon the assumption that student personnel workers must be educators first and student personnel technicians second. The professional seminar is designed to extend educational opportunities beyond those available in usual college settings and not to be a substitute for graduate work. They are high-level staff meetings with attention to general topics rather than routine matters.

Different types of professional seminars have been used with great success and frequency. A topic of professional nature is considered at each meeting with staff members assigned reports on pertinent topics. Assignments may be sequential in nature and planned a semester or longer in advance.

In a different form, an authority is brought in to discuss a chosen topic and answer questions raised by seminar participants. One member is usually responsible for securing the speaker and for distributing a summary of the seminar session to all members later.

Professional seminars help the participants to keep abreast of the changing nature of the student personnel profession, particular academic disciplines and higher education in general. They also provide time for the discussion of new ideas, concepts, and methods for solving existing problems.

Professional conferences provide for the pooling of common problems with the opportunity for each participant to profit from group collective wisdom and experience. Attendance at professional conferences is probably the most popular in-service education activity. Conferences should give participants new insights into problems when discussed outside the context of one's own responsibilities and setting. An opportunity is provided to anticipate issues on campus before they become problems.

These conferences are the means for collective action toward greater professionalism. The ethical standards, the definitions of personnel work, and the relationship of student personnel work to other professions in higher education do much to provide insight which results in more effective student personnel programs on individual campuses.

Directed readings provide a means for stimulating creative thinking and discussion for an entire staff or selected individual staff members. Directed readings assist a staff in consideration of a common problem or area of interest and provide impetus to regular reading of professional literature. Discussions led by staff members have been found to be a useful procedure in maximizing the benefit from directed readings.

Directed common readings are profitable for an entire staff, as well as for individuals, as they explore in depth their specific area of interest or responsibility.

Periodic evaluation and supervision of individual staff members by one's colleagues is a valuable in-service activity. This technique is common in the administration of internships in graduate programs but has not been used to its fullest extent by functioning staff members. Although individual evaluation and supervision are more readily applicable to specific student personnel activities such as counseling and research, there seems to be a need for greater utilization of this procedure between staff colleagues involved in all aspects of student personnel work.

SUMMARY

In-service education should complement an effective student personnel administration. While many divergent viewpoints and even strong disagreement exist regarding the role of student personnel work and staff functions, there is distinct agreement that student personnel administrators are responsible for developing means for constant improvement of individual workers and programs.

Inflexible staff and static programs will not suffice during the period of rapid transition and changing demands on higher education and the profession of personnel work. Demands made on individual students and colleges call for broader and more diversified approaches to student life programs. The need for staff upgrading is further emphasized by the great strides being made in man's knowledge concerning behavior, learning processes, leadership, maturity, and problem-solving methodology.

The preceding in-service education activities are admittedly limited and intended primarily to be illustrative of the nature and potential of the procedures which can assist in developing professional skill and personal growth. Intercollege visitation, research, and case studies have also been used successfully as an integral part of in-service education programs.

Effective personnel administration must devise methods of keeping abreast of professional developments, in education and specifically in student personnel work. A plan is needed to make it possible to meet the increasing challenges facing the personnel administrator in his developing program and responsibility. An in-service education program is one organized means, designed with comprehension and flexibility, to encourage professional improvement and competence.

BIBLIOGRAPHY

Anderson. G. V., and Leona Tyler, "Standards and Training for College Personnel Workers," *College and University,* 24 (1949), 204-212.

Banks, Dorothy J., "In-Service Training for Secondary School Counselors," *J. Na. Assoc. Women Deans and Counselors,* 26 (1963), 10-14.

Beery, J. R., and M. Murfin, "Meeting Barriers to Inservice Education," *Educ. Leadership,* 16 (1960),351-355.

Berdie, R. F., "In-service Training in Counseling and Counselor Evaluation," in Ralph F. Berdie (ed.),*Counseling and the College Program,* Minnesota Studies in Student Personnel Work, No. 6. Minneapolis: University of Minnesota Press, 1954, pp. 11-18.

Bledsoe, Ernestine, "Counselors Plan In-Service Training," *Occupations,* 30 (1952), 495-499.

*Burnett, C. W., "Selection and Training of School and College Personnel Workers," *Rev. of Educ. Res.,* 24 (1954), 121-133.

Camp. N. H., Jr., "A County Studies its In-Service Counselor Training Program," *Personnel and Guidance J.,* 38 (1959), 309-313.

*Primary Resource Material.

Coleman, W., "Motivating Factors in In-Service Training of Faculty Counselors," *Educ. and Psychol. Measurement,* 11 (1951), 747-751.

Collins, D., "An In-Service Training Program for Residence Counselors," *Educ. and Psychol. Measurement,* 7 (1947), 647.

Capehart, B. E., "Try Training Them," *Occupations,* 30 (1951), 198-201.

Cottingham, H. F., "Roles, Functions, and Training Levels for College Personnel Workers," *Personnel and Guidance J.,* 33 (1955), 534-538.

Durkee, F. M., "Organizing for Growth in Service," *Educ. Leadership,* 17 (1960), 336-339.

Feder, D. D., "Selection and Training of Faculty Counselors," in E. G. Williamson (ed.), *Trends in Student Personnel Work,* Minneapolis: University of Minnesota Press, 1949, pp. 288-300.

Froelich, C. P., "Preparation of Teachers and Specialists for Guidance Services," *Rev. of Educ. Res.,* 21 (1951), 159-166.

Future Needs in Student Personnel Work, American Council on Education, Washington, D. C., 1950.

Gilbert. W. M., "Training Faculty Counselors at the University of Illinois, in E. G. Williamson (ed.), *Trends in Student Personnel Work.* Minneapolis: University of Minnesota Press, 1949, pp. 301-312.

Gordon, I. J., "The Creation of an Effective Faculty Adviser Training Program through Group Procedures," *Educ. and Psychol. Meas.,* 10 (Autumn 1950), 505-512.

Gordon, I. J., "Guidance Training for College Faculty," *J. Nati. Assoc. of Deans of Women,* 16 (1953), 69-76.

*Gross, R. F., *"A Study of In-Service Education Programs for Student Personnel Workers in Selected Colleges and Universities in the United States,"* unpublished doctoral dissertation, Michigan State University, 1963.

Hackett, H. R., "University Faculty-Counseling Staff Meetings," *American Personnel and Guidance Journal,* 36 (1957), 125.

Hardee, Melvene D., "A Program of In-Service Training for Teacher-Counselors," *Junior College Journal,* 20 (1950), 453-459.

Henry, N. B. (ed.), *In-service Education,* The Fifty-Sixth Yearbook of The National Society for the Study of Education. Chicago: University of Chicago Press, 1957.

Henry, N. B. (ed.), *Personnel Services in Education,* The Fifty-Eighth Yearbook of the National Society for the Study of Education. Chicago: University of Chicago Press, 1959.

*Hill, G. E., "The Selection of Student Personnel Workers," *J. College Student Personnel,* 2 (1961), 2-8.

*Hill, G. E., and Donald A. Green, "The Selection, Preparation, and Professionalization of Guidance and Personnel Workers," *Rev. Educ. Res.,* 30 (1960), 115-130.

Hood, A. B., "An Experiment Utilizing Residence Counselors to Teach Educational Skills," *J. of College Student Personnel,* 4 (11) (1962), 35-40.

Horle, R. F., and G. M. Gazda, "Qualifications, Training, and Duties of Directors

*Primary Resource Material.

and Staff of Men's Residence Halls," *J. College Student Personnel,* 4 (1963), 231-234.

Houston, C. G., "A Limited Survey of Professional Standards and Training of College Personnel Workers," *Educ. and Psychol. Meas.,* 9 (Autumn 1949), 445-456.

Kelley, W. F., "Twenty Studies of In-Service Education of College Faculty and the Procedures Most Recommended," *Educ. Administration and Supervision,* 36 (1950), 351-358.

Kirk, Barbara A., "Evaluation of In-Service Counselor Training," *Educ. and Psychol. Meas.,* 16 (Winter 1956), 527-35.

*Kirk, Barbara A., "Techniques of In-Service Counselor Training," *Personnel and Guidance J.* 34 (1955), 204-207.

Misner, P. J., "In-Service Education Comes of Age, *J. Teacher Educ.,* 1 (1950), 32-36.

Mueller, Kate Hevner, "Criteria for Evaluating Professional Status, *Personnel and Guidance J.,* 37 (1959), 410-417.

Nonnamaker, E., *"Philosophical Bases for Enrichment Programs,"* Unpublished paper, Michigan State University, 1961.

Norris, R. B., "Administering In-Service Education in the College," *School and Society,* 77 (1953), 327-329.

Ohlsen, M. M., "An In-Service Training Program for Dormitory Counselors," *Occupations,* 29 (1951), 531-534.

Samler, J., "Professional Training: End Goal or Kick-Off Point? *Personnel and Guidance J.,* 31 (1952), 15-19.

Sheldon, Miriam A., T.I.P., "Semiprofessionals as Residence Hall Staff," *J. College Student Personnel,* 4 (1) (1962), 120-122.

Shepard, E. L., "Three-Level In-Service Training Program for Advisers," *Personnel and Guidance J.,* 36 (1957), 48-50.

Shoben, E. J., Jr., "Student Personnel Work: a Worry and a Vision," *Personnel and Guidance J.,* 33 (1954), 152-156.

Silverman, H., "Agency Directors and Professional Growth of Personnel," *Personnel and Guidance J.,* 35 (1957), 391-393.

*Stoughton, R. W., "The Preparation of Counselors and Personnel Workers," *Rev. of Educ. Res.,* 27 (1957), 174-185.

Swearingen, Mildred E., "Identifying Needs for In-Service Growth," *Educ. Leadership,* 17 (1960), 322-335.

Taylor, B. L., "Professional growth—An Aim of In-Service Education," *Educ. Administration and Supervision,* 44 (1958), 349-352.

Trenholme, A. K., "Materials Assist In-Service Growth," *Educ. Leadership,* 17 (1960), 347-350.

Trout, D. M., "Can We Separate In- and Pre-service?," *Educ. Leadership,* 1 (1944), 417-420.

Truitt, J. W., *In-Service Training Programs For Student Personnel Workers,"* paper presented at the American College Personnel Association annual meeting, Denver, Colorado, April, 1961, 14 pp. (mimeo.).

*Primary Resource Material.

Wells, Margaret C., "Training Student Deans at Syracuse," *Educ. Record,* 32 (1951), 96-104.

Williamson, E. G., "The Dean of Students as Educator," *Educ. Record,* 38 (1957), 230-240.

Williamson, E. G., "Professional Preparation of Student Personnel Workers, *School and Society,* 86 (1958), 3-5.

*Williamson, E. G., *Student Personnel Services in Colleges and Universities,* New York: McGraw-Hill Book Co., 1961.

Wilson, Frances M., "What Makes an Effective In-Service Training Program?," *J. Nati. Assoc. Deans of Women,* 16 (1953), 51-56.

Wrenn, C. G., "An Appraisal of the Professional Status of Personnel Work, Part I," in E. G. Williamson (ed.), *Trends in Student Personnel Work,* Minneapolis: University of Minnesota Press, 1949, Part IX, pp. 264-280.

Wrenn, C. G., "Professions and Professional Membership," *Occupations,* 1951, 30, 24-29.

Wrenn, C. G., "The Basis of Training for Student Personnel Work," *J. Higher Educ.,* 19 (1948), 259-261.

Yarborough, J. M., and Mrs. Robert A. Cooper, "The Present Resident Assistant Program," *J. College Student Personnel,* 4 (1963), 246-249.

*Primary Resource Material.

Student Bill of Rights

College administrators have devoted a considerable amount of time to reviewing and adopting a student bill of rights for their campuses. This has been an outgrowth of the student bill of rights which was developed by the joint drafting committee consisting of: Dr. Phillip Monypenny, Political Science. University of Illinois, A.A.U.P. chairman; Dr. Harry D. Gideonse, chancellor, New School for Social Research. (A.A.C.) New York; Mr. Edward Schwartz, national affairs vice-president, (U.S.N.S.A.) Washington, D.C.; Dr. Peter H. Armacost, president, Ottawa University, former program director, (A.A.C.) Ottawa, Kan.; Mr. Earle Clifford, university dean of student affairs, Rutgers. The State University, (N.A.S.P.A.) New Brunswick, N.J.; Dr. Ann Bromley, associate dean of students, Santa Fe Junior College, (N.A.W.D.C.) Gainesville, Fla.; Mr. Robert Van Waes, associate secretary, (A.A.U.P.) Washington, D.C.

Student personnel administrators should be aware of the student bill of rights and use it as a guideline for their campuses. They should not be so naive as to adopt it completely because it is a joint statement and should reflect the uniqueness of each institution. Some administrators have fallen in the trap of accepting the total slate in their anxiousness to have a student bill of rights for their campus.

The original joint statement is as follows:

PREAMBLE

Academic institutions exist for the transmission of knowledge, the pursuit of truth, the development of students, and the general well-being of society. Free inquiry and free expression are indispensable to the attainment of these goals. As members of the academic community, students should be encouraged to develop the capacity for critical judgment and to engage in a sustained and independent search for truth. Institutional procedures for achieving these purposes may vary from campus to campus, but the minimal standards of academic freedom of students outlined below are essential to any community of scholars.

Freedom to teach and freedom to learn are inseparable facets of academic freedom. The freedom to learn depends upon appropriate opportunities and conditions in the classroom, on the campus, and in the larger community. Students should exercise their freedom with responsibility.

The responsibility to secure and to respect general conditions conducive to the freedom to learn is shared by all members of the academic community. Each college and university has a duty to develop policies and procedures which provide and safeguard this freedom. Such policies and procedures should be developed at each institution within the framework of general standards and with the broadest possible participation of the members of the academic community. The purpose of this statement is to enumerate the essential provisions for student freedom to learn.

I. FREEDOM OF ACCESS TO HIGHER EDUCATION

The admissions policies of each college and university are a matter of institutional choice provided that each college and university makes clear the characteristics and expectations of students which it considers relevant to success in the institution's program. While church-related institutions may give admission preference to students of their own persuasion, such a preference should be clearly and publicly stated. Under no circumstances should a student be barred from admission to a particular institution on the basis of race. Thus, within the limits of its facilities, each college and university should be open to all students who are qualified according to its admission standards. The facilities and services of a college should be open to all of its enrolled students, and institutions should use their influence to secure equal access for all students to public facilities in the local community.

II. IN THE CLASSROOM

The professor in the classroom and in conference should encourage free discussion, inquiry and expression. Student performance should be evaluated solely on an academic basis, not on opinions or conduct in matters unrelated to academic standards.

A. Protection of Freedom of Expression. Students should be free to take reasoned exception to the data or views offered in any course of study and to reserve judgment about matters of opinion, but they are responsible for learning the content of any course of study for which they are enrolled.

B. Protection Against Improper Academic Evaluation. Students should have protection through orderly procedures against prejudiced or capricious academic evaluation. At the same time they are responsible for maintaining standards of academic performance established for each course in which they are enrolled.

C. Protection Against Improper Disclosure. Information about student views, beliefs and political associations which professors acquire in the course of their work as instructors, advisers and counselors should be considered confidential. Protection against improper disclosure is a serious professional obligation. Judgments of ability and character may be provided under appropriate circumstances, normally with the knowledge or consent of the student.

III. STUDENT RECORDS

Institutions should have a carefully considered policy as to the information which should be part of a student's permanent educational record and as to the conditions of its disclosure. To minimize the risk of improper disclosure, academic and disciplinary records should be separate, and the conditions of access to each should be set forth in an explicit policy statement. Transcripts of academic records should contain only information about academic status. Information from disciplinary or counseling files should not be available to unauthorized persons on campus or to any person off campus without the express consent of the student involved, except under legal compulsion or in cases where the safety of persons or property is involved. No records should be kept which reflect the political activities or beliefs of students. Provisions should also be made for periodic routine destruction of noncurrent disciplinary records. Administrative staff and faculty members should respect confidential information about students which they acquire in the course of their work.

IV. STUDENT AFFAIRS

In student affairs certain standards must be maintained if the freedom of students is to be preserved.

A. Freedom of Association. Students bring to the campus a variety of interests previously acquired and develop many new interests as members of the academic community. They should be free to organize and join associations to promote their common interests.

1. The membership, policies and actions of a student organization usually will be determined by vote of only those persons who hold bona fide membership in the college or university community.

2. Affiliation with an extramural organization should not of itself disqualify a student organization from institutional recognition.

3. If campus advisers are required, each organization should be free to choose its own adviser, and institutional recognition should not be withheld or withdrawn solely because of the inability of a student organization to secure an adviser. Campus advisers may advise organizations in the exercise of responsibility, but they should not have the authority to control the policy of such organizations.

4. Student organizations may be required to submit a statement of purpose, criteria for membership, rules of procedures, and a current list of officers. They should not be required to submit a membership list as a condition of institutional recognition.

5. Campus organizations, including those affiliated with an extramural organization, should be open to all students without respect to race, creed or national origin, except for religious qualifications which may be required by organizations whose aims are primarily sectarian.

B. Freedom of Inquiry and Expression.

1. Students and student organizations should be free to examine and to discuss all questions of interest to them and to express opinions publicly and privately. They should always be free to support causes by orderly means which do not disrupt the regular and essential operation of the institution. At the same time it should be made clear to the academic and the larger community that in their public expressions or demonstrations students or student organizations speak only for themselves.

2. Students should be allowed to invite and to hear any person of their own choosing. Those routine procedures required by an institution before a guest speaker is invited to appear on campus should be designed only to insure that there is orderly scheduling of facilities and adequate preparation for the event, and that the occasion is conducted in a manner appropriate to an academic community. The institutional control of campus facilities should not be used as a device of censorship. It should be made clear to the academic and larger community that sponsorship of guest speakers does not necessarily imply approval or endorsement of the views expressed, either by the sponsoring group or the institution.

C. Student Participation in Institutional Government. As constituents of the academic community, students should be free, individually and collectively, to express their views on issues of institutional policy and on matters of general interest to the student body. The student body should have clearly defined means to participate in the formulation and application of institutional policy affecting academic and student affairs. The role of the student government and both its general and specific responsibilities should be made explicit, and the actions of the student government within the areas of its jurisdiction should be reviewed only through orderly and prescribed procedures.

D. Student Publications. Student publications and the student press are a valuable aid in establishing and maintaining an atmosphere of free and responsible discussion and of intellectual exploration on the campus. They are a means of bringing student concerns to the attention of the faculty and the institutional authorities and of formulating student opinion on various issues on the campus and in the world at large.

Whenever possible, the student newspaper should be an independent corporation, financially and legally separate from the university. Where financial and legal autonomy is not possible, the institution, as the publisher of student publications, may have to bear the legal responsibility for the contents of the publications. In the delegation of editorial responsibility to students, the institution must provide sufficient editorial freedom and financial autonomy for the student publications to maintain their integrity of purpose as vehicles for free inquiry and free expression in an academic community.

Institutional authorities, in consultation with students and faculty, have a responsibility to provide written clarification of the role of the student publications, the standards to be used in their evaluation, and the limitations on external control of their operation. At the same time the editorial freedom of student editors and managers entails corollary responsibilities to be governed by the canons of responsible journalism, such as the avoidance of libel, indecency, undocumented allegations, attacks on personal integrity, and the techniques of harassment and innuendo. As safeguards for the editorial freedom of student publications, the following provisions are necessary:

1. The student press should be free of censorship and advance approval of copy, and its editors and managers should be free to develop their own editorial policies and news coverage.

2. Editors and managers of student publications should be protected from arbitrary suspension and removal because of student, faculty, administrative or public disapproval of editorial policy or content. Only for proper and stated causes should editors and managers be subject to removal and then by orderly and prescribed procedures. The agency responsible for the appointment of editors and managers should be the agency responsible for their removal.

3. All university published and financed student publications

should explicitly state on the editorial page that the opinions there expressed are not necessarily those of the college, university or student body.

OFF-CAMPUS FREEDOM OF STUDENTS

A. Exercise of Rights of Citizenship. College and university students are both citizens and members of the academic community. As citizens, students should enjoy the same freedom of speech, peaceful assembly, and right of petition that other citizens enjoy and, as members of the academic community, they are subject to the obligations which accrue to them by virtue of this membership. Faculty members and administrative officials should insure that institutional powers are not employed to inhibit such intellectual and personal development of students as is often promoted by their exercise of the rights of citizenship both on and off campus.

B. Institutional Authority and Civil Penalities. Activities of students may upon occasion result in violation of law. In such cases institutional officials should be prepared to apprise students of sources of legal counsel and may offer other assistance. Students who violate the law may incur penalties prescribed by civil authorities, but institutional authority should never be used merely to duplicate the function of general laws. Only where the institutions' interests as an academic community are distinct and clearly involved should the special authority of the institution be asserted. The student who incidentally violates institutional regulations in the course of his off-campus activity, such as those relating to class attendance, should be subject to no greater penalty than would normally be imposed. Institutional action should be independent of community pressure.

VI. PROCEDURAL STANDARDS IN DISCIPLINARY PROCEEDINGS

In developing responsible student conduct, disciplinary proceedings play a role substantially secondary to example, counseling, guidance and admonition. At the same time educational institutions have a duty and the corollary disciplinary powers to protect their educational purpose through the setting of standards of scholarship and conduct for the students who attend them and through the regulation of the use of institutional facilities. In the exceptional circumstances when the preferred means fail to resolve problems of student conduct, proper procedural safeguards should be observed to protect the student from the unfair imposition of serious penalties.

The administration of discipline should guarantee procedural fairness to an accused student. Practices in disciplinary cases may vary in formality with the gravity of the offense and the sanctions which may be applied. They should also take into account the presence or absence of an honor code and the degree to which the institutional officials have direct acquaintance with student life in general and the involved student and the circumstances of the case in particular. The jurisdictions of faculty or student judicial bodies, the disciplinary responsibilities of institutional officials, and the regular disciplinary procedures, including the student's right to appeal a decision, should be clearly formulated and communicated in advance. Minor penalties may be assessed informally under prescribed procedures.

In all situations procedural fair play requires that the student be informed of the nature of the charges against him, that he be given a fair opportunity to refute them, that the institution not be arbitrary in its actions, and that there be provision for appeal of a decision. The following are recommended as proper safeguards in such proceedings when there are no honor codes offering comparable guarantees.

A. Standards of Conduct Expected of Students. The institution has an obligation to clarify those standards of behavior which it considers essential to its educational mission and its community life. These general behavioral expectations and the resultant specific regulations should represent a reasonable regulation of student conduct, but the student should be as free as possible from imposed limitations that have no direct relevance to his education. Offenses should be as clearly defined as possible and interpreted in a manner consistent with the aforementioned principles of relevancy and reasonableness. Disciplinary proceedings should be instituted only for violations of standards of conduct formulated with significant student participation and published in advance through such means as a student handbook or a generally available body of institutional regulations.

B. Investigation of Student Conduct.

1. Except under extreme emergency circumstances, premises occupied by students and the personal possessions of students should not be searched unless appropriate authorization has been obtained. For premises such as residence halls controlled by the institution, an appropriate and responsible authority should be designated to whom application should be made before a search is conducted. The application should specify the reasons for the search and the objects or information sought. The student should be present, if possible, during the search. For premises not controlled by the institution, the ordinary requirements for lawful search should be followed.

2. Students detected or arrested in the course of serious violations of institutional regulations or infractions of ordinary law should be informed of their rights. No form of harassment should be used by institu-

tional representatives to coerce admissions of guilt or information about conduct of other suspected persons.

C. Status of Student Pending Final Action. Pending action on the charges, the status of a student should not be altered, or his right to be present on the campus and to attend classes suspended, except for reasons relating to his physical or emotional safety and well-being, or for reasons relating to safety and well-being of students, faculty or university property.

D. Hearing Committee Procedures. When the misconduct may result in serious penalties, and if the student questions the fairness of disciplinary action taken against him, he should be granted, on request, the privilege of a hearing before a regularly constituted hearing committee. The following suggested hearing committee procedures satisfy the requirements of "procedural due process" in situations requiring a high degree of formality:

1. The hearing committee should include faculty members or students, or, if regularly included or requested by the accused, both faculty and student members. No member of the hearing committee who is otherwise interested in the particular case should sit in judgment during the proceeding.

2. The student should be informed, in writing, of the reasons for the proposed disciplinary action with sufficient particularity, and in sufficient time, to insure opportunity to prepare for the hearing.

3. The student appearing before the hearing committee should have the right to be assisted in his defense by an adviser of his choice.

4. The burden of proof should rest upon the officials bringing the charge.

5. The student should be given an opportunity to testify and to present evidence and witnesses. He should have an opportunity to hear and question adverse witnesses. In no case should the committee consider statements against him unless he has been advised of their content and of the names of those who made them, and unless he has been given an opportunity to rebut unfavorable inferences which might otherwise be drawn.

6. All matters upon which the decision may be based must be introduced into evidence at the proceeding before the Hearing Committee. The decision should be based solely upon such matter. Improperly acquired evidence should not be admitted.

7. In the absence of a transcript, there should be both a digest and a verbatim record, such as a tape recording, of the hearing.

8. The decision of the hearing committee should be final, subject only to the student's right of appeal to the president or ultimately, to the governing board of the institution.

VII. ENFORCEMENT

A separate resolution on enforcement was passed by the final drafting committee but was not included in the documents endorsed by some of the organizations. The resolution reads:

It was agreed that, before becoming party to any joint statement on student rights and responsibilities, the Association should insist that all the parties to such an agreement should undertake:

1. To set up machinery for continuing joint interpretation of the policies and procedures recommended in the agreement.

2. To consult with each other before setting up any machinery for investigating complaints of alleged violation of the agreement.

3. To request the regional accrediting associations to embody the principles of the agreement in their standards for accreditation.

Index

Agitation, student, 61–75
Attitudes of dropouts (Study by William Hannah, 1968), 169
  independence, 169
  reassessment, 170
  return to college, 170
  uncertainty, 169
Attitudes of students, 79
Attrition, 157–169
  causes of, 171
  counseling, need for, 174
  individual differences, 172
  new environment, adjustment to, 172
  potential dropouts, 171
  studies on, 157–169

Behavior therapies: alternatives and additions to traditional counseling approaches, 107–119
  advantages of, 116–117
  cases, 107–108, 112–114
  operant or instrumental conditioning, 114–115
  orientation of behavior therapy, 109
  Wolpe, Joseph, system, 109–111
Behavior therapies—cases
  failure and depression, 114
  fantasies, 108
  fears, 107
  smoking, 107
  teaching, 115
Bill of Rights, Student, 231–239; see also Student Bill of Rights
Black power, 62

Change, revolutionary premise of, 25
Changing role of the counselor in modern society, 86–93
  college student programs, 90
  community work, 91, 92
  counseling process, 89
  future of counselor, 92

Changing role of the counselor in modern society (continued)
  natural resources, 91
  nonprofessional counselors, 89
Civil rights, as a student cause, 76–77
Computer
  affect on people who use it, 145
  role of, 143
Confrontations and disruptive actions, 52–54
Confrontations, anticipation and prevention of, 49–52
Congressional response, 19
Contract theory, 37, 56
Counseling, 5–6
  change of, 86, 88
  junior colleges, 182
  process of, 89
  understanding student, 94
Counselors
  college student programs, 90
  community relationship, 91–92
  future of, 92
  natural resources, use of, 91
  nonprofessionals, 89
"Crisis in the University" (Walter Moberly), 2

Diverse views that contain the basis for student unrest and agitation, 61–75
Dropouts, 13, 156–178
Dropouts: recent studies—implications and observations, 156–178; see also Attitudes of dropouts
  causes of attrition, 171
  counseling—need for improvement, 174
  individual differences, 172
  student adjustment to environment, 172
  studies on college attrition, 157–169

Due process, 37, 54

Economics
  national scene, 38
  university scene, 39
Education
  national scene, 35
  university scene, 35
Eisenhower, Dwight D., 21

Farnsworth, Dana L., M.D., 42
Financial aids, 18
  junior colleges, 185
Future, 19, 28

"Games People Play," 29

Hannah, John, 14
Harrington, Michael, 83
Hearings, 54
Helping the student understand himself,
    94–106; *see also* Self conditions
    of aiding student self-understand-
    ing, 100
Human relationships, 23

Image of today's student, 29–42
  contact theory, 37
  due process, 37
  economics
    national scene, 38
    university scene, 39
  education
    national scene, 35
    university scene, 35
  political
    national scene, 31
    university scene, 32
  religion
    national scene, 39
    university scene, 40
  social
    national scene, 33
    university scene, 34
Information system
  collection of information, 144
  definition of, 140
  research and operations application,
    150
  sensitivity to change, 144
  student research, 147–150
  use of, 146
Information systems in student person-
    nel administration, 139–155
  effect on people who use system, 145
  how system is used, 146
  research and operations application,
    150
  response time, 142
  role of computer, 143
  student research information system
    (SRIS), 147

Information systems in student personnel
    administration (*continued*)
  systems analyst, 141
  systems approach, 141
  what information will be collected,
    144
  what is an information system, 140
Innovation on campuses, 2
In-service education, 3, 209–229
  development of program, 217–221
    common terminology, 219
    determination of objectives, 218
    evaluation, 220
    functionally coordinated program-
      ming, 219
    program planning, 218
    resource material, 220
    staff motivation, 218
    staffing, 219
  general principles of programs, 215–
    217
  nature and scope, 210
  need for in student personnel work,
    212–215
  selected activities
    classroom, 224
    conferences, 223, 225
    meetings, 222
    peer evaluation, 228
    readings, 225
    seminars, 224
    workshops, 221
  status in student personnel work, 210
Instrumental conditioning, 114

Junior colleges, 18, 179–208
  areas of
    admissions and registration, 182
    discipline, 184
    faculty involvement, 187
    financial aid and placement, 185
    guidance and counseling, 182
    health programs, food services, and
      student housing, 186
    student activities, 183
  organization and administration, 188
  philosophy of, 180
  student personnel administration of,
    179–208
  study of student personnel director
    (Campbell, 1969), 190–192

Legislative actions, 56–60
Legislators, 15, 19
Living and learning centers, 128–138
  educational centers, 131
  evaluation of problems, 129
  peer group influence, 132
  role of the student personnel worker
    in living and learning residence
    halls, 135–137
  student community, 131

Michigan State University living and learning centers, 133–135
Ministry, campus, 12, 39, 120–127
structure of, 122–124
student and campus ministry, 125
student personnel administrators view, 120–122, 126
view of university, 124
Moberly, Walter, "Crisis in the University," 2

Nation on the move, 21–28
New dimensions: an overview, 1–20
objectives of student administrative services, 10
of student affairs, 9
of student life, 10
organization and administration of student personnel services, 8–12
New dimensions in junior college student personnel administration, 179–208; *see also* Junior college
areas of junior college student personnel work, 181
organization and administration, 188
philosophy of, 180
study of student personnel director (Jack Campbell, 1969), 190–192
New left, 64

Operant conditioning, 114–115
Organization and administration of student personnel services, 8–12

Policies guaranteeing the right of expression of students, 45
Policies regarding the priorities for use of university buildings and facilities, 47
Policy-making systems, need for change of, 73
Political
national scene, 31
university scene, 32
Private-versus-public-life concept, 67
division of, 68
Protest, 43–60

Radical press, 65
Radical views, 80–81
Reform, 26, 78
Religion
campus ministry, 120–127
national scene, 39
university scene, 40
Research and operations applications for information systems, 150–154
admissions, 150
other functions, 154
registration functions, 154
testing, 152

Residence halls, 128–138
educational centers, 131
peer group influence, 132
student community, 131
student personnel worker, 135–137
Response time, in information systems, 142
Romney, George, 14
Rudd, Mark, 80

Security, campus, 17
Self
consciousness, 96
historical, 96
immediacy of, 97
objective and subjective, 95
public and private, 98
viewed pragmatically, 94
Self-understanding
confrontation with decision making, 103
openness to experience, 101
personal history building, 102
search for personal challenge, 102
self-understanding of the helper, 104
Seventies, future of, 28
Social
national scene, 33
university scene, 34
Student administrative services, objectives of (Indiana State University), 10
Student affairs, objectives of (Indiana State University), 9
Student Bill of Rights, 231–239
in the classroom, 232
enforcement, 239
freedom of access to higher education, 232
off campus freedom of students, 236
preamble, 231
procedural standards in disciplinary proceedings, 236–238
student affairs, 233–236
student records, 233
Student government, 7, 8
Student life, objectives of (Indiana State University), 10
Student personnel administration in junior colleges, 179–208
Student personnel administrators and the campus ministry, 120–127
how does the student personnel administrator look at the campus ministry, 120–122, 126
how the campus ministry views the university, 124
structure of, 122–124
denominational, 122
ecumenical, 122–123
interdenominational, 123–124
student and the campus ministry, 125

Student personnel work
    need for in-service education, 212–215
    status of in-service education, 210
Student personnel worker in residence halls, 135–137
Student power, 69
    need for change, 73
    underlying factors, 69
Student Research Information System (SRIS)
    admissions and related divisions, 148
    physical file or logical files, 149
    registration division, 149
    research and related divisions, 149
    testing and related divisions, 149
Student subcultures, 13, 15, 62–67
Student unrest, 2, 61–75
Student value, judgments, characteristics of, 83–84

Student values–a new approach, 76–85
    characteristics of judgments, 83–84
Students for democratic society, 65–66
Systems approach, 141

Technological revolution, 23, 86
Tension, on campuses, 2
Today's student, 29–42

University posture and student protest— the second round, 43–60
    anticipation and prevention of confrontations, 49
    confrontations and disruptive actions, 52
    due process and fair hearing, 54

Values, 16, 76–85
Vietnam, 22, 24, 77

Wolpe, Joseph, behavior therapist, 109–111